Lyric Incarnate: The Dramas of Aleksandr Blok

Russian Theatre Archive

A series of books edited by John Freedman (Moscow), Leon Gitelman (St Petersburg) and Anatoly Smeliansky (Moscow)

Volume 1
The Major Plays of Nikolai Erdman
translated and edited by John Freedman

Volume 2
A Meeting About Laughter
Sketches, Interludes and Theatrical Parodies by Nikolai Erdman
with Vladimir Mass and Others
translated and edited by John Freedman

Volume 3
Theatre in the Solovki Prison Camp
Natalia Kuziakina

Volume 4
Sergei Radlov: The Shakespearian Fate of a Soviet Director
David Zolotnitsky

Volume 5
Bulgakov: The Novelist–Playwright
edited by Lesley Milne

Volume 6
Aleksandr Vampilov: The Major Plays
translated and edited by Alma Law

Volume 7
The Death of Tarelkin and Other Plays:
The Trilogy of Alexander Sukhovo-Kobylin
translated and edited by Harold B. Segel

Volume 8
A Chekhov Quartet
translated and adapted by Vera Gottlieb

Volume 9
Two Plays from the New Russia
Bald/Brunet by Daniil Gink and *Nijinsky* by Alexei Burykin
translated and edited by John Freedman

Volume 10
Russian Comedy of the Nikolaian Era
translated and with an introduction by Laurence Senelick

Please see the back of this book for other titles in the Russian Theatre Archive series

Lyric Incarnate: The Dramas of Aleksandr Blok

by Timothy C. Westphalen

State University of New York at Stony Brook, USA

Routledge
Taylor & Francis Group
LONDON AND NEW YORK

First published in 1998 by Overseas Publishers Association

This edition published 2011 by Routledge

2 Park Square, Milton Park, Abingdon, Oxon OX14 4RN
52 Vanderbilt Avenue, New York, NY 10017

Routledge is an imprint of the Taylor & Francis Group, an informa business

---

British Library Cataloguing in Publication Data

Westphalen, Timothy C.
Lyric incarnate: the dramas of Aleksandr Blok. – (Russian theatre archive; v. 13)
1. Blok, Aleksandr, 1880–1921 – Criticism and interpretation
I. Title
891.7'23

Cover illustration: Aleksandr Blok in 1907.

ISBN 13: 978-90-5755-021-8 (pbk)

For my grandmothers
Edith Ross and Maurine Westphalen

CONTENTS

CONTENTS

INTRODUCTION TO THE SERIES

The Russian Theatre Archive makes available in English the best avant-garde plays from the pre-Revolutionary period to the present day. It features monographs on major playwrights and theatre directors, introductions to previously unknown works, and studies of the main artistic groups and periods.

Plays are presented in performing edition translations, including (where appropriate) musical scores, and instructions for music and dance. Whenever possible the translated texts will be accompanied by videotapes of performances of plays in the original language.

LIST OF PLATES

(Between pages 86 and 87)

A NOTE ON TRANSLITERATION

Throughout this book, transliteration follows the Library of Congress system. Names, however, constitute a special problem and, within the text, have been dealt with in the following manner: Russian names, whether familiar or not, have been transliterated, while non-Russian names, such as Benois or Meyerhold, have been rendered in their appropriate Western forms. On the other hand, within all references and citations, transliteration has been stringently adhered to, even when this practice has led to the juxtaposition of two different forms of the same name. In such cases, scholarly accuracy has served as a guiding principle.

ACKNOWLEDGMENTS

Although scholarship is often solitary work, no scholar works in isolation. My debt to those who preceded me will be apparent in references to their work. My debt to my contemporaries is no less real, and here, at the outset, I wish to thank colleagues and friends, who helped shape this work.

I am particularly grateful to John Malmstad of Harvard University, who served as advisor for the dissertation from which this book grew. I could not have hoped for a more patient and generous reader, and the present work owes much to him. I am likewise indebted to Jurij Striedter for a sharp and incisive reading that rid the dissertation of much that was extraneous. I owe both men thanks not only for these specific kindnesses, but more largely for their example, and I hope they will see the reflection of their own high standards in the pages that follow.

I have also benefited from intellectual discourse of high order in conversation with friends and colleagues. George Mihaychuk of Georgetown University discussed with me the matter and the manner of Blok's dramas from the inception of this project to its fruition. W. G. Fiedorow of Knox College, first as teacher and then as colleague, has left an indelible imprint on these pages. Nicholas Rzhevsky of the State University of New York at Stony Brook shared generously with me his passion for and his knowledge of Russian drama. To all three I owe a double debt of friendship and scholarly regard.

Several institutions have supported me and my scholarship at key junctures. Knox College, through the good services of then Dean John Strassburger and then Associate Dean Steve Bailey, made possible much of the research on this book through the Faculty Research Fund, the Dean's Discretionary Fund, and the Johnson-Burkhardt Fund for Research in Foreign Cultures. In their attempt to create a community of scholar-teachers, Deans Strassburger and Bailey led an enlightened administration, and it was my privilege to teach at Knox during their tenure.

The editors of the journal *Slavic Review* have also been kind to me: not only did they publish an early version of the first chapter of this book, but they have kindly permitted me to include a revised version here. To the anonymous readers who commented upon that article before its publication, I also owe thanks.

Mere thanks can in no way recompense John Freedman, my friend and editor for the Russian Theatre Archive, for his herculean efforts on this book. He has selflessly read, reread, and commented on numerous drafts, and I have shamelessly exploited his knowledge of Russian drama and theater. My gratitude to him knows no bounds.

I also wish to thank my parents and my wife's parents who have supported us always. Finally, to my wife, who has suffered, but persevered and lived through this, and whose anamorphic image may be detected in these pages, I offer the thanks that love may tender.

If, after all this help and nurture, shortcomings arise as they are bound to, then they must remain very much my own.

INTRODUCTION:

BLOK, HIS DRAMA, AND THE THEATER

Assessing the place of Blok's dramas both within his own corpus and in the history of literature and theater poses a considerable challenge. On one hand, the relative obscurity of Blok's plays and their infrequent production suggest that they belong to the realm of the *Lesedrama*, plays intended to be read rather than acted. On the other hand, every major director of Blok's time expressed the desire to produce his work. Given the differences between them, it is hard to believe that Vsevolod Meyerhold, Vladimir Nemirovich-Danchenko, Konstantin Stanislavskii, Evgenii Vakhtangov, Aleksandr Tairov, and Nikolai Evreinov all could have been mistaken.[1] Add to this list of admirers such actors as Vasilii Kachalov, and Blok's dramas constitute a theatrical force to be reckoned with.

Even so, the fact remains that Blok's theatrical legacy has followed a more twisting path than that of his poetry. In part, this is due to the poetry itself. It is almost a commonplace to say that Yeats the poet overwhelms Yeats the dramatist,[2] and certainly much the same could be said of Blok. In an age of great and widespread experimentation, Blok was a poet of accomplishment, whose innovative rhythms, rhymes and forms helped to transform poetic idiom. The very range of his talent as a poet speaks for itself: from small lyric poems to the cycles Blok arranged them in, from the literary folktale to the verse epic, Blok was master of a broad spectrum of disparate forms. In light of the poetry, the desire to expand the three canonical volumes of Blok's verse to include a fourth that might be subtitled "Dramatic Verse" is an understandable temptation. And despite a number of monographs devoted to the theme of Blok and the theater, his plays have generally been subordinated to his poetry.

In no small measure, Blok's dramatic work has suffered the same fate as Western European Symbolist plays, which traditionally have been regarded as deficient in dramatic action, psychology, and character development and as devoid of dramatic conflict. In a word, the Symbolist drama is anti-drama, at least according to the dictums of theatrical tradition. Such opinions have, of course, a basis: The Symbolists undertook nothing less than an assault on theatrical

---

[1] In fairness, Stanislavskii's attitude toward Blok's work was complex and not always positive. The pertinent point to be made here is that he undertook to stage Blok's last full-length play. For a fuller treatment of this question, see chapters five and six.

[2] The recognition of the importance of Yeats's plays within his oeuvre has grown slowly and should temper any absolute judgment of his poetry's priority.

convention and, in the process, radically redefined the premises of the play. Whereas in realist and naturalist theater the play aided in the creation on stage of the illusion of a reality that existed outside of the theater, in Symbolist theater the play, as an extension of the lyrical persona of the playwright, is the reality the stage is made to bear. As Anna Balakian put it, "Here was an opportunity for the graphic projection of the inner landscape onto the external reality of the world of objects, and animate beings, none of whom would have any autonomous character but would represent the various shadings and fluctuations of the author's mood" (Balakian, 124).

Herein lie both the possibilities and the limitations of Symbolist theater, at least as it developed in Western Europe. The poet's persona, no longer restricted to the printed page, was free to reify itself not only in the characters, but also in the manifold devices theater exploits. In this way, synaesthesia, an ideal in Symbolist poetry, became a focal point for Symbolist theater. Acting, lighting, stage design, music, costuming, and makeup combined with words, tempo, and blocking to create a concomitant sensation, often a mystical intuition of another world. Mallarmé, for instance, dreamed of "a play written in the folio of heaven and mimed with the gesture of his passions by man" (Mallarmé, 294).[3] At its best, Symbolist theater delivered a unified, unadulterated experience of the poet's vision. At its worst, the single and unitary vision eschewed dramatic development altogether and devolved into mere stasis.

Here, however, Russian Symbolism diverges from its French counterpart. Although they bear the same name, the relation between them would be clearer if they did not. Russian Symbolism itself belied the unity its name suggests. According to a longstanding convention, scholars divide Russian Symbolism into two generations. Although recent studies have demonstrated the shortcomings of this generational approach, the disparateness of the poets who made up the Russian Symbolist movement can hardly be questioned. Nowhere is this more important than in assessing the influence of French Symbolism in Russia. For some, the example of French Symbolism is pivotal. Valerii Briusov's work, for example, is hardly imaginable without Baudelaire, Mallarmé, and Verlaine. The influence of French and Belgian Symbolism permeates even his personal life: He cherished his friendship with Émile Verhaeren to the end of his days (see Kogan, 15 and Donchin, 20).

For others, and especially Blok, French Symbolism exerted a weaker influence than native Russian ones, Pushkin, Solov'ev, and Fet, for example. At first glance, this is surprising, given that his mother was an accomplished translator from the French and that she expressed a lively interest in and translated Baudelaire and Verlaine long before it was fashionable to do so. For Blok himself, though, the Russian romantic tradition proved to be his formative experience of literature. Describing his mother's family, Blok once wrote, "To put it vulgarly, in Verlaine's manner, *éloquence* held sway here [...]. To this dear, old-fashioned *éloquence* I am indebted to the grave that literature began for me not with Verlaine and not with decadence in general" (Blok 1960-63, 7: 12).[4] Zhukovskii, Pushkin, Polonskii,

---

[3] See also, however, J.C. Ireson's caution against the distortion of Mallarmé's dictum (Ireson, 135).

[4] All future references to Blok's *Collected Works* (Blok 1960-3) will include only the volume and page numbers.

and Fet all loomed much larger than any of the French Symbolists in Blok's development.

The influence of French Symbolism on Blok's drama was further attenuated because Blok wrote his first play when he had already reached maturity as a poet. By that time, influence of any kind had been sublimated to Blok's own organic evolution. While a full consideration of Blok's poetry lies far beyond the scope of the present study, a few words about the relation between his poetry and drama are in order. Critics have followed Blok's lead in dividing the his career into three periods that correspond to the three volumes of verse in his *Collected Works*. The collection *Verses About the Beautiful Lady* [*Stikhi o Prekrasnoi Dame*] dominates the first period. The influence of Vladimir Solov'ev and his conception of Sophia, or the Divine Wisdom, manifests itself particularly in Blok's image of the Beautiful Lady. Not unlike the Dante of *Vita Nuova*, Blok records now the timidity, now the jealousy of his love for the Beautiful Lady. The poems tend toward the monologic and document a growing sense of remove between the persona and the Beautiful Lady.

The idealism of the first volume gives way to disillusion in the second, and it is at this juncture that Blok turns to drama. The rarefied air of worship for the Beautiful Lady evaporates in the face of a sometimes almost naturalistic preoccupation with the fallen world. Under the spell of Briusov's urban poetry, Blok finds in the city a wide range of voices counterposed to his own. The strictly monologic contours of the earlier poetry loosen, and Blok begins to compose in noncanonical forms with innovative techniques, an experiment that comes to fruition in such cycles as *The Snow Mask* [*Snezhnaia maska*]. Blok's interest in drama, then, coincides with the ever expanding dialogic potential of his lyric poetry. Drama and theater offered, Blok thought, "an exit from lyric isolation" (8:170).

The organic development in the work to move beyond the restrictions of the lyric stance and into drama lagged decidedly behind Blok's lifelong love for and involvement in the theater. Perhaps the most surprising aspect of Blok's drama is that it took him so long to get started. From the time he saw his first play when he was thirteen, Blok was fascinated by theater. When only a little older, he and his cousins would spend much of their summer vacation at Shakhmatovo, the family's country estate, staging what Blok's English biographer Avril Pyman has described as a "positive orgy of private theatricals" (Pyman 1979, 1: 44). From the comedies of Koz'ma Prutkov, Blok quickly graduated to Pushkin's *Little Tragedies* [*Malen'kie tragedii*] and Shakespeare. Hamlet especially caught his imagination. In the summers that followed, Blok joined in amateur productions at the neighboring estate of Boblovo, where the woman who would be his wife spent her summers. Liubov' Mendeleeva, the daughter of the great chemist who formulated the periodic table, and Blok put on *Hamlet*, Pushkin's *Boris Godunov*, and Griboedov's *Woe from Wit*, among others.

Acting held a special charm for both Mendeleeva and Blok. In time, Mendeleeva would become a professional actress. Blok too embarked on this path, although he would question his own sincerity in retrospect. As he remarked in his autobiography, "In a superficial way I was preparing to go into acting" (7: 13). Other evidence, however, suggests that he may have been more ardent than he gave himself credit for. During the 1899-1900 theater season, Blok joined the St. Petersburg Gogol Drama Circle, arguably the foremost amateur theater group in the capital (Galanina, 35). The importance of Blok's participation in an amateur theater group may appear paltry; however, at the time such groups played a significant part in theatrical and cultural life and sometimes gathered enough momentum to become independent theaters. The Moscow Art Theater is perhaps the most famous theater to grow out of an amateur theatrical circle. Blok's decision, then, to join a dramatic circle suggests seriousness of purpose, and his acceptance by the circle in turn suggests that Blok displayed some talent as an actor. In the end Blok's pursuit of an acting career came to nought. His aunt and biographer, Mariia Beketova, recounts how distasteful the intrigues behind the scenes were to Blok (Beketova 1922, 69). Playing alongside lawyers and the occasional police agent may also have dampened his spirits (7: 340.) This distaste becomes apparent in most of his later comments about this experience. As he wrote to the poet Zinaida Hippius, "... for several years in a row I prepared assiduously for the stage and even played in a repugnant circle in Pavlova Hall in Petersburg. Mainly it was this that drove me away" (8: 42).[5] Whatever his disappointment, his experience in and knowledge of theatrical life had important ramifications for the dramas he was to write later. Blok, after all, called the published collections of his plays *Theater*, not *Dramas*.

Blok's interest in drama and theater was echoed by that of his coevals. Other Symbolists and their sympathizers may not have matched, but nonetheless shared Blok's interest in theater. The Russian Symbolists devoted an extraordinary amount of attention to the theater in the course of the first decade of the twentieth century. Article followed article, and eventually programmatic pronouncements issued forth. Fyodor Sologub's "Theater of Will", the counterposed attempts of Viacheslav Ivanov and Innokentii Annenskii to revive Greek tragedy, and Blok's own articles on theater and drama were integral to the growth and dissolution of Russian Symbolism as a movement. The Symbolists' ideas about theater were rescued from the abstraction of the ivory tower that French Symbolism strove for by directors sympathetic to them. Vsevolod Meyerhold, in particular, engaged the Symbolist poets in an ongoing dialogue, and although the lines of influence become murky, the fact of their existence lies beyond doubt.

What the Symbolists shared with directors such as Meyerhold was a fervent desire to renew art in general and theater in particular. A reaction against realism and naturalism bound them together. Such a reaction would have remained nihilistic, had it only sought to destroy the conventions of the preceding epoch. However, their reaction was profoundly positive, and they sought to expand the possibilities of the theater. In so doing, they cast back over the history of theater for forgotten, and therefore in their own era, new forms. In this sense, Osip Mandel'shtam's characterization of Blok as a "collector of Russian verse, which had been scattered and lost by the historically broken nineteenth century" aptly describes a determining trait, not just of Blok's, but of his age (Mandel'shtam, 2: 347). This quest into the past is perhaps nowhere more evident than in Nikolai Evreinov's Starinnyi, or Antiquarian Theater, whose express credo was historically accurate staging in the manner of particular theatrical traditions. In successive seasons Evreinov and his associates hoped to mount productions of medieval

[5] Blok's published comments about the circle are few, but see a letter from Blok to his father, dated January 22, 1900, in which he describes his participation in the circle (8: 10-11). The best work presently available on Blok's participation in theater circles is Galanina's.

miracle plays, the classics of the Spanish Golden Age, Greek choral tragedy, and the *commedia dell'arte*. In fact, Blok's translation of the trouvère poet Rutebeuf's *Le Miracle de Théophile* saw light of day in a production at the Starinnyi.

Blok's distinctiveness as a playwright in no small measure derives from the conjunction of such large cultural forces and his personal, practical experience in the theater. His drama, though recognizably Symbolist drama, displays an innovative stageworthiness that sets it apart from the dramatic work of most of his contemporaries. At the same time, however, the demands it makes on the theater necessitated a search for new forms. The chapters that follow examine Blok's reckoning with literary and dramatic tradition in each play. Questions of dramatic form and genre and the connection between them, Blok's own work, and theatrical tradition come to the fore. It is in light of such considerations as these that the structure of the chapters that follow should be understood. Each chapter opens with an examination of the course of Blok's work on the play in question and then turns to consider his first readers' and audience's response. The genesis and reception of each play highlight Blok's struggle with and against prevailing norms. The analysis that then follows assesses the play in terms of the new aesthetic Blok sought, not in terms of traditional norms. Since several of Blok's plays did not reach the stage during his lifetime, only three chapters expand the scope of this study to examine the specifically theatrical challenges posed by the plays and their resolution by the directors who undertook their production. The plays are treated in the chronological order in which they were written: *A Puppet Show*, *The King on the Square*, *The Stranger*, *The Song of Fate*, and *The Rose and the Cross.* Since Blok's first three plays constitute a trilogy, a separate chapter has been devoted to them as a trilogy.

Not all of Blok's dramatic works, however, warrant separate consideration, and perhaps a word or two about such works is in order. His dramatic dialogue *Of Love, Poetry, and Government Service*, which grew out of *The King on the Square*, is treated together with that play. Then too, Blok's sixth and last play *Ramses* garners no attention until the conclusion largely because its narrowly construed didactic aims set it apart from his other work. Written in 1919 in connection with "Commission on the Compilation of Historical Tableaux," *Ramses* is an anomaly in Blok's work and will be treated as such. Blok's articles on and reviews of drama and theater, his verse translations, and his unfinished dramas do not receive attention in separate chapters, but are treated in relation to his major plays. My aim throughout has been to do justice to the singularity of Blok's achievement in drama, to examine, on one hand, his contributions to literature, drama, and theater, and, on the other, to acknowledge the limitations of his achievement, whether inherent or imposed by shifts in literary and theatrical norms or by such cataclysmic historical events as the Russian Revolution.

CHAPTER ONE

OF PUPPETS AND CARNIVAL: *A PUPPET SHOW*

> Si tant de poètes ont été attirés par la forme dramatique, ce n'est pas parce que celle-ci leur donne la joie un peu grossière (et généralement cher payée) de réaliser leurs conceptions en chair et en os dans une atmosphère de carton peint, mais parce qu'elle leur permet précisément de laisser parler les voix profondes qu'ils entendent dans leurs coeurs.
>
> -Edouard Dujardin

I

Origins and Reactions

"It is impossible to imagine a more barbarous impression than that which remains from *A Puppet Show*. ... The public could not make anything out" (Kotrelev and Timenchik, 3: 265). It was to such rousing fanfare as this that Aleksandr Blok's first play, under the direction of Vsevolod Meyerhold, opened on 30 December, 1906. This reaction is all the more striking because the talents involved were so considerable: Blok, who had already established himself as a leading light of Russian Symbolism, made his debut as playwright that evening; Meyerhold, having broken away from his mentor and sometime nemesis Stanislavskii several years earlier, was establishing himself as a director to be reckoned with at the theater of Vera Komissarzhevskaia, a legendary actress in her own right. Yet, what should have delighted the audience elicited no small measure of controversy and strife.[1]

---

[1] The motley makeup of the audience undoubtedly explains part of the ensuing controversy, but since its exact composition remains a matter of some dispute, it cannot provide by itself an entirely satisfactory explanation. According to the actress Vera Andrushevich [Polevaia] who attended that evening's performance, "This was an alien audience, not friends of the decadents" (Kotrelev and Timenchik, 3: 265). In contrast, the diary of Blok's aunt and eventual biographer, Mar'ia Beketova, suggests

Reaction mirrored the makeup of the audience itself, and no one, not even Blok's friends, could ignore the contentious reception that met the play. Blok's best friend, Evgenii Ivanov, jotted down this note in his diary that night: "The first performance of *A Puppet Show* — Whistles and clapping" (Ivanov, 415). Another friend, Georgii Chulkov wrote to his wife, "*A Puppet Show* went off with a 'little scandal': they both clapped and whistled" (Kotrelev and Timenchik, 3: 264). In a review that appeared three days after the premiere, Chulkov went into more detail: "The audience's reaction to *A Puppet Show* was far from indifferent and not unanimous. There was applause, and there were protests. During the loud calls for the author, someone's whistle sounded persistently, and in the front rows were heard the phrases: 'No, you explain what this is to me'" (T-ch [Chulkov], 6).

The newspaper reviews echo Chulkov's anonymous theatergoer and form a monotonous litany of complaint. The outraged reviewer for one paper wrote, "No one needs this... This is pretentious, affected, and false ... Is *A Puppet Show* not a satire of the public itself?" (Beliaev, 13). Another reviewer opined, "(T)he beautiful production exposes all the more the inner poverty of the 'lyrical scenes'" (Avel', 4). A third ranted, "To attempt to find sense in this farcical Foolery is beneath the dignity of a man of common sense" (Smolenskii, 6). Yet another went so far as to dub Blok's little play a "bedlamlet" (Azov, 5). As Leonid Dolgopolov has aptly remarked, "In regard to the newspaper responses, a blank wall of incomprehension awaited Blok" (4: 571). Positive appraisal proved the exception, not the rule.

A Puppet Show fared little better amongst Blok's relatives. Several days after the first performance, Mar'ia Beketova, reported that her uncle "said that this is impudence, ... that this is literature for a small circle, nonsense not needed by anyone, and so on" (Beketova 1982, 621). In fact, a note of trepidation runs through all of Beketova's diary entries that deal with *A Puppet Show*. She was especially concerned about how the relatives would react. There is an almost perceptible sigh of relief in her statement, "The relatives did not quarrel ..." the first night (Beketova 1982, 620).

The outrage and sheer consternation implicit in such comments were not limited, however, to a conservative public and older members of Blok's family. Even from the Symbolists, who ostensibly understood it, the play drew a heated response. Before the play ever opened, the poet Nikolai Minskii wrote, "What an insult that they are putting on a play of that idiot Blok at Komissarzhevskaia's. They will kill their own theater!" (Kotrelev and Timenchik, 3: 260). Indeed, the play cost Blok dearly. The Muscovite Symbolists — and in particular, the "Argonauts" Sergei Solov'ev, Èllis, and Andrei Belyi — reacted violently. As the editors of the correspondence between Blok and Sergei Solov'ev have noted, "After the appearance of *A Puppet Show* Solov'ev refused to have any contact whatsoever with Blok" (Kotrelev and Lavrov, 1: 314). Èllis wrote to Blok, referring to *A Puppet Show* as a "conventional thing for a small circle" (Èllis, 2: 282). Within

---

that the audience was somewhat more diverse: "The audience of the first performances: writers, artists, and musicians of the new. Several ladies involved in the arts and, of course, relatives. There were relatively few students..." (Beketova 1982, 620).

several months, Èllis would break off their correspondence, saying, "(I) consider our inner relations broken" (Èllis, 291).[2]

It was also at this point that Blok and Belyi entered into one of the most strained periods in their friendship. Belyi, in fact, was still fuming two years later when he reviewed the collection in which Blok gathered together his lyrical dramas, which of course included *A Puppet Show*. At one time, wrote Belyi, Blok's poems had seemed like roses, but then added, "(W)hen the cover flew off his muse (the roses opened) — in each rose sat a caterpillar..." (Belyi, 66). And at the end of the review, Belyi tends toward condescension: "... now with painful love, with love-pity I take in the lament of a sick soul for itself and the laughter of a sick soul at itself: Lament and mockery from a pure heart" (Belyi, 68). Perhaps because of the personal nature of Belyi's comments, the editors of the journal in which his review appeared felt obliged to disassociate themselves from them. In a note at the bottom of the first page of the review, they wrote, "The editorial staff, subscribing to the opinion of the author of this notice that the dramas of A. Blok are a 'not commonplace phenomenon of our literature,' does not share all the judgments expressed by A. Belyi about the work of A. Blok" (see Belyi, 65). It is perhaps a testament to their friendship that relations between Blok and Belyi were not severed for good.

In most instances, such a mountain of criticism would be damning. However, as Konstantin Rudnitskii has pointed out, Blok and Meyerhold's contemporaries failed to ascertain the significance of the production: "None of their contemporaries turned out to be in a position to comprehend the full scale and the full significance of the event that was taking place. No one appraised at its true worth either A. Blok's play or Vs. Meyerhold's production, which elicited the poet's complete approval" (Rudnitskii 1978, 172). Blok himself seems to have been one of the few who understood that this was to be a defining moment. It is striking that in the face of all of the criticism, coming as it did from all sides, Blok remained strangely nonplussed. In fact, he seemed almost to enjoy the controversy that stormed over his little "fairy play," the term he adopted in a foreword when his trilogy of lyrical dramas first appeared in book form (4: 434). In his notebook, he remarked, "Yesterday, 30.XII, of December [sic, TW], I went out on the stage four times. Nothing but a piercing whistle and applause. I bowed to the former and the latter" (Blok 1965, 91). While this behavior might conceivably reflect Blok's usual diffidence and composure, a remark he made to his friend, Aleksandr Gippius, suggests otherwise. He said that *A Puppet Show*"... is playing at Kommissarzhevskaia's (right at this minute for the fifth time already) with, I would say, success because they called me out a lot and whistled and hissed abundantly at the first and second performances" (8: 176). Georgii Chulkov's comments to his wife after the first performance further enhance this impression. He wrote, "Blok went out to bow with a silly little smile. He was terribly funny, and touchingly pressed to his heart a tiny bouquet thrown by a woman's hand" (Kotrelev and

[2] Èllis wrote this final letter because Blok had defended Chulkov during a skirmish over the latter's idea of "mystical anarchism," which would prove to be one incident among many as Russian Symbolism entered a period of crisis. *A Puppet Show* was not the sole reason Èllis broke off contact. However, it was arguably the single most important incident in a series of misunderstandings and arguments.

Timenchik, 264). Taken together, these comments conjure up the picture of someone who, at the very least, had anticipated and, in all likelihood, had desired a mixed reaction. Paradoxically, it would seem Blok considered the opening night a success because of the heated response. An echo of Blok's response is audible in that of his aunt, who wrote, "At the end of the play hissing and a piercing whistle resounded, but everything was covered by loud and friendly applause. ... Hissing, a whistle, and the thunder of applause." She concludes in a similarly paradoxical tone, "In general, a success" (Beketova 1982, 620).

Success then meant something other than mere approval. Controversy could be success only if it were Blok's aim. Indeed, this was the case. *A Puppet Show* grew out the desire to create a new, Symbolist theater. It arose from the work of a group that had originally formed at one of Viacheslav Ivanov's so-called "Wednesdays." Ivanov, a poet and classical scholar who had studied with Theodore Mommsen, brought together a wide range of the Petersburg intelligentsia at these gatherings. At Ivanov's "tower," Blok met not only with fellow Symbolists, but also with philosphers, academics, and politicians. (For more on Ivanov's Wednesdays, see Pyman 1979, 1: 228-31). Quite naturally, smaller alliances formed.

It was precisely in this way that a group interested in creating a new theater came into being. In January of 1906, Chulkov, one of the more enterprising members, proposed that they form a new theater in conjunction with a new literary miscellany. Both were to be called *Torches* [*Fakely*]. Of the two projects, only the miscellany got off the ground. *A Puppet Show*, though directed by Meyerhold, would run in the theater of Vera Komissarzhevskaia. As they divided up the tasks, it fell to Blok to write the first play and to Meyerhold to direct it. At Chulkov's behest, Blok transformed his poem "A Puppet Show," which he had written in July of 1905, into a play. Chulkov's suggestion, however, was only one factor in Blok's choice of theme. His decision also appears to have grown out his earliest theatrical experience. A preeminent Blok scholar has argued, in fact, that as a child Blok saw puppet show presentations first hand in Petersburg (Mints 1986, 44-53, especially 46). Moreover, the presence of the same motifs, imagery, and even some of the same scenes in works by Blok's contemporaries — in the memoirs of Aleksandr Benois, for example — leads the same scholar to conclude, "These images, undoubtedly were contained in the harlequinades of the Petersburg puppet shows in the period of Benois and Blok's childhood" (Mints 1988, 403). These impressions ran deep, and Blok returned to the puppet show and those images related to it time and again in his poetry. Blok's familiarity with these motifs and the freedom he exercised with them may help to explain why the poem and the play appear to have so little in common at first glance. Despite superficial differences, however, the poem anticipates important aspects of the play.

II

From Poem to Play

Perhaps the most surprising aspect of the poem "A Puppet Show" is the absence of the *commedia dell'arte* figures and motifs that dominate the play. The *commedia dell'arte* figures, while absent from "A Puppet Show", do appear in a number of other poems written between 1902 and 1905. Critics have found that a number of them, in fact, incorporate key elements of the future play. The most important include: Another, but not diminutivized "A Puppet Show" ["Balagan"], "You dress me in silver", "Light staggered in the window", "He appeared at an elegant ball", "They were all yelling around round tables", and "At the hour when narcissuses get drunk" (2: 123, 37; 1: 210, 227, 252, 322). (See in this regard: Rodina, 128-9; Clayton, 140-1; Shelud'ko, 105.) Yet by themselves, they cannot explain how the *commedia dell'arte* figures arose in Blok's work in the first place. The most likely conduit appears to be the artists who were associated with Diaghilev's *World of Art* group. Their advocacy reawakened interest in Watteau, whose paintings of *commedia dell'arte* figures found a new and receptive audience in Russia at the turn of the century. Some critics have also argued stridently, if not always convincingly, that Verlaine's treatment of the *commedia dell'arte* influenced Blok (Jones, 185-6). Surprisingly, no theatrical source has yet been discovered. Although Blok knew Meyerhold at the time, the latter's interest in the *commedia dell'arte* appears to have been ignited by Blok's play. Certainly the writings in which Meyerhold examines the *commedia dell'arte* belong to a slightly later period.

As important as the *commedia dell'arte* is in and of itself to *A Puppet Show*, it by no means sets the parameters for the relationship between the poem and the play. The poem proves to be connected to the play in subtle ways, and it is here that inquiry into the play should begin:

A PUPPET SHOW

Look, a puppet show opened
For good, happy kids who behave.
A boy and a girl are hoping
To see kings with their ladies, and devils.
And this music from hell can be heard:
A doleful bow howls.
The devil who caught that little boy roly-poly is horrid,
And cranberry juice trickles down.

THE BOY

He will be saved from the rage of the black one

With a wave or the sleight
Of a white hand. And look: little lights
Approach from the left.
Do you see smoke? Do you see torchlights?
That certainly must be the queen, herself.

THE GIRL

Oh no, why do you tease me?
This is the devil's own retinue...
The queen, she comes out in the middle of the day,
Laced all around with garlands of roses.
Swords clanking, a retinue sighing,
Knights carry her train.

All of a sudden a fool suddenly leans across the footlights
And shouts: Help!
I'm hemorrhaging cranberry juice!
I'm bandaged with rags!
On my head, there's a helmet of cardboard,
And in my hand, a sword made of wood.

The girl and boy burst into tears,
And the fun puppet show closes down. (2: 67-8)[3]

The poem and play share few themes and motifs. To begin with, they bear the same title, one that has proven recalcitrant to satisfying, or even satisfactory translation. Blok's title "Balaganchik" has been translated in a variety of different ways, including such renderings as "A Puppet Show," "The Puppet Show," "The Puppet Booth," and "The Fairground Booth." A problem not solved by any of these variants issues from the Russian word "balaganchik" itself, a diminutive of "balagan," which means a show or a show-booth. Of these alternatives, "A Puppet Show," though by no means ideal, is the most accurate in the context of the works in question because Blok dismantles in his works the puppet show, not the puppet booth. In the end the spectator is left with puppets and their strings, not with timber and nails. The question of whether to use the definite, indefinite, or no article also proves to be a thorny issue. In the final analysis, the indefinite article best reflects Blok's purpose. As we shall see, the particularity granted by the definite article is at odds with the generalizing tendencies of the play: Pierrot, we are told, is "like all Pierrots", and the play itself is one puppet show among many. Aside from their problematic titles, the poem and the play have in common a procession of lights, a fool who bleeds cranberry juice, and knights. A number of images, however, do not survive the transition: the boy and the girl appear only in

[3] For a radically different translation, see Pyman 1979, 1: 205-6.

the poem, and the queen, king, and devil are replaced by figures from the *commedia dell'arte*.

More important than the motifs that poem and play share or do not share is a certain generic overlapping, however odd such a characterization may appear in comparing a play with a poem. Both can be described as serio-comical, as that term was understood by Bakhtin (1984b, 108). Both place a premium on "familiar contact with the open-ended present" (Bakhtin 1984b, 108). Although this trait is far sharper in the play, it is very much in evidence in the poem, where the boy and girl work out their feelings about the puppet show right before the reader's eyes. Their immediate reactions are very much bound up with the second characteristic of serio-comical works, namely a critical relation to legend, in this case the legend of the "fun puppet show". Their gradual disillusionment with the puppet show borders on what Bakhtin calls a "cynical exposé" (Bakhtin 1984b, 108). The same kind of disillusionment will prove to be pivotal in the play as well. We should note in this regard that Blok lays bare the artifice of his creation in both works. Thus, the image of the fool who bleeds cranberry juice acquires significance not merely because it occurs in both the poem and the play, but because the fool reminds both the reader of the former and the spectator of the latter that the proceedings are neither real, nor intended to be. The attempts by the boy and the girl to make sense of the puppet show serve a similar purpose in that they mimic the reader's own attempts to interpret the poem. Blok reminds the reader of the poem's artifice by drawing attention to interpretive stategies. Finally, both poem and play are, in Bakhtin's term, "multi-styled" (Bakhtin 1984b, 108). They exhibit traits of the high and the low, the serious and the comic, and so forth.

This latter characteristic deserves special attention because both poem and play are unorthodox in their formal features. For instance, the poem, a mere twenty-eight lines in length, contains an odd mixture of narration and dialogue. It opens and closes with narration, but this is broken up by an exchange between the boy and the girl, who are each given a six-line stanza. Thus, narration and dialogue appear to be separated and distinct until the fifth stanza, in which the fool breaks into the narration and takes up over four of the stanza's six lines with his speech. The resulting pastiche of narration and dialogue makes for a motley generic fabric. On one hand, the dialogue tugs at the parameters of the lyric in the direction of the dramatic. Yet, on the other hand, the action, if it can be called that at all, bears little trace of drama. It sets the scene, but no more. The poem is perhaps best described as a hybrid lyric.

Similar tensions become apparent at the level of rhythm and meter. The poem may be described as "basically anapaestic in structure, nineteen of the twenty-eight lines being pure anapaests of one kind or another" (Kemball, 439). We should also note that three of these nineteen lines have a monosyllabic, rather than the expected disyllabic, anacrusis. The remaining nine lines, or nearly one third of the poem, display irregularities if we take the anapaest to be the poem's basic foot. In an anapaestic line, the number of interstitial syllables between ictuses, that is the syllables that ordinarily may be stressed, should be two. In nine of the lines of "A Puppet Show," however, this number varies. It dwindles to one in three instances and balloons to four in five others. This latter phenomenon, tetrasyllabic substitution, is relatively uncommon in syllabotonic meters and should give us pause. Taken together with the poem's other non-standard features — such as the six non-standard anacruses and the variable number of feet per line (nineteen have three, seven have two, and two have four) — this problem of tetrasyllabic substitution suggests that "A Puppet Show" cannot be treated simply as a poem written according to the standards of syllabotonic verse. Examining "A Puppet Show" in the context of several other poems from Blok's middle period, one scholar concludes, "We instinctively feel that the limit has been reached to that type of verse which may still fairly be considered *syllabo*-tonic in basic structure and that we are already on the threshold of *pure*-tonic (accentual) verse" (Kemball, 240).

The historical significance of these structural observations may not be apparent immediately. The lyric poem in the practice of nineteenth-century Russian poets had adhered, with a few notable exceptions, to syllabotonic meters. The most notable include Pushkin's evocation of accentual folk verse forms in such works as his *Songs of the Western Slavs* and his *The Folktale about the Fisherman and the Little Fish.* Aside from such forms inspired by folklore, another and distinct accentual form arose in logaoedic meters and in the hexameter line, the latter employed in the translations of the Homeric epics by such poets as Zhukovskii and Gnedich. While these forms veered toward accentual verse in the eighteenth century, by the nineteenth the hexameter had solidified into a dactyllic line. Overall, Russian verse was ruled by syllabotonic meters and would remain so until the dawn of the so-called Silver Age, when the Symbolists began to experiment with accentual verse and free verse forms. Thus, when Blok wrote purely accentual verse or, as in "A Puppet Show," interspersed accentual lines amongst lines that could be scanned as ternary syllabotonic lines, he implied a polemic with traditional syllabotonic forms. Accentual and free verse forms, in fact, are sometimes referred to as "nonclassical" in Russian practice. This opposition in Blok's poetry anticipates a similar polemic with traditional dramatic and theatrical structures that become apparent in his dramas.

These similarities notwithstanding, the play developed into an utterly unique creation. A brief synopsis of the play may give some small indication of the play's uniqueness and originality.[4] The curtain opens to reveal a group of Mystics, who await the mystic revelation of Death and who speak in verse, but in such a way that they continue one another's lines. Then enters Pierrot, one of three masks from the *commedia dell'arte* in the play. Pierrot cannot fathom the Mystics' intent, since he is merely waiting for his fiancée, Columbine. A character named the Author breaks in to protest that this is not what he intended, that the actors are taking liberties with his work. The Author suddenly becomes embarrassed and slinks offstage. At this point, Columbine enters, hailed as Death by the Mystics and as a Fiancée by Pierrot. The Chairman of the Mystics tries to persuade Pierrot that Columbine is Death and, as evidence, points to the scythe [kosa] behind her shoulders. Much hinges on how the word "kosa" is understood, since it has two distinct meanings. The Chairman understands the word in its first meaning. Pierrot, on the other hand, understands the word to mean a "braid," such as that worn by Columbine. The resulting confusion about whether Columbine is Death or just Pierrot's fiancée is, of course, critical to any interpretation of the play. At this juncture in the play, Pierrot hesitates, even though Columbine tells him that she will not abandon him.

[4] Numerous translations of the play exist. See, for example, Bennett 1982b, Green, Reeve, and Vogel 1990.

Suddenly Harlequin appears. Her earlier protestations of devotion notwithstanding, Columbine allows Harlequin to lead her away.

The curtain falls and the Author appears on the stage to assure the spectator that this is not what he had in mind. His play, a most realistic play, concerned star-crossed lovers, who surmount all obstacles to be together. Just as he finishes uttering these words, however, a hand yanks him offstage. When the curtains open again, we see a ball in progress. Masks, knights, ladies, and fools whirl around on the stage. Pierrot is alone. He comes to the front of the stage and enters into a soliloquy, in which he tells how he followed Harlequin and Columbine. Out on the streets in a snowstorm, he tells the audience, Columbine suddenly turned to cardboard. Pierrot relates how he and Harlequin danced over her fallen figure and how they became friends.

As Pierrot finishes his soliloquy, a procession of couples begins. A couple dances to the front and pretends to be in a church. They look up at the cupola and speak of their holy love. The woman notices "someone dark" standing by a column. A second couple comes forward, the man chasing the woman who holds him in sway. They speak of their passion, and, as they leave, they are pursued by a double. The third and final couple to come forward consists of a man and woman, who repeats the last word of whatever the man says. Suddenly, a Fool challenges the man, who hits him with a wooden sword. The Fool falls over the footlights and cries, "I'm bleeding cranberry juice!" Next comes a procession of torches, at the head of which is Harlequin, the coryphaeus, who laughs over all that he has done and all that has happened. He then leaps through the scenery into what the stage directions describe as a void. With Harlequin's demise, Columbine reappears, her scythe becoming a braid. The Author comes forward to reunite Columbine and Pierrot. But just as he does so, the scenery flies up. The Author, once he realizes what has happened, makes a run for it as do all the other characters. Pierrot alone remains. As the play ends, he sings a sad sang about his unhappy love.

III

The Carnival-Grotesque and Noncoincidence

Although the play's originality is clear even in such a brief synopsis and must have been clear to Blok in retrospect, he was skeptical about the prospect of writing a play in the beginning. The dynamics of the group at Ivanov's tower left him somewhat reluctant and more than a little annoyed. He wrote to Andrei Belyi, "... (I)t turned out that I will have ... to write a play, 'developing the poem 'A Puppet Show.' All this building of such highly cultured people, like Viach. Ivanov, and such highly enterprising people, like Georgii Chulkov and Meyerhold, is beginning to torment me" (8: 146). Despite such initial misgivings and internal resistance, he finished the play quickly, in less than a month. Such a short gestation period, together with originality and mastery of the completed work, suggests that Blok very quickly ascertained precisely the qualities he sought in a new, Symbolist theater. Few have been so perceptive in their appraisal of what those qualities were as the man who would direct it. Strangely, however, Meyerhold's comments about *A Puppet Show* have been ignored in the scholarship on the play. This omission is particularly striking, given Meyerhold's close association with Blok at the time.

In their quest for a new theater, Blok and Meyerhold sought to bring dramatic and theatrical convention into question. Although he would later turn to Stanislavskii with *The Song of Fate* and *The Rose and the Cross*, Blok chose to work with Meyerhold on *A Puppet Show*, and, as Avril Pyman has argued, Meyerhold and Blok were well matched for their work on the play. Pyman writes, "In their work on 'The Puppet Booth,' however, Blok and Meyerhold understood one another perfectly within that 'sphere of irony' in which the action of the play takes place, and Meyerhold's own performance as Pierrot had a quality of eerie solemnity which safeguarded the delicate lyricism of the play" (Pyman 1979, 1: 267). Blok praised Meyerhold for his innovations throughout this period. For instance, less than a month before the first performance of *A Puppet Show*, Blok contrasted Stanislavskii's iron-fisted rule with Meyerhold's methods. Meyerhold, according to Blok, gives his actors a general plan, but then slackens the reins, and "throws (their) individual gifts to the mercy of the stage, like a sheaf of sparks. They are free, they can burn down the ship of the play, but they can also ignite the auditorium with sparks of true art" (5: 97). Blok found in Meyerhold's direction a technique which answered the needs of a new kind of theater. Nor were his expectations frustrated. Blok was exceptionally pleased by Meyerhold's production. In his own words, "The production of *A Puppet Show* makes me happy" (8: 174). As he wrote to Meyerhold before the opening, "The general tone, as I have already said to you, was so pleasing to me that new perspectives on *A Puppet Show* have opened up for me: it seems to me that this is not only lyricism, but there is already in it the frame of a play" (8: 170). Blok went even further in the foreword to the first collection of the lyrical trilogy, which included *A Puppet Show*, *The King on the Square*, and *The Stranger*. He wrote, "I am indebted to V.È. Meyerhold, his troupe, M.A. Kuzmin, and N.N. Sapunov for an ideal production of (my) little fairy-play *A Puppet Show*" (4: 434).[5] Far from a mere pleasantry, this comment reflects Blok's conviction. As he explained it to Meyerhold before the first performance, "Believe me that it is necessary to me to be around your theater, it is necessary that *A Puppet Show* play under your direction; for me in this there is a cleansing moment, an exit from lyrical isolation" (8: 170).

On Meyerhold's side, *A Puppet Show* held an ongoing fascination: He would produce *A Puppet Show* again in 1908 and 1914. *A Puppet Show*, according to Meyerhold, forced both director and actor to return to the origins of theater, and its author was "a true magician of theatricality" (Meierkhol'd 1968a, 1: 208). The basis for such praise becomes apparent in Meyerhold's theoretical writings. Meyerhold, whose own art has been described as grotesque, understood Blok's work in like terms. (See, for instance, Symons). *A Puppet Show*, in fact, proves to be a pivotal work in Meyerhold's definition of the grotesque in his article "A Puppet Show," where he suggests that Blok followed in the footsteps of Goya,

[5] Mikhail Kuzmin had composed the music and Nikolai Sapunov had created the scenery for Meyerhold's production.

Poe, and Hoffmann. Citing Harlequin's final jump through a window into nothingness and the Fool's cry that he is bleeding cranberry juice, Meyerhold argued that "Blok went along the path of the grotesque in the spirit of these masters" (Meierkhol'd 1968a, 1: 227).

Meyerhold, in fact, appears to have been the first to suggest that *A Puppet Show* was fundamentally grotesque. (The only other commentators to even mention the term are Fedorov, Frolov, Gromov, and Pollak.) Through its unresolved oppositions, *A Puppet Show* takes on an almost paradigmatic significance for Meyerhold. "The grotesque," he writes, "does not know only the low or only the high. The grotesque interferes with opposition, consciously creating the sharpness of contradictions and playing only with its own originality" (Meierkhol'd 1968a, 1: 225). Despite the programmatic intent of this definition, it is consonant with later definitions of the term. In a similar vein, one scholar has written, "In the grotesque, life passes through all degrees, from the lowest, inert and primitive, to the highest, most mobile and spiritualized, bearing witness in this garland of various forms to its oneness. Bringing together what is distant, combining elements which mutually exclude each other, disrupting all habitual conceptions, the grotesque in art is related to the paradox in logic. At first glance, the grotesque is merely witty and amusing, but it contains great potentialities" (Pinskii, 119-20; see also Bakhtin [1968] 1984a, 32 and Bakhtin [1965] 1986, 39).

Yet, in order to adequately understand how the carnival-grotesque operates in *A Puppet Show*, special reference to Mikhail Bakhtin's conception of the term becomes necessary since in *A Puppet Show*, the grotesque became an organizing principle. First, we should note, as we did in relation to the poem "A Puppet Show," that *A Puppet Show* exhibits the three characteristics that Mikhail Bakhtin has described as common to all carnivalized serio-comical genres. First, the play's relation to the reality that surrounds it is immediately apparent. *A Puppet Show*, in fact, is almost topical. The apocalyptic overtones of the mystics' discussions invoke Mæterlinck's dramas, and the Author's implicit criticism of Symbolism echoes discussions of the movement in the world outside the theater. Secondly, *A Puppet Show* emphasizes experience at the expense of all official, unitary languages as will become apparent later. The debunking of the mystics, in fact, borders on what Bakhtin aptly calls "cynical exposé." And finally, *A Puppet Show* demonstrates a rejection of stylistic unity, in the sense of the unity of a single unitary language. Blok's mixing of poetic and prosaic speech is typical of the stylistic diversity found in carnivalized works (Bakhtin 1984b, 108).

In order to understand how the carnival-grotesque precipitates out of the serio-comical, it is essential that neither the destructive nor the productive aspect of the carnival-grotesque should fall outside the purview of critical inquiry. (See in this regard Bakhtin 1984a, 45). In its destructive aspect, carnival overturns all social convention. As Bakhtin puts it, "(W)hat is suspended first of all is hierarchical structure and all the forms of terror, reverence, piety, and etiquette connected with it" (Bakhtin 1984b, 123). And in its productive aspect — and by means of this destruction — "a new mode of interrelationship between individuals" arises (Bakhtin 1984b, 123). Blok speaks metaphorically of this in his famous letter to Meyerhold about *A Puppet Show*: "In the embraces of the fool and the puppet show the old world will grow prettier, will become young ... " (8: 169-70).

Commentators, including Blok's contemporaries, have generally recognized the destructive, satirical aspect of *A Puppet Show*. (See Belyi, 67 and Bazarov, 72). They concentrate, however, on the satire to the exclusion of all else. (This tendency mars even the fine work of Zelentsova). Only a handful of commentators have seen anything positive in the play at all. (See, however, Chulkov 1907, 53). Yet only by understanding the positive aspect of the carnival-grotesque can we ascertain why Blok turned to the masks of the *commedia dell'arte*. First and foremost, the masks suited Blok's desire to redefine himself and his position in the world. As Blok wrote to Andrei Belyi, "In the face of present conditions, when everything is confused everywhere, my biggest wish is to be myself" (8: 167). The masks afforded Blok the opportunity for redefinition.[6] By simultaneously combining irreconcilable opposites within themselves, they undermine the normally unambiguous and inflexible quality of the tragic hero and effect "a new mode of interrelationship". As Bakhtin has argued, "Outside his destiny, the epic and tragic hero is nothing; he is, therefore, a function of the plot fate assigns him" (Bakhtin 1981b, 36). Bakhtin continues, "On the contrary, popular masks — Maccus, Pulcinello, Harlequin — are able to assume any destiny and can figure into any situation..., but they cannot exhaust their possibilities by those situations alone" (Bakhtin 1981b, 36). He concludes, "Therefore these masks can function and speak independent of the plot" (Bakhtin 1981b, 36). What is most important about such popular masks is their "noncoincidence with themselves, and with any given situation — the surplus, the inexhaustibility of their self" (Bakhtin 1981b, 36). The masks become the means by which this potential becomes manifest. The unified personality, as rendered in the realist drama, has no place in *A Puppet Show*.

It is precisely because the masks offer the potential for constant redefinition that Blok turned to the *commedia dell'arte*. His decision to incorporate the *commedia dell'arte* figures into the play was not arbitrary, but carefully considered. As Medvedev has demonstrated, Pierrot and Columbine were originally called Somebody and Fiancée (Medvedev, 18-19). Blok's decision to use masks in *A Puppet Show* takes on then an almost paradigmatic importance. As Bakhtin has suggested, "The mask is connected with the joy of change and reincarnation, with gay relativity and with the merry negation of uniformity and similarity; it rejects conformity to oneself" (Bakhtin 1984a, 39-40). The one who wears the mask is both himself and not himself.

Blok, however, achieves such "noncoincidence" through means different than those of the *commedia dell'arte* itself. Whereas in the *commedia dell'arte*, a mask remains noncoincident with itself by assuming a variety of roles in scenario after scenario, in *A Puppet Show* masks become noncoincident with themselves through Blok's consistent characterization of them through negatives, through what they are not. Rather than describe what is, Blok exploits negative constructions that show absence or lack to underline what is not. For example, Blok uses negative particles, prefixes, and prepositions to describe most of Pierrot's actions. Pierrot is described as "moustache<u>less</u>" and "eyebrow<u>less</u>" in the stage directions. The other

[6] Konstantin Rudnitskii makes an analogous point in regard to Meyerhold's production of the play: "At the very dawn of the history of theater of the twentieth century, Blok and Meyerhold introduced the images of Harlequin, Pierrot, and Columbine into a new theatrical system by linking Symbolist drama with the more vital tradition of improvised performances of the public square" (Rudnitskii 1978, 172-3).

dramatis personae are characterized similarly. Columbine, at least for Pierrot, turns out to be "faithless ". When Harlequin runs off with Columbine, the mystics "all hang lifelessly on their chairs" Their sleeves cover the bones of their hands "as if there were no hands". Even the speech of the Author brims with negatives. When he first steps out on stage, he tells the audience, "I wrote my drama not for a puppet booth". During his second speech he insists, "I never decked my heroes out in jester's clothing". He complains that everything that has gone on up to this point has happened "without my knowledge". All told, negative particles, prefixes, and prepositions recur no fewer than thirty-five times in the course of twelve pages. Positive description is almost entirely absent.

The use of negatives is not restricted, however, to negative prefixes, particles, and prepositions. It extends into semantics, which has a telling effect on characterization. Here, the conventions of the *commedia dell'arte* abet Blok's negative, open-ended, potential characterizations. Blok's semantic choices underscore precisely those elements in the *commedia dell'arte* that further the principle of noncoincidence. For instance, Pierrot and Columbine are described as "pale". Within the tradition of the *commedia dell'arte*, the word "pale" suggests the white makeup worn by the players. This makeup serves to cover or diminish any particular characteristics the players may have. What result, then, are concrete manifestations of general types, whose coherence does not stem from the particular and unique characteristics that serve as the basis of realist characterization.

In this sense, the few, negative characteristics Pierrot has are not his alone; he is "like all Pierrots". Other words used to describe Pierrot also point to the negative, to what he does not have. The Chairman refers to Pierrot as "our poor friend", suggesting that Pierrot is lacking in some way. In particular he casts aspersion on Pierrot's mental faculties, suggesting to him at one point, "You have lost your mind". Others join the Chairman's chorus, and Pierrot is described variously by both himself and others as a "simpleton", a "blockhead", and an "unhappy madman". By the end of the play, the best that Pierrot can say for himself is that he is a "poor thing".

Similar semantic implications apply to the other characters. Columbine is described as pale or white. One of the mystics comments, "Her features are pale, like marble." And regardless of whether she Columbine or Death, her clothes are white: As Columbine, "she is in white," and as Death, she is "in long white shrouds." The color white, however, is not the only one of Columbine's attributes that suggest a lack. Such emphasis at the semantic level on what she lacks necessarily affects the overall characterization of Columbine. She is never what others expect her to be. When she first appears, the mystics expect Death, but she is simply a girl. When she runs off with Harlequin, she ceases to be even a girl, turning into a "cardboard girlfriend." And in her final incarnation, she appears in the stage directions as "Death." However, before she can utter a word, she once again becomes Columbine in the morning mist. We will return to Columbine's various incarnations, but for now let us merely note the consistency of her unresolved malleableness, the emphasis on the negative from the lexical level to the descriptive to the symbolic.

The use of negatives also has significant ramifications for the characterization of Harlequin. Ostensibly, he is Pierrot's enemy, a rival for

Columbine's hand. And in fact, he does turn out to be a rival, but only to a point. After he has stolen Columbine away from Pierrot and she turns to cardboard, no animosity arises between Pierrot and Harlequin. Instead, the two of them dance over her cardboard figure. Pierrot even goes so far as to say that Harlequin did not offend Columbine in any way. Harlequin, in his turn, calls Pierrot his brother. While the durability of this friendship may be in question, the fact of its existence, no matter for how short a time, is not. At once Harlequin and Pierrot are both friends and enemies. Such ambivalence pervades Harlequin's demise, which is also characterized by negatives. In his last speech, Harlequin speaks of going forth to greet the world. However, when he jumps through the window, the distance he expects to jump into turns out to be mere stage design. Something more ominous opens up before him: "Harlequin flew head over heels into emptiness." Nothingness, emptiness lies behind the set. Not coincidentally, Death, a metaphorical negation, appears precisely when Harlequin jumps into this emptiness.

All the negatives Blok employs serve to destabilize meaning and to underscore underlying ambivalence. The voice of the mask sounds notes that are seemingly alien to it. (See in this regard Kristeva's comments about the carnival word in the novel. Kristeva, 165). By this means, Blok sought to break out of monologism. Since Harlequin is as likely to be Pierrot's friend as his rival, he is, in Bakhtin's terminology, noncoincident with himself. Where a tragic hero would be static, represented as either a friend or a rival or one of these changing into the other *over time*, Harlequin is *at once* both and neither. At any given moment in time, he encompasses the potential to be either one, but his character is not exhausted by this potential. He contains within himself any number of other contradictory dualities: He is both tragic and comic, both happy and despairing. As Meyerhold put it, Harlequin is both an "imbecilic simpleton" and a "powerful magician, wizard, and sorcerer" (Meierkhol'd 1968a, 1: 218). He continues, "The mask is capable of hiding beneath itself not just two such contrasting images. The two faces of Harlequin are two poles. Between them there is an infinitely large quantity of different variants, nuances" (Meierkhol'd 1968a, 1: 218). Nor is attention to the voice of the other limited to Harlequin. No single quality defines Pierrot, for instance. He is as likely to cry over Columbine as to laugh at her cardboard demise, as likely to be convinced that Columbine is his finacée as to doubt it. Sophie Bonneau, in fact, sees in Harlequin and Pierrot not only simultaneously contradictory polarities, but also "... two parallel chains, one the inferior faces and the other of the superior faces of the Double, which compose what has been called the Multiple in Blok" (Bonneau, 91). With the double comes new potential. The image of the mask affords the poet great freedom. Through it he can express "the very process of the development of a given quality or condition" (Zarovnaia, 134). And since the lyrical drama deals with development and not stasis, it "contains within itself ... the possibility of a new knowing, a new appraisal, a new understanding and interpretation of it" (Zarovnaia, 135).

IV

Doubles and Masks

A corollary to the theorem of Pierrot and Harlequin as doubles suggests that they "contain in themselves contrary principles" (Zarovnaia, 135). In other words, the doubles contain contrary principles not only within themselves, but also in relation to one another. Critics have generally recognized the presence of doubles in *A Puppet Show*, and the conception of Harlequin and Pierrot as doubles has long been a basic tenet of the scholarship on the play. The critics took their cue in this from Blok who stated quite explicitly in the drafts: "1. In Pierrot's story — doubles (Pierrot and Harlequin)" (Medvedev, 20). In their search for predecessors, traditionally critics have pointed to the influence of Tieck, Hoffmann, and to Romanticism generally. In addition, Zinaida Mints's study of Dostoevskii and Blok suggests that the novelist's influence was of seminal importance throughout this period in Blok's development (Mints 1971, 217-47 passim).

This importance of doubles is sometimes obscured by critics who emphasize the importance of Blok's biography in explicating the play. They see a biographical love triangle, not a literary double. The issue is further clouded by critics like Gromov, who focus so narrowly on particular borrowings that they miss the forest for the trees. Gromov, for example, argues, "... (T)he basic situation of *A Puppet Show* in many respects resembles the dramatic knot of relations of the main heroes of *The Idiot*, the coupling of the fates of Rogozhin, Myshkin, and Natas'ia Filippovna" (Gromov, 459-60). Without a doubt the comparison is justified. Gromov, however, fails to complete the comparison. Just as the theme of the love triangle is structurally subordinate to the theme of the double in Dostoevsky, so too is it subordinate in *A Puppet Show*. Despite such missteps, critics generally recognize that Blok's use of the double, both as a theme and more importantly as a technique, is widespread and intricate. (For the development of the doubles through the drafts, see Medvedev, 21-2). However, that recognition has not penetrated into the analyses of how doubles and doubling function in *A Puppet Show*. Doubles inform almost every aspect of the play. Besides the obvious example of Pierrot and Harlequin, nearly every character in *A Puppet Show* is pursued by a double, a characteristic of the play that is apparent already in the drafts (Medvedev, 20). Pierrot meets his double not just in Harlequin, but in each of the three men who come forward with their love interests during the ball. In their turn each of these three men has a double. It is the woman in the first couple who first draws our attention to this: "... Someone dark is standing by the column..." (4: 16). Later, the man in the second couple talks explicitly about his "black double," and as he and his lady exit, they are in fact followed by this double (4: 17). The Fool serves as a double for the knight in the last couple, and as one critic has put it, "The duality of the knight-Fool is subtly underlined by Blok" (Volkov, 32-3). And just as Pierrot is doubled by the men, Columbine is doubled by each of the three women. Among the other characters, we can also point to the doubling of the Author and the Chairman of the Mystics, who echo each other in their own overblown, self-assured rhetoric.

This technique of doubling, however, is not just limited to individual characters. The three pairs of lovers, for instance, are perhaps better understood as doubles for the pair of Pierrot and Columbine. Blok implies as much by listing the three couples as couples and not individuals in the dramatis personae. Moreover, if we include each man's double, each couple becomes a triplet that doubles the threesome of Columbine, Pierrot, and Harlequin. The implications of such doubling have generally been understood as thematic. For instance, Mochulsky's interpretation of the couples as three variations on the theme of love clarifies the thematic ties between the ball and the early part of the play, but does not elucidate their structural relationship. The two appear to be merely contiguous. A proper understanding of doubling as a technique, however, reveals more than just the recapitulation of a theme. Blok reintroduces the structural elements that carry the theme.

The importance of the double consists in its capacity to undermine its referrent. The single most important structural manifestation of the double in *A Puppet Show* is the fool, an image which is surprisingly intricate, given the confines of such a short play. The structural significance of the fool is as a "dialogic category" (Bakhtin 1981a, 405). In general the fool can assume three guises: that of the fool proper, the simpleton who fails to understand what is said to him; that of the rogue, who engages in what Bakhtin terms "gay deception", a lie directed at liars and the official lie; and finally, that of the clown, who is something of a hybrid, combining the fool's lack of understanding and the rogue's "gay deception" into a malicious distortion of the official language (Bakhtin 1981a, 400-10 passim). In *A Puppet Show* all three — the fool, the rogue, and the clown — play a critical role.

Blok utilizes the image of the fool in both Pierrot and the Author, although the nature of their individual failure to understand is radically different. Pierrot is unable to comprehend the dark and foreboding language of the mystics. Where they await the incarnation of death in a woman's figure, Pierrot is waiting for his fiancée. In fact, when the Chairman accuses him of having lost his mind, of not being able to understand the full significance of what is transpiring, Pierrot replies matter-of-factly, "I am a simple person" (4: 13). His failure to understand calls the mystics' language into question; that is, the reader would accept their language as authoritative, were not doubt cast upon it by Pierrot's polemical failure to understand a language that is ostensibly self-evident. It is this undermining of the mystics' language that separates Blok from other Symbolist playwrights, including Maeterlinck, for instance.

The Author outdoes Pierrot by failing to understand not only the mystics, but everyone else as well. What separates the two is that Pierrot's remarks are directed to other characters, such as the mystics, whereas the Author's remarks both are and are not. The Author's is a failure to understand the play which is going on before his very eyes. He attempts to apply standards to it that are not applicable. "I wrote a most realistic play," he cries (4: 14). His remarks, then, are aimed not at the other characters, but rather at a larger question that exists outside the narrow limits of the stage: What should a play be like? The Author implicitly addresses the writer of *A Puppet Show* as a representative of a literary movement, which the Author fails — and again, polemically — to understand. In this sense, "The Author is Blok's double" (Frolov, 138).

In contrast to the image of the fool, the image of the rogue plays, at first glance anyway, a small part. The only rogue in the play is a character, who is identified as a Fool. The Fool proves to be no fool at all and understands all too well the world around him. He operates, in fact, at two levels in the play. First, he makes fun of the last couple in the ball and their stilted romantic vocabulary by sticking his tongue out at them. In his malice the Fool betrays his kinship with the mask of the Fool. However, what happens next demonstrates that the Fool is a rogue and not a Fool. Hit in the head by the man's wooden sword, he leans over the footlights and hangs down. A stream of cranberry juice spurts out of his head, and he piercingly shouts, "I'm bleeding cranberry juice!" (4: 19). His cry partakes of the rogue's "gay deception" more than it does of the Fool's "malicious distortions." He happily pretends to be hurt, only to call theatrical convention into question by so doing.

More important than the image of the rogue in *A Puppet Show* is the image of the Clown. And the most important clown is not the Fool, but Harlequin. Harlequin maliciously distorts the language of romantic love by leading Columbine away from Pierrot. After befriending Pierrot, he mocks the language of friendship, calling Pierrot a blockhead. His final soliloquy, in which he hails the world, parodies the mystics' speeches, in which they hail death. Perhaps most importantly, Harlequin's appearance as coryphaeus mocks the Greek tradition of the chorus, in which the coryphaeus is a respected leader in the community. In each of these cases, Harlequin distorts the clichés of an official language, turning it into something other than what its speaker intended.

The ability of the clown to distort official language, of the rogue to lie to those who espouse the official lie, and of the fool to call the official language into question by not understanding it has deep structural implications. Because they call all official, unitary languages into question, they expand the usual monologic limits of discourse in drama. But the images of the fool, the rogue, and the clown, are not exhausted by what they are as characters. Blok employs a second and entirely different level of the fool image in *A Puppet Show*. The playwright himself dons the mask of the clown, who first fails to understand prevailing norms and conventions and then distorts them beyond recognition. We have already noted that the Author directs his discourse toward the playwright. The entirety of the play in a sense represents the discourse the playwright directs at the Author, who serves as a representative of the official theater. The playwright refuses to understand the Author's realistic expectations, fails to take for real the illusion of reality that is ordinarily the aim of realistic theater.

In this regard, a few words about the play's structure, viewed as part of the playwright's discourse, are in order. Commentators point out that *A Puppet Show* is anti-dramatic in a number of ways. (On Symbolist theater as anti-theater, see Balakian, 131.) In contrast to the traditional and most conventional meaning of the term dramatic, the most important action of the play, Columbine's transformation into cardboard and Pierrot and Harlequin's subsequent carousing, occurs off stage. We do not learn about it until Pierrot's second soliloquy, at which point Pierrot relates the whole sequence of events. One critic remarks, "Instead of developing relationships in struggle and dynamics, Blok prefers to give them in the guise of a story" (Volkov, 30). Blok actually puts this second soliloquy to a different purpose than that which a soliloquy usually serves. A soliloquy is ordinarily lyric and contemplative in nature. In it, the character mulls over some question of great importance. Such is the nature of Pierrot's first soliloquy, which is a complaint of love. The second, though it has lyric overtones, serves a narrative function in the play. One commentator, in fact, describes Pierrot's speech as a monologue, "... which has been stripped of striking dramatic emotions" (Rodina, 140).

The second way in which the play is anti-dramatic lies in its tendency to break down conventional dramatic forms. As Volkov puts it, "Blok took a traditional scenario [the love triangle — TW] for the sole purpose of consciously distorting and deforming it. The device of deformation is that device which gave Blok the possibility of creating a subtly orchestrated play from a simple situation — 'two are bothered by a third'" (Volkov, 27). Andrei Fedorov's comments about theatricality in *A Puppet Show* bear particular importance here. Fedorov sets *A Puppet Show* in the context of the European dramaturgy contemporary to Blok and argues that an undercurrent of anti-theatricality ties these plays together. According to Fedorov, *A Puppet Show* is more extreme in its anti-theatricality than its western counterparts. In this respect, "*A Puppet Show* is the most ironic play of both Russian and western European Symbolism" (Fedorov, 50). Blok had numerous predecessors in anti-theatricality and theatrical illusion, among them Fedorov cites Koz'ma Prutkov and Ludwig Tieck. To these we should add Vladimir Solov'ev's *The White Lily* , which heavily influenced *A Puppet Show* (Westphalen 1992, 435-51 passim). One of the more important instances of such anti-theatricality is, according to Fedorov, Blok's use of authorial remarks. Blok is innovative in broadening the function of the authorial remark. In this way, the play's structure, and hence the playwright's discourse, should be understood to be polemical in nature. The playwright, in this sense, is a clown.

The ability of the images of the fool, the rogue, and the clown to destabilize meaning and to renew old themes explains, in large measure, why the *commedia dell'arte* was so attractive to Blok. Although these images also exist outside of the dramatic tradition, Blok sought a specifically theatrical form that contained within itself these images. The *commedia dell'arte*, as Bakhtin has suggested, remained closely tied to the carnivalesque. Bakhtin, for instance, writes, "(T)he contents of the carnival-grotesque element, its artistic, heuristic, and unifying forces were preserved in all essential manifestations during the seventeenth and eighteenth centuries: in the *commedia dell'arte* (which kept a close link with its carnival origin), ..." (Bakhtin [1968] 1984a, 34). Precisely because it is a highly carnivalized dramatic form, the *commedia dell'arte* provided Blok with many of the requisite techniques for overcoming the monologic parameters of his art.

V

The Carnival Queen

The *commedia dell'arte* by itself, however, cannot explain the breakdown of these parameters and constitutes only one element of the carnival-grotesque in *A Puppet Show*. As in any other carnivalized work of literature, the positive aspect of the carnival-grotesque manifests itself in *A Puppet Show* most significantly through a number of carnival acts. The most important of these is "the mock crowning and subsequent decrowning of the carnival king" (Bakhtin 1984b, 124). In *A Puppet Show* carnivalization, in part, is enacted through the ritualistic crowning and decrowning of Columbine. A female figure in the role of carnival king may be surprising at first glance, but is not uncommon. (See Bakhtin's comments about Mar'ia Aleksandrovna Moskaleva in Dostoevsky's "Uncle's Dream," Bakhtin 1984b, 162.) Such a contention, though, flies in the face of existing *A Puppet Show* scholarship, which practically disregards Columbine. A closer look, however, reveals that she is the central figure in the play and that she exhibits the requisite characteristics of a carnival king.

Structural considerations make Columbine's central position apparent. The tendency for important actions to occur offstage, coupled with the narrative function of some of the monologues mentioned above, suggests a structure that is at odds with the structural model usually set forth by critics. Ordinarily, critics maintain that *A Puppet Show* falls into two scenes: The mystics' scene and the ball. Critics base this model on the fact that the only time the curtain falls is between these two "scenes" and at the end of the play. In its essentials, this model is not wrong, but rather oversimplified. Underneath this schema a more highly symmetrical structure unfolds.

A Puppet Show is composed of three scenes, a contention that is confirmed by the first draft which was divided into three acts (Medvedev, especially p. 21). Volkov understood the play's structure in similar terms: "*A Puppet Show* ... consists of two scenes and Pierrot's monologue, which links them" (Volkov, 27). Each of the three scenes contains within itself two parts that flow into each other. (See also Zarovnaia, 142 and Gromov, 437). The first scene traditionally has been identified as the mystics' scene, which is something of a misnomer, since the first scene is not limited to the mystics and includes a second section, in which the main players are Pierrot, Columbine, and Harlequin. The only one of the mystics who figures into this second section at all is the Chairman, who plays a bit part. An obvious objection to such an interpretation is that the mystics are still on stage during this second part. However, the mystics do not interact with Columbine and Harlequin, nor do these two interact with the mystics. We need not insist on a strict separation of the two sections of the first scene, only on their polarization: In the first, the mystics hold sway, while the figures associated with the *commedia dell'arte* dominate the second.

The last scene shows a similar polarization. It opens with a procession of couples and ends with Harlequin jumping out the window and with the failed reunion of Pierrot and Columbine. Again, as in the first scene, the boundaries between the two parts overlap, and we can speak only of the first part being predominantly a ball and the second predominantly an arena for Harlequin, Pierrot, and Columine.

Of course, both of these scenes, and all of their parts, are subject to the Author's interruptions. His biggest interruption, however, opens the middle scene. The curtain has fallen, and he comes out to deny any responsibility for the play. He is yanked off stage, and the curtain opens again. Pierrot's entrance marks the second part of the middle scene. In his soliloquy, as mentioned before, he informs the audience of all the action that has gone on offstage. His narration describes offstage events that are as important as anything that happens on stage.

Such an interpretation puts the offstage events at center stage. Columbine's transformation into cardboard thus becomes the hinge on which the play swings. Such a view is at odds with most of the criticism on the play, which sees Pierrot as the central character. We should keep in mind, however, that Blok lists Columbine, not Pierrot, first in the dramatis personæ. Only Zarovnaia and Rodina adhere to the former point of view, relegating Pierrot to a subordinate position. According to Zarovnaia, Columbine "fullfills the role of the compositional center of the play" (Zarovnaia, 142). Though less precise about the structural implications of this observation, Rodina comes to the same conclusion: "In the triangle of Pierrot-Columbine-Harlequin, the image of Columbine is the apex" (Rodina, 138). By insisting on the centrality of the image of Columbine, Zarovnaia made a major contribution to the scholarship on the play.

Once Columbine's structural importance is understood, her carnival crowning and uncrowning become readily apparent. As the play opens, the mystics await and then meet her with all the solemnity and awe royalty deserves. On the other hand, Pierrot, as a fool, is important here for his inability to understand the gravity of the situation, which undercuts the mystics' attempt at seriousness. The coronation is further debased by the fact that her royal sceptre is perhaps a scythe, or maybe only a braid. This pun on the word "kosa" adds to the frivolousness of the coronation and holds within itself the seeds of her subsequent decrowning. As a symbol of authority, the scythe, like all carnival sceptres, "become(s) ambivalent and acquire(s) a veneer of joyful relativity" (Bakhtin 1984b, 124).

The act of decrowning brings this debasement to fruition. Bakhtin describes decrowning in the following manner: "The ceremonial of the ritual of decrowning is counterposed to the ritual of crowning: regal vestments are stripped off the decrowned king, his crown is removed, the other symbols of authority are taken away, he is ridiculed and beaten" (Bakhtin 1984b, 125). In *A Puppet Show* the decrowning takes place offstage. Pierrot, in his second soliloquy, relates how Columbine turned to cardboard. His description of his own reaction is especially telling: "I could not restrain my laughter" (4: 15). In view of the carnival-grotesque nature of *A Puppet Show*, Pierrot's utterance takes on a paradigmatic significance. He goes on to tell how he and Harlequin then danced over her prostrate figure. The ridicule they heap on Columbine is part of the ritualistic decrowning.

This, however, is not the end of crowning/decrowning ritual in *A Puppet Show*. Blok weaves in a variant of the ritual, resurrecting Columbine one more time before the end of the play. She arises seemingly in full regalia: She is Death. But no sooner is she identified as Death than she ceases to be Death. As Pierrot approaches her, she once again becomes Columbine. This metamorphosis is signalled in the stage directions: "The silver scythe [kosa] disappears in the drifting morning mist." With the carnival sceptre gone, Columbine's reign as carnival queen ends. Where her arrival had been the focal point of the proceedings, Columbine is now again debased. The former queen becomes just another player in the Author's banal love story. The very ease with which she moves between these two polarities emphasizes the duality of her nature in particular and the duality of the carnival king in general. In the end, however, even the small consolation of a happy love story is denied her as the scenery flies up, and the artifice of the play itself is upended. It is from such considerations as this that one critic argues,

"Blok's theater is oriented futurologically toward the spectator of the future or toward that intellectual elite which, in the author's assumption, ought to understand not only the sense of what is going on on the stage in *A Puppet Show*, but also the meaning of theatrical art..." (Chałacińska-Wiertelak, 56). At this moment, Columbine's identity, as well as the identities of all the other characters, are overturned and are revealed to be artificial creations. In the act of Columbine's final decrowning, the illusion of the play as a play is unmasked. *The Puppet Show* moves beyond the mere enactment of the carnival ritual to become a meditation upon the very mutability of the ritual itself. Thus, the play offers not so much ritual, as meta-ritual.

In this way, the carnival-grotesque systematically dismantles all single, unitary languages within the play, including that of the playwright. Viewed against the background of realist or neo-classical drama, such dismantling would be a detriment since, as Bakhtin acutely observed, "any weakening of the monolithic quality leads to a weakening of dramatic effect" (Bakhtin 1984b, 17). However, Blok sought to break with the realist tradition and consciously eschewed dramatic effect by allowing no single voice to predominate. (The playwright's polemical relation to the Author is telling in this regard.) What resulted, within the confines of this one-act play, was a polyphonic drama, that is, a drama whose chief characteristic is a "plurality of independent and unmerged voices and consciousnesses" (Bakhtin 1984b, 6). In its polyphony, *A Puppet Show* stands as perhaps the seminal work of Blok's second period, in stark contrast to the monologic parameters of the poetry of his first period. To a significant extent, *A Puppet Show* represents a renaissance in creative method.

CHAPTER TWO

STASIS AND REVOLUTION: *THE KING ON THE SQUARE*

I

Genesis and Reception

Where *A Puppet Show* exhibits a subtle mastery of dramaturgy and stagecraft and marks the period 1906-7 as seminal in Blok's career, *The King on the Square* represents an achievement of a different order, fraught with creative tension, pregnant with unrealized potential.[1] Blok set to work on his second play within months of finishing his first, and it was done by the end of the summer of 1906. At its best, the finished product presages the growing importance of social themes, particularly revolution, in Blok's work. At its worst, it suffers from a laxity in dramatic organization, as when, for instance, the main characters fail to appear until the second of the play's three acts. The forces of carnivalization and a concomitant tendency to undermine all single, unitary voices, forces which figure so prominently in *A Puppet Show*, do battle in *The King on the Square* with a monologic, official "dream." What results is not the victory of one or the other, but an unhappy and unresolved admixture of the two.

These problems are already palpable in the manuscripts of the drafts, which eloquently bespeak the play's contradictoriness.[2] They reveal a great deal of tension, much of it reflected and only partially resolved in the printed text. In the course of the play's evolution, three different plans emerged. The printed play, which consists of a prologue and three acts, shares relatively little with the first plan, which contains seven basic scenes that are not as yet divided into acts. The remainder of Blok's work on the play turned out to be a series of radical revisions. In the second version, Blok deleted from the first plan entire scenes, such as a scene involving socialist conspirators (Medvedev, 30). In turn, enormous cuts took place between the second and third plans. Blok removed a conversation between two characters, the Poet and the Fool, that runs to twenty-nine manuscript pages. With minor revisions, this conversation became a separate and independent

[1] *The King on the Square* has been translated once into English. See Vogel 1987b.

[2] In respect to the manuscripts of the play, terminology assumes an importance greater than usual. Medvedev identifies three plans in the manuscripts, but only two drafts, the first plan consisting almost entirely of notes. In the following discussion of the drafts, I rely on Medvedev. (See Medvedev, 25-50 passim).

work, namely *A Dialogue about Love, Poetry and Government Service.* Only after such cuts and further revisions did the third version reveal the same three-act structure the printed version has. However, even with such drastic cuts and revisions this version was not definitive. In the printed version, "The division into three acts remained, but the make-up of each of them and the sequence of scenes turned out to be different" (Medvedev, 45). The definitive plan thus appears to have taken shape only in the final version.

Given the radical nature of Blok's revisions, his emotional response to the play is perhaps not surprising. Throughout the course of its development, *The King on the Square* elicited a certain ambivalence from Blok. Upon finishing the first full draft, he wrote to his friend Evgenii Ivanov, "After your departure I started to write a play, wrote it all in prose, rather a lot. While I was writing, I was happy and cheerful. When I read it aloud, everybody (and I in that number) saw that it is no good at all — just a sketch. ... [I] have to redo it and set it in verse" (8: 159). Further work, however, failed to assuage his discontent. Indeed, the whole course of Blok's work on the play reflects a great deal of doubt, which was entirely absent from his work on *A Puppet Show.* As he told Briusov a week after finishing the second draft, "I don't know how you would regard it. I myself am not entirely satisfied with it both from the formal and the internal sides. It's a three-act [play], and there are places little tied to the action. I still haven't mastered the technique" (8: 164). Later in the same letter, though, he turned around and vehemently defended the play: "Generally, I myself wanted what they reproach me for, and I did it not from want of skill" (8: 164). Years later, however, in the summer of 1916, he referred to it again as "very doubtful" (Blok 1965, 309-10).

Blok was not alone in his ambivalence. His doubts find an echo in the reactions of those close to him. His family categorically rejected the play. His mother, herself a professional translator, was generally supportive of her son's literary endeavors, but she did not shield her son from sometimes acute criticism. In the midst of helping Blok rewrite a clean copy of *The King on the Square* for the censor, she wrote to Evgenii Ivanov, "I am rewriting *The King* and am going into despair from the immaturity of this work and from the flimsiness of the third act" (Kotrelev and Timenchik, 3: 260). Blok's aunt echoed her sister. She noted her dislike of the play and did not mince words in describing how much she disliked it: "In my opinion, the drama is naive, uneven; the idea is crumpled; the end doesn't fit at all and is unmotivated; but the details are beautiful" (Beketova 1982, 3: 619).

Despite the family's cool reception, the play attracted admirers. Blok's friend Evgenii Ivanov reacted positively. In his diary, he noted, "[We] heard *The King on the Square* in its entirety. An enormous impression. According to its strength it is completely on a par with the works of musical drama. ... It is good, the King, the Poet, and the Architect's Daughter" (Ivanov, 412). The play created a great deal of excitement when Blok read it at the first of Vera Kommissarzhevskaia's literary "Saturdays".[3] Blok's aunt noted in her diary, "The youth are in ecstasy from it." She went on, "It was read at Komissarzhevskaia's club, and it produced a storm. The actors are delighted, the writers not only criticize [it], but hiss and fume" (Beketova 1982, 3: 619). Valentina Verigina, an

[3] The dates of these "Saturdays" are a matter of some dispute because some of the participants contradict one another in their memoirs. For a fuller treatment of this issue, see Westphalen 1991, 76, footnote 19 and Rudnitskii 1978, 143.

actress in Komissarzhevskaia's troupe, wrote, "I think that the delight I felt at the essential harmony between the poet, his appearance, voice, way of reading, and the poetry itself, was shared by all those who were present" (Verigina 1961, 311-12. See her similar appraisal in Verigina 1974, 89).

The response from publishers echoed Verigina's enthusiasm. Briusov, as editor of the journal *The Scales* [*Vesy*], wrote to Blok on October 13, "Have you earmarked it anywhere? Won't you give it to *The Scales*?" (Briusov and Blok, 1: 497). Nikolai Riabushinskii, the editor of the rival *Golden Fleece* [*Zolotoe runo*] had long been interested in Blok's work, and Blok told Briusov, "Riabushinskii has been asking for the drama for a long time already" (8: 164). Commenting on Blok's good fortune with the play, Avril Pyman exaggerates only slightly when she writes, "It was disputed by three publishers: Bryusov for *Vesy*, Sokolov for *Grif*, and Ryabushinsky for the new Symbolist journal *Zolotoye Runo* (also, at that time, edited by Bryusov), to which it finally went" (Pyman 1979, 1: 261).[4]

The *King on the Square*, like *A Puppet Show* before it, made a strong impression on Meyerhold. Blok told his mother, "I received a letter from Meyerhold yesterday. He writes that they have decided to stage *The King on the Square* this season" (Blok 1927-32, 1: 157-8). Pyman adds that both "Meyerhold and Kommissarzhevskaya wanted to stage it" (Pyman 1979, 1: 261). The play, however, never even went into production because, as Blok told his friend Aleksandr Gippius, "the theatrical censor prohibited my other play, *The King on the Square*" (8: 176). In fact, despite an abortive attempt by Komissarzhevskaia's brother, Fedor Komissarzhevskii, in 1918, *The King on the Square* never made it to the stage in Blok's lifetime. Meyerhold tried to mount a production again in 1923, but met with no success. (See Blok 1965, 420, 425, and Dolgopolov, 4: 574).

II

Ideologies

Had a production of the play materialized, it would likely have received the same stormy reception that *A Puppet Show* encountered. Like its predecessor, *The King on the Square* challenged existing theatrical norms. The setting, for instance, begins to break down the distance between the audience and the stage. The stage is dominated by a city square. In the background is the facade of a palace with a high and wide terrace. On a massive throne sits the gigantic King. At the very bottom, by the footlights, under the high parapet of an embankment is a bench, to which stairs lead from two sides. The bench is on the shore of the sea, which comes in in the shape of a narrow strip from afar, skirting the cape with the square and the palace from the left. It flows together with the orchestra and the theater in such a

---

[4] Pyman overstates Briusov's involvement in *The Golden Fleece*. As one commentator has observed, after the resignation of the editor Sergei Sokolov, "Briusov, while not formally accepting the title of literary editor, did offer more help to *Zolotoe runo*" (Richardson, 43).

way that it presents but an island, "a random sanctuary for the characters" (4: 23). As the prologue begins, the Fool paddles in from sea to the shore.

The prologue most clearly betrays the play's debt to such theatrical traditions as the *commedia dell'arte*. This debt was a conscious one, attested to by the transformations that the prologue underwent in the course of numerous drafts. Initially, one the main characters, the Architect, was to deliver the monologue. Already in the second plan, however, Blok wrote a new one with a Fool in mind. (See Medvedev, 27-9). The design of the new prologue, according to Rubtsov, "is taken from the traditional *commedia dell'arte*" (Rubtsov, 46). Blok's borrowings from the *commedia dell'arte* become apparent only gradually as the prologue unfolds. It begins as would a traditional prologue. In the first four stanzas, the Fool acquaints the spectator with the central features of the setting and the action. For instance, he indirectly remarks on the coming dawn and the sea he has sailed to reach this shore. He points directly at the King on the throne. However, in his speech, in the way that he speaks, he draws attention to a more common feature of the *commedia dell'arte* prologue. As Allardyce Nicoll has suggested, the *commedia dell'arte* prologue is "almost always spoken by one of the comedians in character, with words not related to the drama which is to follow but rather designed amusingly to be an exhibition of Pantalone's, Graziano's or Franceschina's qualities" (Nicoll, 125). In his choice of words, the mockery that the Fool revels in shines through. Anyone who wants to rest may stroll in front of the palace, he tells the audience; however, he avows that the path is shown to neither dog nor democrat.

Despite such convergences with the *commedia dell'arte*, however, Blok fashioned the prologue after his own designs. As one critic has observed, Blok changed the design of the *commedia dell'arte* prologue “in a fundamental way” (Rubtsov, 46). Medvedev likewise argued that the Fool's prologue is "curious mainly for its untraditional character" (Medvedev, 31). However, Medvedev appears not to have had the *commedia dell'arte* prologue in mind. He noted that the prologue had changed in character from a device for introducing the play's main action and themes to a lyrical piece. Where a prologue ordinarily acquaints the spectator with the meaning or the general character of the play's action, the Fool's words go beyond this function, in Medvedev's opinion. He asserts that this break with tradition was not unconscious and developed very gradually: "From the rough drafts, it is apparent that he [Blok — TW] originally proposed to give a wholly traditional, canonized type of prologue" (Medvedev, 32). The uniqueness of Blok's conception shapes the last three stanzas of the prologue particularly. It is in these stanzas that the Fool systematically breaks down the artifice of the play. First, he draws attention to the prologue itself. Speaking of a public bench, the Fool says that "only by the rights conferred by the Prologue" does he sit on it. In so doing, he reminds the spectator that the prologue is an agreement of sorts between playwright, actor, and spectator. The Fool reinforces this awareness of artifice: "Before me — in the orchestra — is the sea." The very absurdity of such a proposition foists an acknowledgment of the artifice of the scenery on the spectator. It also endows his following remarks with double meaning: "If the sun rises shortly, I will see everything to the bottom." Whether he means the bottom of the sea or the artifice of the play remains open to question. Likewise, when in the last stanza he coyly remarks, "My duty was only to force you to look at the view," his words suggest two different ideas (4: 24). First, as is consistent with the function of the traditional prologue, the Fool has acquainted the spectator with the main features of the scenery and action. Secondly and perhaps most importantly, he has forced the spectator to gaze on the artifice of this view. With this inference the Fool undermines what follows and sets a precedent for every other word uttered in the play.

Time and again Blok acknowledges traditional formal values, but in a polemical manner that calls into question the very tradition from which they spring. For instance, *The King on the Square* observes only two of the three classical unities. The unity of time is observed as the action of the play does not exceed the requisite twenty-four hours: The first act takes place in the morning, the second in the middle of the day, and the third at night. Likewise, the unity of place is strictly observed since the city square serves as the setting for all three scenes. However, the most important unity, the unity of action, the only one of the three that Aristotle sponsors explicitly in the *Poetics*, finds no place in *The King on the Square*. Some of the characters seek to revive the King, some seek to maintain the status quo, and still others await ships which they believe will bring deliverance. As a result of these unresolved oppositions, the action of the play is stratified, and this stratification allows for anomalies in the play's structure. For example, as mentioned above, all of the main characters are absent from Act One. Nor do any of the main characters exhibit a tragic flaw that might organize the action. And despite the cataclysmic finale, little is changed at the end. As the Architect observes, "Tomorrow the world as before will be green, and the sea will be just as calm" (4: 60). Thus, the formal unities fail to lead to catharsis.

Rather, the play becomes an arena for a clash of opposing ideologies. It is only a slight exaggeration to say that the play is a succession of arguments heard from different points of view. A synopsis of the play will serve to make this point. The first act opens with three characters, two visible and one hidden, who debate the nature of the malaise that afflicts the town. They reject as "madness" the popular belief in the imminent arrival of ships bearing the town's salvation. The greater danger they perceive emanates from two of the main characters, the Architect and his Daughter. The former represents a lesser danger because "the crowd is too petty to obey the will of a titan." But the Architect's Daughter is dangerous because she espouses a great dream, calling the crowd to religion, poetry, beauty. This too is dismissed as madness by the three discussants, and they disperse (4: 30-2). With these three broad ideological positions outlined, the rest of the first act consists of a series of encounters that highlight the social unrest in the town. The second of two workers remarks that a revolutionary visited the building site of a structure for meeting the ships and forbade them to continue building (4: 32). Next, a Girl tries to assuage a Youth's melancholy by reminding him of their love and of the ships that will bear them happiness. Their conversation, beautifully set in verse, is rudely interrupted by the Seller of Roses: "I will suffocate you with flowers," she says, "if you do not give me bread" (4: 33). The Girl gives the Seller of Roses money for some flowers, and then she and the Youth leave. Above them, the Second of two dandies suggests that the government could disperse the madness of the people "with energetic measures" (4: 34). Then the Girl and the Youth reappear; however, this time it is the Youth who tries to dispell the Girl's melancholy. Despite the Youth's efforts to console her, the Girl insists, "I no longer believe in my ships" (4: 35). Her disillusion ends the first act.

The second act begins with two conversations, the first between two workers, the second between two dandies. Again, the ships are dismissed as “nonsense”. As in the first act, the voice of a third, the Fool this time, underscores what is said. He complains that everyone has gone crazy, that he cannot hook anyone on common sense, but that he pins his hopes on "the very craziest," the Architect and the Poet, who make their first appearance at this juncture. The Architect upbraids the Poet for his moral weakness and tells him, "You are sick. Live more simply. You are a poet, a senseless melodious being...." Moreover, the Architect treats the Poet’s faith in the ships with disdain (4: 38-9). News that the scaffolding at the building site has collapsed and ten people have fallen into the sea interrupts their exchange. Red Rumors scatter in all directions, and Voices in the crowd cry out that the King is sick, that he has been taken into custody. From out of the crowd emerges the Architect's Daughter. She begins to talk with the Poet, and the Fool interjects that he has just hooked a big one. The Architect's Daughter inspires the Poet with her dream of reviving the King: Where the Poet spoke in prose with her father, he and the Architect's Daughter now speak in verse. As the Architect's Daughter disappears, contradictory opinions about the king and the ships erupt again. Then the Fool, barely able to control his laughter, tells the Poet that must decide where he stands. Two bird-like figures, one Black and the other Golden, appear from behind the Fool's back. The first asks the Poet to sing of freedom and the death of the king, and the second asks him to be faithful to the king. The Poet pledges for the king, and the Fool rejoices in his common sense. The act ends not with the Fool's rejoicing, however, but with the Poet’s confusion: "Everything is as in a dream" (4: 45-6).

The third act begins as night falls. Like the other acts, it begins with a conversation between two men about the ships (4: 48). A Beggarwoman interrupts it, asking for bread for her baby, and then the Fool makes his entrance. The First man, who has slumped to his knees, is found to be dead. The Fool, who identifies himself as a “spiritual doctor,” is recognized by the Second man: "I cannot remember where, — I have seen a lot in my time: In court, where you suggested death penalties to jurors; or in church, where you preached resignation; or ... yes! here, on the shore you demonstrated to people that they do not need freedom." Enraged by the Fool's duplicity, the crowd turns on him. Eventually he not only extricates himself, but makes the people submit. He promises to tend his "flock" with "an iron staff" (4: 50-1). The crowd leaves to greet the ships. In the now empty square, the Architect meets the Poet and tells him not to follow the crowd, but to sing of love. The Architect departs, and his Daughter appears. She declares herself "the poor daughter of the crowd" and leaves to carry out her duty (4: 53-6). The crowd then hears a false report of a sighting, and the Architect's Daughter begins her ascent to the King, for whom she will sacrifice her body and her youth (4: 57). A moment of peace descends on the square, and the Fool decides that emigration is the last sanctuary left to Common Sense. The cries of a dying baby break the peace, and the crowd rebels. The Golden one announces that the ships have arrived, but to no avail. The Black one bemoans their abandonment by Common Sense. The Poet, however, trumpets the arrival of the ships and ascends to meet the Architect's Daughter. The enraged crowd starts up the stairs after him. The terrace gives way under the weight, and the King, the Architect's Daughter, the Poet, and part of the crowd go down with it. In the aftermath, the Architect appears on top of the rubble and castigates the crowd for destroying the son, daughter, and creation he has bestowed upon them (4: 59-60).

Faced with such opaqueness, critics, especially orthodox Soviet critics, turned to the realia of Blok's life and Russian society as a means of elucidating *The King on the Square*. This interpretative strategy emphasizes three factors in Blok's development: the 1905 revolution, Blok's "crisis of solitary lyric consciousness," and his relationship to what is often derisively termed "Petersburg mysticism." Numerous objections present themselves. As one scholar has assessed the situation, "Our objections begin when these reliable premises are projected onto the concrete image-bearing structure of the play" (Lenchik, 206). For example, the argument that mysticism impairs the play proves unproductive. The modern critic, according to Lenchik, understands mysticism to denote something vague and confused. This, however, was not Blok's understanding of the term. Roman Jakobson more generally has defined such tendencies in criticism as "biographism, which takes a literary work for a reproduction of the situation from which it originated and infers an unknown situation from a work" (Jakobson 1987, 320). The first task of literary interpretation then is to articulate the literary nature of the work at hand.[5]

The recognition of this problem constitutes the first step toward properly orienting a fuller interpretation of *The King on the Square*. The most important of the literary processes at work in the play is carnival, a term first introduced by Lenchik in what remains the best single work on the play. The term may seem surprising at first glance, particularly given the serious tone of the play. However, upon careful examination, *The King on the Square* betrays the necessary prerequisites of all carnivalized works.

Like *A Puppet Show* before it, *The King on the Square* exhibits all three characteristics of the serio-comical, as mapped out by Bakhtin. The first characteristic of these genres is their direct relation to the present. Characters "... act and speak in a zone of familiar contact with the open-ended present" (Bakhtin 1984b, 108). In this respect, critics have been absolutely correct in emphasizing the importance of the 1905 Revolution for *The King on the Square*. Dolgopolov aptly argues that "... in contrast to *A Puppet Show*, the psychological and social subtext of *The King on the Square* is already tied not just with the themes of Blok's spiritual experiences, but also with contemporary events of real life" (Dolgopolov, 4: 558).

The second characteristic of serio-comical genres is that they "do not rely on *legend* and do not sanctify themselves through it, they *consciously* rely on *experience* (to be sure, as yet insufficiently mature) and on *free invention*; their relationship to legend is in most cases deeply critical, and at times even resembles a cynical exposé" (Bakhtin 1984b, 108). The failure of the legend of the King, of

[5] We should also note here that this emphasis on politics has often obscured how Blok characterized himself as a political being at the time. At the very end of 1905, Blok wrote to his father, "I will never become either a revolutionary or a 'builder of life,' and not because I do not see sense in the one or the other, but simply because of the nature, quality, and theme of my spiritual experiences" (8: 144). Since Blok neither renounces nor affirms political commitment in this statement but rather defends the integrity of his own development, this statement alone should caution against a narrowly political reading of his work.

course, is at the heart of *The King on the Square*. If it were not, the efforts of the Architect's Daughter to resuscitate the legend would be superfluous. As we shall see later, the legend of the King is intimately bound to the processes of carnival at work in the play. Moreover, the Architect's attitude toward the legend borders on cynicism. His concluding remarks, in which he tells the crowd that he sent his Daughter and the Poet to them, knowing full well that they must perish, bespeak a duplicitous use of power.

The play's style reflects the third characterisic of serio-comical genres, their "deliberate multi-styled and hetero-voiced nature" (Bakhtin 1984b, 108). "They reject the stylistic unity (or better, the single-styled nature) of the epic, the tragedy, high rhetoric, the lyric. Characteristic of these genres are a multi-toned narration, the mixing of high and low, serious and comic; ... in some of them we observe a mixing of prosaic and poetic speech ... " (Bakhtin 1984b, 108). One of the most striking qualities of *The King on the Square* in this regard is the way in which Blok mixes prose and poetry. The admixture of the two does not even preserve unity within the speech of individual characters. The Fool delivers the prologue in verse but speaks in prose the rest of the time. Likewise, the Poet speaks in verse only when addressing the Architect's Daughter. The rest of the time, as when he speaks with her father, he speaks in prose.

This question of the play's "multi-styled and hetero-voiced nature" assumes particular importance because it informs the larger question of ideology. Every character in the play is an ideologist in the sense that everyone has an opinion about the King. Lenchik also emphasizes this clash of ideologies: "The social polyphony of *The King on the Square*, the technique of direct projection of 'voices' of the street onto the artistic canvas anticipated the structure of the poem *The Twelve*" (Lenchik 1972, 217). In this, Lenchik follows Dolgopolov's commentary on Blok's "many-voicedness." Dolgopolov remarks that *The King on the Square*" is one of the first attempts in Blok's work to reproduce the polyphony of the street" (Dolgopolov, 4: 558). Some believe, some do not, but everyone expresses an opinion; and depending on the character's orientation, the expression may be high or low. The Architect's Daughter, for instance, speaks only in verse. The lofty ideal of her dream seems to allow no other mode of discourse. She tells her "fairy tale" to the Poet in a solemn tone:

> I know a great book on a radiant land,
> Where a beautiful maiden ascended
> To the bed of the tsar who was dying
> And breathed into his then decrepit heart youth!
> There over the blossoming land
> Rules the tall King!
> Youth has to him been returned!
>
> (4: 43)

So long as he speaks to the Architect's Daughter, the Poet matches her elevated verse. The symbolism of his imagery creates an atmosphere of mystery about the Architect's Daughter. "Above the sea you move, / And the shadow of the ships arises after you" (4:41). Even in the presence of the Architect, the Poet is capable of ecstatically proclaiming this dream of salvation, even if only in prose: "The ships will come!" (4: 38). Ostensibly, the Poet believes in his beloved's dream. However, the Poet wavers as he himself admits quite frankly to the Architect's Daughter. "I am weak when your father speaks," he tells her.

The Poet's faltering faith does not stem from weakness, as it would appear at first glance. Rather, it stems from the subordination of the ideology of the Architect's Daughter to another ideology, namely romantic love. The Poet's belief in the arrival of the ships or the resurrection of the King ultimately arises out of his love for the Architect's Daughter. His self-perception, in fact, hinges on this love. As he tells the Architect's Daughter in their first conversation, "Be with me! My wings grow!" (4: 41). Perhaps no one understands the Poet better than the Architect who in the last act tells the Poet to sing of his love. Nowhere, however, does the predomination of romantic love in the Poet's belief system become so clear as when he approaches the Architect's Daughter when she sits at the feet of the King. "I am coming to you!" he tells her. She contradicts him: "You are going to the Father!" On the last step, the Poet cries, "Hello, heaven!" The Architect's Daughter fails to understand his love and tells him, "Higher! Higher! Passing me, you are going to the Father" (4: 59). Having reached the Architect's Daughter, the Poet has attained his goal.

The other characters fail to understand the Poet's ideology of romantic and spiritual love and take it as sign of the Poet's malleable nature. In particular, the political ambiguity of the Poet's ideology makes him the object of other, more overtly political ideologists. In turn, the Architect, the Architect's Daughter, and the Fool, along with the latter's intermediaries, attempt to persuade the Poet of the truth in their respective positions. At stake is the Poet's talent, by means of which each of these ideologists hopes to sway the crowd. As the First person suggests at the beginning of the play, "At the hour of death the beautiful that was forgotten will come back to all" (4: 30). Potentially, the Poet could herald any of these three positions, whether it be the status quo, the resuscitation of the King, or Common Sense. The Poet's ultimate failure to herald any of them suggests that his ideology is independent and self-contained, even if imperfect politically. The other characters, however, understand the political shortcomings of the Poet's ideology as moral failure. The Architect implies as much when he says to the Poet, "I believe only those who distinguish good and evil" (4: 39). Although the Poet's beliefs need not be regarded as moral failure, the political shortcomings of his ideology have dangerous consequences. Because of his political naiveté, other characters attempt to coopt the Poet's ideology to their own ends. This extends even to the linguistic level. For instance, the Poet refers to the Architect's Daughter as "Heavenly Rose" at the end of the play (4: 59). Earlier, when telling the Poet not to heed rumors, the Architect encapsulates the Poet's appellation for his beloved in his own phrase for the destruction of the rumors and those who listen to them. "A heavenly thunderstorm" will descend, says the Architect. Although the words "rose" [roza] and "thunderstorm" [groza] differ in stress, the two phrases are identical typographically, except for the extra "g" in the Architect's term. The Poet, who should be acutely aware of language, remains strangely unaware of the coopting of his own language.

The Poet's ideological stance assumes a position of importance because he is not alone in his belief in romantic love. The Youth and the Girl also believe in it. As the Girl tells the Youth, "... (L)ook into my eyes. / Read the happiness of my meeting with you" (4: 32). And after the Seller of Roses has threatened to suffocate the Girl with flowers, the Youth tries to comfort her with their dream of love by saying, "We will forget the flowers. Look into my eyes" (4: 35). Like the Poet, the Girl and the Youth believe in the ships. The Girl, for instance, exclaims, "For joy! For joy! The seas are setting the tune! / I hear, far away the ships are coming!" (4: 33). As in the Poet's case they subordinate that belief to the ideology of romantic love. For them, love conquers all, even social discord.

Other characters speak in a banal, everyday language that becomes polemical in relation to both romantic love and the dream of the Architect's Daughter. For example, the Beggarwoman appears twice in the third act and asks the onlookers to give something so that her dying child can have bread. Her cry, "My child is dying!," points to the failure of both romantic love and the King to provide for even her child's most basic needs (4: 58). Other characters echo her. The threat by the Seller of Roses to suffocate the Girl, for example, expresses the same ideology, but in a more vulgar fashion (4: 33).

Still other characters move beyond such an implied polemic and openly espouse revolution. In the course of the conversation that opens the first act, the First man, overcoming the objections of his interlocutors, asserts, "All the same, everything will burn down" (4: 29). The King, according to him, will come down. "We will scatter (him) to the wind. We will throw (him) into the sea" (4: 29). Other characters weave variations on this theme. As the Fool tells the Poet after the latter's conversation with the Architect Daughter in the second act, "While you were having a talk, a whole political coup was prepared here" (4: 44). The Black one, the first of the two bird-like men who are trotted out by the Fool, illustrates the Fool's point. When asked by the Poet if he opposes the King, the Black one replies, "Death to him!" (4: 45). By the beginning of the third act, the revolutionary spirit is everywhere apparent. The First member of the crowd says, "All night they will burn and pillage" (4: 48). Perhaps the most eloquent of the revolutionaries, though, is the one in Black, who makes his second appearance just before the Architect's Daughter ascends to the King's throne. He says, "In your hands, insulted people, is vengeance against that one who looks indifferently on your destruction, that one there above my head!" (4: 56).

At the head of yet another camp stands the Fool, who parodies, though often in a muted way, the notion of romantic love, the dream of the Architect's Daughter, and the status quo. Some critics dispute this point. Fedorov, for instance, believes that the Fool does not function in his traditional role, but is reduced to the role of an ordinary sceptic. "His buffoonery is very conventional," he remarks (Fedorov 1972, 62). The speech of the Fool suggests otherwise, however. His speech tends to deflate the official line. A good example of this arises in the Fool's response to the Poet's espousal of love for the Architect's Daughter. The Poet says to the Architect's Daughter, "My heart is open only to you — / my soul is given over to its dark melodies" (4: 42). The Fool takes the air out this confession, saying, "Indeed, all this is too well known. No matter what she said, he would like it all because he is a love-stricken fool" (4: 42). He further deflates the official dream through his sideswipes at the government. When the Poet asks if the ships are near, the Fool replies, "What ships? Have you gone mad? Join the party!" (4: 44). The Fool, in fact, pokes fun at all official languages through his parodies of particular official languages. For instance, the Fool parodies biblical language, as when he tells the Poet, "I am a fisher of men" (4: 44). In the third act, the Fool, a self-appointed "spiritual doctor," gaily blasphemes,

"You need truth? Here's the truth! Throng together, people! Look at me from the roofs, hail me on the streets, bow down to the ground to me" (4: 50).

The Architect's speech, on the other hand, cynically subverts his Daughter's dream. He all but mocks her dream and her efforts to resurrect the King when he tells the Poet, "While the sea washes this shore, while the king rules the city, nothing will change, besides your wandering thoughts" (4: 37). Moreover, apparent contradictions plague his utterances. As one critic has noted, the second conversation between the Architect and the Poet differs from their first. In their first conversation, "the Architect emerges as a defender of the common people, but his position is reversed in his next encounter with the Poet" (Vogel 1987, 327). Particularly in the Architect's speech to the crowd at the end of the play, an almost Machiavellian duplicity emerges: "I sent you my beloved son, and you killed him. I sent you another consoler, my daughter. And you did not spare her" (4: 60). Knowing full well their folly, he nonetheless allowed them to be sacrificed for his purposes.

III

Masks, Subtexts, and the Carnival King on the Square

The various ideologies are in no way so self-contained as in the preceding exegesis. Because they are in competition, each battling with the others for supremacy, they constantly attempt to undermine each other. Perhaps the most important means of undermining any given ideology are the three images of the fool discussed above in relation to *A Puppet Show.* For instance, the deflating, parodic overtones of the Fool's speech mark him as a rogue. His speech embodies "a gay and intelligent deception, a *lie* justified because it is directed precisely to *liars*" (Bakhtin 1981a, 401). The Fool's role as a rogue, in fact, points to the importance of the various images of the fool in *The King on the Square*.

The image of the fool, with its mask of incomprehension, becomes manifest in both the Poet and the Architect's Daughter. Like the Poet in *Of Love, Poetry, and Government Service*, the Poet in *The King on the Square* betrays himself as a fool in what appears to be merely his moral spinelessness, in his vacillations between the party, the status quo, and the dream of the Architect's Daughter. Even at the end of Act Two, when he embraces the status quo, he fails to understand both the issues involved and the bird-like men who present them. The Black one, who supports the party, speaks harshly, mostly in imperatives: "It's time! Follow us! Sing us songs!" (4: 45). The Golden one, who represents the King and the status quo, conducts himself more gracefully and speaks politely. "I am happy to speak with you. One must not lose a minute. The crowd is in your hands" (4: 45). Flattered, the Poet follows the path of the Golden one. However, because he is flattered into joining, because he fails to understand, the Poet's support becomes, from the standpoint of the work as a whole, polemical.

The Architect's Daughter, too, dons the mask of the fool. Her failure to comprehend becomes even more apparent than the Poet's and manifests itself on two levels. First, she maintains that the resuscitation of the King will alleviate all evil. But the death and squalor that surround her are omnipresent: The Seller of Roses says, "I am dying from the hot sun, from dust, from fatigue, from hunger" (4: 33). A beggarwoman pleads, "Good people, help (us) for the sake of my child" (4: 49). People even die right on the stage. As noted above, the First of two men involved in a conversation suddenly expires at the beginning of Act Three (4: 49). And yet, the Architect's Daughter propounds her dream, her "fairytale," not acknowledging the people she plans to help. The dream itself thus becomes polemical. Secondly, by abandoning the Poet for the King, she turns the dream into a polemic with the notion of romantic love. In her failure to understand that she cannot love a statue, she mocks the language of romantic love.

The third image of the fool, the clown, also finds expression in *The King on the Square* in the character of the Architect. In many respects, the Architect is like the Fool. Both practice deception, justifying their lie on the grounds that they direct to liars. The Architect goes one step beyond the Fool, though, by masking his deception with a facade of incomprehension. Like his Daughter, he does not acknowledge the world around him, but outdoes his Daughter, who simply does not see the people. Her father, on the other hand, not only sees them but, at certain points, steps forth as their defender. He berates the Poet for endorsing the dream of the arrival of the ships, saying, "You castigate their families; you castigage their banality! But they are all better than you" (4: 38). Later in the same exchange, he continues, "They will labor, starve, and die side by side with you, and you will come to from your delirium only towards evening" (4: 39). His sympathy, however, masks condescension. Like an admonishing father, he tells the crowd at the end of the play, "You have smashed my creation, and there your house remains empty" (4: 60).

Dismissing the Architect as merely cynical would be possible, were a literary subtext not apparent, were the mode of his discourse not reminiscent of another literary figure. In the Architect's every utterance reverberates an echo of Dostoevsky's Grand Inquisitor. The similarities between Blok's play and Ivan Karamazov's poem, in fact, run the gamut from general likenesses in setting and character to very specific likenesses in terms and phraseology.

In the most general terms, *The King on the Square* mimics certain aspects of the setting of "The Grand Inquisitor," which takes place, as Ivan Karamazov himself notes, in sixteenth-century Seville. In this regard, it is significant that Blok did not situate *The King on the Square* in Russia. Instead, he chose an unspecified, generic Western European kingdom. The very choice of the King's title is telling: He is a king, not a tsar. The historical setting, like that of "The Grand Inquisitor," is medieval. The court system, even if in decay, remains apparent. Though the King and his Fool may be but remnants of a more vital system, the system itself has not disappeared entirely. However, like the Spanish crown during the Inquisition, the royalty of *The King on the Square* has weakened enough for real power to have been usurped. In both instances, it is a powerful old man who has taken control.

Striking similarities in ideology between the two old men emerge. For example, the Grand Inquisitor and the Architect both hold the mob in contempt. The vast majority of people are, in their eyes, weak and rebellious. The Grand Inquisitor refers to them as rebels. A similar attitude makes itself felt when the Architect admonishes the Poet for paying heed to rumors. Rumors, says the Architect, "are born in the dry and yellow dust, and they penetrate along with it into rebellious hearts" (4: 52). The Architect then enjoins the Poet, "Don't go after the crowd. Don't sing rebellious songs for it" (4: 53). Both the Grand Inquisitor and the Architect see themselves as part of an elite that is superior to the crowd and that, because of its superiority, holds dominion over the great mass of humanity. For the Grand Inquisitor, this superiority consists of the knowledge of good and evil, a burden from which the ruling elite frees the masses. The Architect suggests much the same thing. "I am alien to all of you," he tells the Poet in the third act. "I look through your heads and see clearly my blue path" (4: 52).

Where this proud elite is strong, the mob is weak and unable to grapple with the demands that freedom makes of them. The Poet's predicament is perhaps paradigmatic in this regard. Faced with the choice between the blind idolatry of the mob and the exalted faith of the Architect's Daughter, he suffers in his indecision. "I am weak when your father speaks," he admits to the Architect's Daughter (4: 41). The crowd's first concern is not spiritual freedom, but bread. This, of course, is one of the Grand Inquisitor's fiercest arguments. It is in these terms that he interprets the first temptation for Christ. The devil, in the Grand Inquisitor's paraphrase, points to some stones and says, "Turn them to loaves and humanity will run after you like a herd, grateful and obedient, though also eternally trembling that you will remove your hand and your loaves will cease" (Dostoevskii, 14: 230. I have aimed at a very literal translation here. For another translation, see Dostoevsky, 252). True to form, Blok's crowd at every turn expresses its concern about bread. In Act One the Seller of Roses threatens to suffocate the Girl if the latter does not give her bread. In Act Two the first comment about the collapse of the scaffolding and the presumed drowning of ten workers comes from another worker, who says, "A family without bread!" (4: 38). And in Act three the Beggarwoman appears seeking bread for her child.

Yet the connection between *The King on the Square* and *The Brothers Karamazov* would be relatively weak, were the parallels to remain at such a general level. However, a very specific paraphrase, almost a quotation, occurs at the very end of the play. With the King demolished, the crowd expresses its anxiety about where its bread will come from. "Who will feed us?" they ask the Architect (4: 60). Significantly, the verb they use [nakormit'] is the same verb used by the crowd in the Grand Inquisitor's prediction of the downfall of Christ and his temple. The Grand Inquisitor argues that humanity will say that there is no crime or sin, only the hungry masses. Turning against Christ, they will try to be free and will attempt to build another Tower of Babel. They will fail, however, according to the Grand Inquisitor. Then they will search out the Grand Inquisitor and his like, saying, "Feed us, for those who promised us fire from the heavens did not give it" (Dostoevskii, 14: 230-1; compare to Dostoevsky, 253).

Again, the occurrence of the verb "to feed" in utterances of crowds in both texts would be little more than intriguing if other similarities did not reinforce it. Other repetitions, in this case syntactical, arise in relation to this verb in utterances by the Architect and the Grand Inquisitor. In both texts, a construction involving the pronoun "he" and the relative pronoun "who" are combined syntactically with the verb "to feed". The Grand Inquisitor, in the course of describing to Christ the downfall of His teaching, says that the people will not complete their new Tower of Babel. "And then already we will finish building them their tower, for he who will feed them will finish building it, and only we will feed them, in your name, and we will lie that it is in your name" (Dostoevskii, 14: 231; compare to Dostoevsky, 253). It is, of course, the phrase "he who will feed them" that interests us since it is that phrase which the Architect repeats. To the crowd's question, "Who will feed us?" the Architect replies, "He who moves the stars will feed you" (4: 60). The only difference between the Architect's and the Grand Inquisitor's phrases lies in whether the verb is subordinated to "he" or "who." These correspondences are further enhanced by the motif of building in both texts. The Grand Inquisitor says that he and his kind will finish building a new Tower of Babel and will lie that it and the feeding of the people are done in Christ's name. Likewise, the Architect openly admits that he hewed the King with his own hands, and his duplicity is barely veiled when he explains in whose name he acts. His last words, which are the last words of the play, are: "The Father will feed you" (4: 60).

Closely tied to this Dostoevskian subtext is the extensive use of doubles, which pervade the play. One critic, for instance, in discussing the images of the Architect's Daughter, the Poet, and the Fool, argues, "Each of these images is correlated with the image of the Architect as his double" (Lenchik 1972, 210). The Fool, in fact, is integrally related to the Grand Inquisitor subtext. Early in Act Three, for instance, the Fool in effect parodies the speech of the Architect that ends the play: "I will tend you, my herds, with an iron staff!" (4: 51). Instead of the Father, however, Common Sense is the greater good that the Fool works for. Fundamental to the speech of both the Fool and the Architect is a mockery of biblical language, which they employ to duplicitous ends. More generalized parallels, parallels less dependendent on the Dostoevskian subtext, also arise. For instance, both battle for the Poet's soul. Through sarcasm, the Architect attempts to persuade the Poet to abandon his poetic dreams and to believe simply in the King. The Fool, as mentioned above, persuades the Poet to believe in the King through flattery. In passing, we should also note that the vehicle of that flattery, the Golden one, is an obvious double of the Black one.

Doubling, although perhaps inspired in some measure by Dostoevsky's example, is not limited to the Dostoevskian subtext. It often assumes other, rather complex forms. Not only does the Youth double the Poet, but the Girl doubles the Architect's Daughter; and the Youth and the Girl, as a couple, double the Poet and the Architect's Daughter, as a couple. As shown above, the Poet and the Architect's Daughter, as a couple, provide ironic commentary on the theme of romantic love. The Youth and the Girl provide ironic commentary not only on the theme of romantic love, but on the Poet and the Architect's Daughter as well. Where the Architect's Daughter shows herself to be morally stronger than the Poet, creating a legend that comforts him, the Youth proves to be the comforter of the Girl after the encounter with the Seller of Roses.

Doubling also accounts for the otherwise random parade of characters across the stage. Each of the three acts, for instance, opens with a discussion between two men. In Act One, the two men introduce the theme of the ships. The First man says, "They build their happiness on some crazy dream. They expect something from the ships, which will arrive today" (4: 27). The Second expresses his dismay, saying, "After all this is madness!" (4: 27). Such doubling gives way to further bifurcation at the beginning of the second act. The two workers who open it echo the sentiment that waiting for the ships is madness. The First Worker says, "Every moment they await the ships" (4: 36). The second chimes in, "One would like to ask what they are waiting for from them" (4: 36). Two dandies replace the workers, but continue the theme. The First says, "Who thought up all this nonsense, I'd like to know?" (4: 37). The two men who start the third act pick up the theme. The First asks, "Will the ships really not arrive today too?" (4: 37). The Second later comments, "To believe in this means to grasp at straws" (4: 48).

Moreover, a third voice, most often sinister, joins into these conversations or comments on them. The third voice becomes the vehicle, in its positive aspect, of the theme of imminent destruction, and, in its negative aspect, of the theme of deceiving the people into believing that the destruction is not imminent. In the first act, the Second person remarks, "What happiness to die!" (4: 27). The Voice of the Third states the theme of destruction in its positive aspect, saying, "He talks about happiness. We will go only to burn and destroy" (4: 27). In the second and third acts, however, the Fool is the vehicle of this theme, and he states it first in its negative aspect. Fast on the heels of the two workers, who remark on the absurdity of believing in the ships, comes the Fool, who laments, "No one wants to go for the bait of common sense. Everybody has gone crazy" (4: 37). Seen in light of our comments about the Fool's function as a rogue, this comment betrays his ulterior motive. He attacks the dream of the ships on the basis of common sense because he supports the Architect, who defends the status quo. Status quo and common sense become, in the vocabulary of the play, synonyms. Thus, when the Golden one persuades the Poet to sing in favor of the King at the end of act two, the Fool exclaims, "I've caught one! I've caught one!" (4: 46). His deception of the people thus becomes polemical. In the third act, the Fool weaves the positive and negative aspect of the theme of destruction together. The positive expresses itself in the Fool's morbid parody. Coming upon the First man, who has just died, the Fool asks, "Drunk?" (4: 49). The negative aspect of the theme finds expression in the Fool's grand deception of the people, when he proclaims himself to be the truth. It is consistent, in this respect, that toward the end of this proclamation, the Fool tells the people, "Clear the corpses from off your streets!" (4: 51).

The use of doubles, coupled with the three images of the fool, destabilizes meaning in *The King on the Square*. This carnivalesque upending of words points to larger elements of carnival in the play. The play's setting, for instance, is a city square, which seems no accident since, in Bakhtin's words, "The main arena for carnival acts was the square and the streets adjoining it" (Bakhtin 1984b, 128). Moreover, the image of fire and references to things burning recur throughout the text. The deep foreboding, to which all the characters give expression, reflects crisis and points to a "threshold" atmosphere. Finally, the day, during which the play takes place, is no ordinary day. Any sense of normal life — merchants selling their goods, children going to school, people shopping — is absent. The only people at work "are raising some kind of structures for meeting the ships" (4: 32). Thus, a rather perverse carnival atmosphere fills the play.

These elements of carnival, however, merely prepare for the ritual carnival crowning and decrowning of the King takes place (Bakhtin 1984b, 124). This crowning and decrowning represents the fabric that makes *The King on the Square* cohere. The King is not a real king. Bakhtin says much the same thing about the carnival king: "(H)e who is crowned is the antipode of a real king, a slave or a jester" (Bakhtin 1984b, 124). In *The King on the Square*, he is not even a slave or a jester, but just a statue deprived of animacy. Precisely because the King is a statue, not only his regal vestments, but he himself becomes ambivalent. This ambivalence centers not just around the illusory nature of his power, that is, around the negative, but also around what is for the people his very real existence. Witness their shouts when the statue breaks apart: "Cries of horror are heard: 'A statue!,'

'A stone idol,' 'Where is the King?" (4: 59). The decrowning of the King is spectacular.

Once established, the act of decrowning points to a parallel between the endings of *The King on the Square* and *A Puppet Show.* In both, the world, whether understood as a stage or a seat of governmental power, crashes down upon itself. This parallel has been described by one scholar in the following terms: "It is of essence that the 'harlequinade' and irony are conceived of as a power of eschatological destruction of the *world in its entirety* (the finale of *A Puppet Show* with its collapse of the world — of the puppet show right before the spectators' eyes) and that to this destruction, it is easy to assign the meaning of revolutionary (rebellious) eschatology (the finale of *The King on the Square*)" (Mints 1988, 403). Of course, eschatology in *A Puppet Show* is transformed by carnival: the end of the world proves to be the beginning of a new one. Columbine arises from cardboard to live a new life as death. Pierrot emerges from the debris of what had been the stage to sing a song about its demise. The puppet show ends in order to begin again. However, such is not the case in *The King on the Square.* Here, eschatology is not transformed by carnival: the end of the world proves to be merely the end of the world and promises no renewal or rejuvenation.

In fact, the failure of *The King on the Square* stems not, as some Soviet critics argued, from the relative maturity or immaturity of Blok's political views in the late summer and early autumn of 1906. Rather, the shortcomings of the play center around the tension between the monologic dream espoused by the Architect and the relativistic crowning and decrowning ritual which forms the base of the play.[6] In Bakhtin's words, "Carnival celebrates the shift itself, the very processs of replaceability, and not the precise item that is replaced" (Bakhtin 1984b, 125). What should be replaced in *The King on the Square* is the monologic official dream, and in a more purely carnivalized work, it would be. In this sense, carnival "absolutizes nothing, but rather proclaims the joyful relativity of everything" (Bakhtin 1984b, 125). In the case of *The King on the Square*, however, the laughter of this joyful relativity is reduced, even impaired: the official dream does not change, and the carnivalistic upending that is implicit in the Fool's soliloquy in the prologue never bears fruit. The King is dead, but as the Architect tells the crowd, "You will be fed by Him, Who moves the stars, Him, Who waters the black earth with rains, Him Who gathers clouds over the sea. You will be fed by the Father" (4: 60). This image of the monologic state the Architect creates at the end of the play is at odds with the carnival that has already undermined it.

The King on the Square nonetheless reveals within itself the workings of carnival as a highly complex literary process. Erring in the direction of narrow autobiographism by denying the influence of poet's environment poses a great danger. As great, if not greater danger is posed by erring in the direction of biographism, as some commentators have. They attribute the changes in Blok's poetics to the political vicissitudes of his day. While the 1905 Revolution certainly

[6] This tension is missed by those critics who would see the play as "simple allegory" (Rodina, 150; but see also Zelentsova, 38 and Fedorov, 62). Such critics reduce the clash of ideologies to the victory of one or another of those ideologies. In the end, however, even the ostensible winner, the Architect, loses, since his duplicity, in the guise of the stone King, has been unmasked and demolished. In this sense, the sacrifice of the Architect's Daughter is not in vain.

had a major impact on Blok, that impact was refracted through the lens of both cultural and literary processes, carnival being predominant among them.

IV

Carnival and the Dramatic Dialogue

No commentary on *The King on the Square* can claim to be comprehensive to any degree without a thorough consideration of *Of Love, Poetry, and Government Service*, a dialogue which grew out of the play. Because it was once part of the play and is thus intimately tied to the genesis of the play itself, the dialogue was subject to the same creative forces that shaped *The King on the Square*. Carnivalization is woven deeply into the fabric of Blok's work, regardless of genre. Analysis will demonstrate that,though it belongs to a different genre, the dramatic dialogue, just as much as the play, reflects very deep carnivalization.

Like *The King on the Square*, the dialogue belongs to the realm of the serio-comical. It displays all three of the the characteristics that distinguish any serio-comical genre. First, the "starting point for understanding, evaluating, and shaping reality, is the living *present* " (Bakhtin 1984b, 108; italics in the original). The very topicality of *Of Love, Poetry, and Government Service*, in fact, has led to much misunderstanding. Not only have commentators seized on it as a reflection of the 1905 Revolution, but many saw in it a commentary on Russian society as the two reprints of it after the 1917 revolution testify.

Secondly, *Of Love, Poetry, and Government Service* reflects a very critical attitude toward legend. As Bakhtin points out, the relationship of the serio-comical genres to legend " ... is in most cases deeply critical, and at times even resembles a cynical exposé" (Bakhtin 1984b, 108). True to form, Blok's dialogue reveals a very deep vein of cynicism where government is concerned. This cynicism shines most brightly through the speech of the Courtier to the crowd of hungry beggars, as when he says, "Standing guard on the interests of the country, we, the courtiers, listen keenly to the people's voice. I ask you to state your thoughts as succinctly and precisely as possible" (4: 66). It is also reflected in the Fool's duplicitous attitude toward the government, to which we will return later.

Finally, "A third characteristic is the deliberate multi-styled and hetero-voiced nature of all these genres" (Bakhtin 1984b, 108). In *Of Love, Poetry, and Government Service*, the most obvious instance of this multi-styled quality manifests itself in the remnants of dramatic forms, which saturate the dialogue form itself. The very presence, for instance, of stage directions suggests that Blok intended for the dialogue to be performed and not merely read. Moreover, as the play progresses, action, albeit extremely delimited action, interrupts what, strictly speaking, constitutes a dialogue. For example, The appearance of the Courtier with the crowd of beggars around him cuts short the first series of exchanges between the Poet and the Fool. The ending of *Of Love, Poetry, and Government Service* also reveals the dramatic underpinnings of the dialogue. The stage directions apprise the reader of a "desperate brawl," which takes place "offstage" (4: 71). The

Fool returns to the stage to deliver several lines and then falls silent while he starts searching for his fishing rod.

Not only does *Of Love, Poetry, and Government Service* belong to the realm of the serio-comical, it shows marked parallels to the Socratic dialogue. While the interference of the dramatic elements mentioned above prevent *Of Love, Poetry, and Government Service* from being a Socratic dialogue in the strict sense of the term, the similarities between its structure and the form of the Socratic dialogue merit closer examination.

Bakhtin notes five essential traits of the Socratic dialogue, all of which are observed to a greater or lesser extent in *Of Love, Poetry, and Government Service.* First, "At the base of the genre lies the Socratic notion of the dialogic nature of truth, and the dialogic nature of human thinking about truth" (Bakhtin 1984b, 110). Very significant in this regard are those junctures where one character complains that his interlocutor has not fully understood him. For instance, when the Poet and the Fool discuss the former's beloved, the Fool wonders if she does not "suffer from an inclination toward liberalism?" (4: 64). In response, the Poet protests, "I am convinced that she is higher than all passing formulas. But freedom is dear to her — did you not want to express yourself thus?" (4: 64). Their roles are reversed when the Poet paraphrases the Fool's belief that "literature should be social" (4: 65). The Fool replies, however, "You nonetheless are interpreting my words incorrectly" (4: 65). He finds social literature to be injurious to the masses.

Because of such interaction, no single view predominates. Bakhtin argues, "The dialogic means of seeking truth is counterposed to *official* monologism, which pretends to *possess a ready-made truth*, and it is also counterposed to the naive self-confidence of those people who think that they know something, that is, who think that they possess certain truths" (Bakhtin 1984b, 110). Consequently, the ideas with which the characters enter the dialogue change. The Fool enters the play espousing a very cynical brand of common sense, which he believes will solve all problems. He tells the Poet, "Anyone, who will follow me, will enjoy equality, satisfaction, and health because on my banner is inscribed: common sense" (4: 63). By the end of the play, though, common sense has failed him, and the Poet pulls out a clump of his hair. The Poet's thought too undergoes a shift. At the beginning of the dialogue, his beliefs are well-worn clichés. He is in love with a beautiful, but unattainable woman, and he suffers from melancholy. In the course of ten pages, however, he embraces civic poetry and a career in the diplomatic corps, only to renounce them at the end of the play.

The second important characteristic of the Socratic dialogue rests on two technical devices, syncrisis and anacrisis. According to Bakhtin, "Syncrisis was understood as the juxtaposition of various points of view on a specific object" (Bakhtin 1984b, 110). In *Of Love, Poetry, and Government Service*, each character brings a different point of view to bear on the question of what role poetry has or should have in society. The Poet, as mentioned above, begins as a proponent of art for art's sake. At one point, the Fool advises the Poet to try his hand at "civic verses" (4: 65). The Courtier, on the other hand, suggests that poetry is only for the elect. He says, "The subjective lyric ... gives the chosen hours of aesthetic relaxation and allows them, if only for a minute, to forget the capricious voice of the mob" (4: 69-70). Similarly, each of them offers a different opinion of the other two topics of the dialogue, love and government service.

The second of these devices, anacrisis, guarantees that the characters express their disparate opinions fully. In Bakhtin's definition, "Anacrisis was understood as a means for eliciting and provoking the words of one's interlocutor, forcing him to express his opinion and express it thoroughly" (Bakhtin 1984b, 110). Anacrisis arises in several different guises in *Of Love, Poetry, and Government Service*. We have already seen anacrisis at work at those junctures, when one character complains that his interlocutor has not fully understood him. Because of this misunderstanding, the character who complains that his ideas are not being grasped must express himself more fully. Anacrisis also finds expression in the Fool's unabashed flattery. By calling the Poet a "beautiful youth", the Fool appeals to the Poet's vanity and thereby wins his confidence (4: 64). As a result, the Poet confides in him, telling the Fool about his fears, anxieties, and melancholy. This confidence motivates the fuller expression of the Poet's ideas.

In somewhat attenuated form, *Of Love, Poetry, and Government Service* also exhibits what Bakhtin identifies as the third characteristic of the Socratic dialogue. "The heroes of the Socratic dialogue are *ideologists*" (Bakhtin 1984b, 111; italics in the original). Each of the characters is, or becomes, an exponent of a particular creed. The Fool espouses "common sense," while the Poet tacitly believes in art for art's sake, and the Courtier defends government service and what he calls the "consciousness of sacredly fulfilled duty" (4: 69).

The collision of these ideologies becomes the proving ground for the relative truth of each of them. In Bakhtin's words, "(T)he very event that is accomplished in a Socratic dialogue (or, more precisely, that is reproduced in it) is the purely ideological event of seeking and testing truth" (Bakhtin 1984b, 111). The Poet's ideological wandering takes special significance in this regard. When confronted with common sense, the Poet begins to question the exclusively aesthetic concerns of his creed. Art for art's sake fails to encompass the Fool's objections to a predominantly aesthetic ideology. This failure forces the Poet to investigate other avenues, although his attack on the Fool at the end of the play implies that he never completely abandons art for art's sake. The full force of the characters as ideologists in *Of Love, Poetry, and Government Service*, however, remains somewhat attenuated because of the intractability of both the Fool and the Courtier. The fight at the end of the play suggests that the Fool will have to reconsider his common sense, but this comes to pass because the Poet physically attacks him, not because his word is tested by the Poet's word.

This fight, however, points to another characteristic of the Socratic dialogue. According to Bakhtin's formulation, "In the Socratic dialogue, the plot situation of the dialogue is sometimes utilized alongside anacrisis, or the provocation of the word by the word, for the same purpose" (Bakhtin 1984b, 111). The Poet's attack on the Fool is one manifestation of this. A more important one arises in the Poet's doubts about the further course of his life. He stands, in Bakhtinian terms, "*on the threshold*" (Bakhtin 1984b, 111; italics in the original). While the threshold in *Of Love, Poetry, and Government Service* does not represent a life-and-death situation as it so often does in Socratic dialogue (as in Plato's *Apology* and *Phaedo*, for instance), it does mark the potential death of the Poet as a poet. Throughout the play, the Poet appears ready to abandon poetry and the "beautiful." Only at the end, when he tears out the Fool's hair and screams that he does not want to be a diplomat, does this "threshold" situation resolve itself.

Finally, and perhaps most importantly for our purposes, each of the characters has a personal stake in his ideology. Bakhtin writes, "In the Socratic dialogue the idea is organically combined with the image of a person, its carrier (Socrates and other essential participants in the dialogue)" (Bakhtin 1984b, 111). This characteristic, in fact, explains why the Poet resorts to physical violence at the end of the play. Not only are his ideas threatened, he himself is threatened. As Bakhtin suggests, "The dialogic testing of the idea is simultaneously also the testing of the person who represents it" (Bakhtin 1984b, 111-2). Each of the characters has something to prove. Each eagerly awaits an opportunity to convert the others. As the Fool tells the Poet, "I gladly cast my fishing rod in order to speak with you" (4: 63). As a consequence of the personal stake each of them has in their ideology, when they engage their interlocutor in conversation, their ideas and those of their interlocutor " ... are not quoted here, not paraphrased, but are presented in their free and creative devlopment against a dialogizing background of other ideas" (Bakhtin 1984b, 112). Because of this interconnection of character and idea, "We may therefore speak here of an embryonic *image of an idea* " (Bakhtin 1984b, 112; italics in the original).

Of Love, Poetry, and Government Service thus reveals a close kinship with the Socratic dialogue. The two, however, are not identical. Bakhtin's notion of the "image of an idea" suggests where the major differences lie. While the "image" of Socrates in the Socratic dialogue is certainly carnivalized, the "image" of the Fool in *Of Love, Poetry, and Government Service* reflects more specifically the lingering influence of the *commedia dell'arte* and Blok's use of it in *A Puppet Show* and *The King on the Square*. *Of Love, Poetry, and Government Service* incorporates carnival elements that are not necessarily characteristic for the Socratic dialogue. These elements, in part, pass through the conduit of the *commedia dell'arte*. In particular, the *commedia dell'arte* and its relation to "low" genres exerts a powerful influence on the image of the Fool.

Bakhtin has suggested, "It is precisely here, on a small scale — in the minor low genres, on the itinerant stage, in public squares on market day, in street songs and jokes — that devices were first worked out for constructing images of a language" (Bakhtin 1981a, 400).[7] Bakhtin identifies the three most important as the images of the rogue, the fool, and the clown, a coupling of the first two. Literary forms absorbed in abstracted form the specific images that were worked out in the low genres. Thus, a character called the fool becomes part of the general literary vocabulary and passes into Blok's dialogue *Of Love, Poetry, and Government Service*.

In fact, nearly all the characters in *Of Love, Poetry, and Government Service* manifest the images of the rogue, fool, and clown. The Fool, for instance, is a clown,who issues from "the category of *gay deception*" and "deliberate stupidity" (Bakhtin 1981a, 401, 403; italics in the original).[8] He perpetrates "a gay and intelligent deception, a *lie* justified because it is directed precisely to *liars*," but

---

[7] As in *The King on the Square*, the setting is crucial. *Of Love, Poetry, and Government Service* takes place on a "city square" (4: 62), which serves as a carnival square.

[8] The vitality of the Fool's approach to life gives the Poet pause: "Your joy of living forces me to think" (4: 63).

often masks it behind the mask of the fool, as at those junctures when he fails to understand the Poet (Bakhtin 1981a, 401; italics in the original). Indeed, one of the most important manifestation of carnivalization in *Of Love, Poetry, and Government Service* lies in the very ambivalence of the characters' speech in general and in the parodic orientation of their language to any and all official languages. Nowhere is this quality more visible than in the Fool's speech, as evidenced in the opening exchanges between the Fool and the Poet. A relativistic and blasphemous undercurrent cuts through the Fool's speech. For instance, in speaking of a fish, he says, "I taught it common sense and political economy for a long time" (4: 62). The Poet responds, "I do not understand you. You speak about fish, as though about people" (4: 62). The Poet implicitly acknowledges that the Fool is toying with the "official" humanistic vision of man. This theme becomes even more pronounced in the Fool's parody of biblical language. The Fool gives his assent to the Poet's comment that he speaks about people as about fish by saying, "I am a fisher of men" (4: 62).

In sharp contrast to the "malicious distortions" of the Fool as clown, the Poet, is actually the fool in the dialogue (Bakhtin 1981a, 405). In the Poet's speech, "The naiveté of a simpleton who does not understand pathos (or who understands it in a distorted way, wrong side out), is counterposed to a false pathos, which together with gay deception has the effect of 'making strange' any pretensions to lofty reality a discourse of pathos might have" (Bakhtin 1981a, 402). As the Fool tells the Poet, "Your straightforwardness astonishes me" (4: 67). Seen in this light, the Poet's gullibility, his eagerness to embrace every new idea, takes on polemical overtones. This polemicism becomes manifest when he attacks the Fool at the end of the play. This attack in no way disrupts the image of the fool in the Poet. The fool's sudden realization of having been taken in often provides convenient resolution to the action of a given work. Especially significant for our purposes is the fact that the Poet's attack is physical, not verbal.

The Courtier, who shows no signs of failing to understand, plays the part of a rogue. He directs his "gay deception" at the conventional conception of the humane function of government. For instance, though he tells a crowd of beggars that the government will listen closely to their complaints, this attention proves to be merely formal. A beggar says, "I am hungry." The Courtier replies, "This is concise, but imprecise" (4: 66). Later, he tells the Poet that "to bury talent is a sin," but is only too happy to take the Poet away from poetry when the latter expresses interest in government service (4: 69). The Courtier says, "That is all I wanted to hear from you, young man. ... I hope you won't refuse to accept my proposals. Your speeches about duality created in my mind a brilliant combination: we will prepare you for a diplomatic career" (4: 70-1).

An image of the author as a rogue also emerges. The chief means through which this image materializes are anti-dramatic, distancing devices, which serve, in *Of Love, Poetry, and Government Service* as they did in *A Puppet Show* and the prologue of *The King on the Square*, to make the reader or spectator aware of the artifice of the work at hand. As in *A Puppet Show*, stage directions provide one channel for this image. Characters sometimes direct their lines to someone other than their interlocutor, someone offstage. When the Fool says, "My science is an infectious, gay science," the Poet remarks "to the side" that the Fool has read Nietzsche (4: 63).

More often, however, there are no stage directions, and the character just utters his distancing words to the consternation of his interlocutor. At one point, for instance, the Fool tells the Poet, "I feel my responsibility before the reader. If you are going to prolong our conversation with useless hesitations, the anger of the readers is going to fall on me" (4: 63). The Poet, however, looks for some hidden meaning in this "allegorical" speech. He says, "This man speaks with a hidden design" (4: 63). Later the Fool refers directly to the author. Commenting on the conversation between the Courtier and the beggars, the Fool says, "The composer of this dialogue, which I have wormed myself into, will go apparently along a well-trodden path. It is advantageous for him to show any courtier in a stupid light" (4: 68).

The author thus adds another voice to the fray. The implication of the Fool's remark is that the voice of the author contributes to the dialogizing background, against which every comment in *Of Love, Poetry, and Government Service* appears. The Fool implies further that the author's intent at times is parodic. In other words, the author serves as a rogue who parodies the conventions — the "official" conventions, which prohibit authorial intrusion — of the theater, on the one hand, and of realism, on the other.

Blok's concern with the image of the author reveals the kinship of *Of Love, Poetry, and Government Service* and another piece of carnivalized literature, Pushkin's "The Conversation of the Bookseller with the Poet." Both take the form a dialogue, and in both a poet enters into a conversation with someone who represents the world of business and politics. Both poets confront the question of their position in the world. For the Poet in "The Conversation of the Bookseller with the Poet", the question centers around his status as a professional writer. Until Pushkin's time, the writer who made his living through his writing was a rarity. But precisely during Pushkin's lifetime, writers began to make a living off of their work. For the first time, the question of how to reconcile inspiration with material needs arose. In the words of the Bookseller, "In an instant we replace the verses of the favorite of the muses and graces with rubles." The Poet laments that the days when he wrote only for inspiration are gone. He has become famous, but he wonders what that fame is. "Is it the whisper of a reader? Is it the persecution of a lowly ignoramus? Or the admiration of an idiot?"

Such considerations become one of the subtexts of *Of Love, Poetry, and Government Service*. References to the differences between the poet and mob arise constantly. When the Poet is pondering civic poetry, the Fool asks, "Would it really be more pleasant for you to act on the low instincts of the crowd, than to delight the taste of the chosen?" (4: 65). As noted earlier, it is the Courtier's opinion that poetry is for the elite. Like the Poet in "The Conversation of the Bookseller with the Poet," the Poet in *Of Love, Poetry, and Government Service* understands that the cure for his melancholy lies in the resolution of this polarity.

The difference between the two poets ultimately defines itself historically. The Poet in "The Conversation of the Bookseller with the Poet" worries about his place in the bookseller's world because his position is as yet tenuous and still in the making. By the turn of the century, the position of the writer as a professional, however, was no longer tenuous. The Poet in *Of Love, Poetry, and Government Service* understands that he is part of this society. However, because his work provides no material benefit, he must define what the benefits of his art are. In *Of Love, Poetry, and Government Service* the Poet approaches this question negatively and denies his art any value whatsoever, seeking a career with more tangible benefits. Of particular importance in this regard is the fact that both "The Conversation of the Bookseller with the Poet" and *Of Love, Poetry, and Government Service* end with reconciliation of the poet with the world of business and politics. The Poet in "The Conversation of the Bookseller with the Poet" comes to terms with the bookseller, and the Poet in *Of Love, Poetry, and Government Service* accepts the Courtier's offer of a diplomatic post.

In both works the poet relates to the world as a double, on the one hand inspired by the muses, and on the other dealing with the "rabble." More importantly, because of the pact they make with the world, they themselves call into question the "truth" of the dreams they had earlier espoused. In other words, they come to believe in what are for them two mutually exclusive truths: the truth of the world and the truth of poetry. In Bakhtinian terms, they become non-coincident with themselves. As a result, everything they say ceases to emanate from a single and closed-off voice. Their voice becomes more complicated and colors everything they seek to express, giving it overtones a pure monologic voice would not.

These comments apply, of course, only to the two poets as characters. However, as demonstrated above in the discussion of the image of the author that arises in *Of Love, Poetry, and Government Service*, an analogy between the voice of the author and the voice of the Poet becomes apparent. Both voices expand beyond strict, monologic boundaries. Just as the Poet's voice is polemical in the world of the dialogue, so too the voice of the author states its relation to the world polemically. It cannot represent the world; it must refract it.

This breakdown of monologic boundaries unites *Of Love, Poetry, and Government Service* and *The King on the Square*. Blok sought in both to expand his voice by pitting mutually polemical voices against each other. The resulting approach to human social order defies narrow political definition. The image Blok created is multivalent. No single interpretative approach exhausts it. It is equally true, however, that because of the flaws in these works, Blok failed to achieve true polyphony in either work. Nonetheless, he depicts here, for the first time on a large scale, social process in carnivalized form. The impact of carnival and the carnivalized images developed here would define Blok's treatment of social questions, particularly revolution. While his definitive statement of this theme would wait until *The Twelve*, his approach, albeit in embryonic form, is already apparent in *The King on the Square* and *Of Love, Poetry, and Government Service*.

CHAPTER THREE

CARNIVAL AND EROS: *THE STRANGER*

I

Poem and Play

In contrast to the well-documented beginnings of the first two plays of Blok's lyrical trilogy, the genesis of *The Stranger* remains something of a mystery. In their letters, notebooks, diaries, and reminiscences, Blok and his circle discussed the origins of *A Puppet Show* at length. And while it is true that Blok referred to *The King on the Square* less often than to *A Puppet Show*, the outlines of Blok's work on his second play are still apparent in what remarks he did make, especially in correspondence with his friend, Evgenii Ivanov. In contrast, there are no references in any of the published letters or diaries or reminiscences of either Blok, his family, or friends to when or why Blok transformed the poem "The Stranger" into a play. The trilogy, as it were, describes an arc from the social and communal beginnings of *A Puppet Show*, as a statement of the Symbolist theater "Torches," to *The King on the Square*, which Blok openly discussed with only his closest friends and relatives, to the very personal and private *The Stranger*.

Nor do the manuscripts shed any light on the play's genesis. Pavel Medvedev, who has studied the evolution of the manuscripts of all of Blok's plays, has noted that there is little to say about the manuscripts of *The Stranger* because the first copy apparently turned out to be a fair copy. Medvedev remarks, "These forty-six pages of rough drafts of *The Stranger* will remain mute but, for all that, eloquent witness to the strength and clarity of the creative thought, to the ease of the mastery of the material, to the harmony and elegance of the creative process itself. It seems that Al. Blok wrote *The Stranger* as though joking and playing" (Medvedev, 53).

The ease with which Blok transformed his poem into a play is all the more striking for the glaring differences between the two. While the play is one of the most formally innovative of the Symbolist era, the poem is quite traditional in form. Its meter, iambic tetrameter, was favored by Pushkin and is the most common of all Russian meters. The poem's quatrains too were bequeathed by a long and rich tradition. Perhaps only the rhyme scheme, alternating masculine and dactyllic rhymes, might raise eyebrows. Yet even this rhyme scheme had been firmly established and canonized by the end of the nineteenth century. If the poem "A

Puppet Show" anticipated the innovations of the eponymous play, the same can hardly be said of "The Stranger."

Nonetheless, the poem merits attention before we turn to the play:

THE STRANGER

In the evenings the ardent air
Over the restaurants is wild and hollow;
A corrupt and vernal spirit
Rules with the shouts of alcoholics.

Beyond, above the crossroad dust,
Above the boredom of suburban dachas,
There glows a baker's gilded pretzel,
And you can hear the children screeching.

And every evening beyond the turnpike,
The tried and tested wits,
Cocking their slanting derbies,
Stroll with their ladies out amongst the ditches.

Above the lake, the locks are creaking,
In the sky, to all inured,
though you can hear a woman's shriek,
A disk inanely glowers.

And every evening my only friend
Is reflected in my glass.
Like me, he is subdued and stunned
By liquid that is tart, mysterious.

Beside the neighboring tables, close by,
The waiters hang out and "get lost,"
And drunks with rabbit eyes
Cry, "In vino veritas!"

And every evening at the appointed hour
(Or am I only dreaming this?)
Swathed in silks, a woman's figure
Moves in the window laced with mist.

Always without escort, alone,
(The drunks remain where she has passed),
By the window she sits down
Slowly, breathing in perfume and mists.

From her resilient silks there wafts
Ancient knowledge as if winnowed.

Her hat — all plumage and mournful tufts.
Her hand, adorned in rings, is narrow.

Fettered by her estranging nearness,
I look beyond her dark veil's haze
And make out an enchanted shore
And an enchanted distant space.

Obscure, these mysteries are given in trust
To me, along with someone's sun;
And my soul is pierced in all its twists
And turns by sharp, tart wine.

And in my brain there sway
Those lilting feathers from an ostrich,
And blue, unfathomable eyes
On some distant shore are blossoming.

In my soul there lies a treasure,
With the key to me alone entrusted.
Yes, you are right, you drunken horror!
Now I know: In wine — the Truth.
(2: 185-6)

What poem and play share, most importantly, is a number of motifs: the Stranger herself, a bar, alcohol, the inebriation of the persona of the poem and of a character called the Poet in the play. Still, these motifs will appear in a different configuration in the play. Perhaps only in their general thematic contours do the poem and play share very much. In both the arrival of the Stranger is set against a naturalistic backdrop. However, beyond this, they have little in common. In fact, "The Stranger" is only one of several poems that display motifs similar to those in the play. Among the more important are "There in the night's howling cold," "Her train strewn with stars," "Your face is paler than it was," and "Ladies flaunt their fashions there" (2: 81, 105, 183, 187). Yet despite such similarities in imagery, the play is quite distinct.

A synopsis will suggest the degree to which the play developed independently of the poem. It is divided into "visions," rather than acts, and the first opens in a bar. On the wallpaper "exactly identical ships with huge flags" cut through "blue waters." At the counter stand the Owner and his brother, who look exactly alike except for their mustaches: that of the former turns down, while the latter's goes up. Snippets of conversation can be heard. Two men argue about how much one of them paid for his hat, while a third man tries to reconcile them. Another man rises from his seat and makes his way unsteadily to tub of crayfish. The Owner tells him not to pick them over. The scene then shifts to another conversation, this one involving a Seminarian, who goes on at length about a woman who danced so wonderfully he "could have kissed her, I tell you, right on the lips." His boon companions tease him about his infatuation, calling him a dreamer. At a nearby window sits "the spitting image of Verlaine," who mumbles over and over to himself, "To each his own. To each his own...." A red-haired man and a woman enter at this point, and the woman orders a bottle of porter. She rambles on about a commotion that broke out when one of the girls caught a man going through her dresser. When she notices her companion's lack of interest in her anecdote, she asks him what the matter is. "Drink and shut up," he replies. Nearby, at a second window, sits "the spitting image of Hauptmann." A young man runs in and informs him that a woman is waiting for him. Hauptmann, however, does not get too excited; instead, he tells the young man to let her wait. Verlaine again mumbles loudly to himself, and finally one of the main characters, the Poet, makes his entrance. He tells the Owner how he wandered the streets, seeing the eyes of hundreds of women. Then he came upon the "beautiful face of the Stranger." At this point, Verlaine begins mumbling yet again, the Seminarian waxes rhapsodic about his dancer, and Hauptmann tells the Young Man to let the woman wait a little while longer. A Man in a coat enters, trying to sell a cameo that depicts the Woman who Rules the World. The Poet is enchanted and buys it. Then two of the bar's patrons are heard to laugh over the insipid jokes from a humor magazine. In turn, the Poet and then the Seminarian go into raptures, the first over the cameo, the second over his dancer. Then the Man in the coat begins arguing with another man about cheese and connoisieurship. The first "vision" comes to an end with Verlaine once more mumbling to himself, Hauptmann telling the Young Man to let the woman wait, the Girl bidding her escort farewell, the Seminarian praising his dancer, and the Poet conjuring the Stranger to appear. As the action of the "vision" ends, the whole bar seems to be diving somewhere: the walls part and the ceiling opens up to reveal a cold and blue winter sky.

As the second vision begins, the bar has disappeared, and in its place the audience finds "the end of a street at the edge of the city." A dark, deserted bridge spans a large river, and ships can be seen on either side. Beyond the bridge, an avenue lined with streetlights stretches out seemingly endlessly. On the bridge is an Astronomer, who marvels at the infinity of stars above him. He disdainfully watches as doormen throw the drunken Poet in the snow. The Astronomer again looks up and sees a falling star. The star falls to earth, and a moment later the Stranger walks onto the bridge.[1] She is met there by the Blue one. They talk, and it becomes apparent that the Stranger seeks earthly passion, while the Blue one can only worship her with an otherworldly love. The Blue one disappears from the bridge, and a Gentleman appears. He offers the Stranger the physical passion she seeks. When they have departed, the Astronomer reappears and mourns the fallen star he has named "Mariia." The Poet joins him, asking if he has seen the Stranger. The Astronomer is insulted by what he, in the face of the loss he has just suffered, deems coarseness. To the Poet's sadness, he does confirm seeing a woman with a "blue gentleman." However, the snow has covered their tracks. The second vision ends with the Poet and the Astronomer attempting to prove whose loss is greater. As the action ends, the snow becomes heavier and forms out of the distance white walls that thicken.

These white walls become those of a large drawing room, the setting of the third vision. As it begins the Host greets a guest and, in the course of the small talk that ensues, inquires about the cost of his hat. The Hostess tells the guest to come

---

[1] Nikolai Volkov has traced the image of the star back to a poem by Apollon Grigor'ev, several lines of which serve as an epigraph to Blok's collection *The Earth in Snow* [*Zemlia v snegu*] (Volkov, 54-5).

in. While the hostess talks to the newcomer, two young men, Georges and Misha, argue about a dancer they have seen. Misha goes into raptures over her "classical figure." Georges will have none of it and is soon joined by the Hostess, who expresses her disapproval. An Old Man sitting across from the Hostess suddenly bursts out, "Whorehouse." The Hostess blushes and turns to one of the other guests. In the meantime, Georges and Misha continue their argument, and Georges calls Misha a dreamer. Suddenly the Old Man tells the Hostess that one of her buttons has come undone. The Hostess tells the Old Man not to say such things in front of everyone. She is saved from this embarrassing situation by the entrance of a Lady and her fiancé, a Red-haired Gentleman. The Lady entertains the Hostess with a delicious little morsel of gossip to which the audience is not privy. She then turns to her fiancé to inquire if anything is wrong. "Drink and shut up," he tells her. A Young Man runs up to a man, in whom "it is easy to recognize the one who led off the Stranger." The Young Man says that she is waiting. Then, according to the stage directions, "everything becomes uncommonly strange. It is as if everyone suddenly remembered that somewhere the very same words had been pronounced and in the same order." At this juncture, the Poet enters. As the Hostess greets him, the Old Man says, "It's exactly as if somebody died. Gave his soul up to God." The Hostess reprimands him and then asks the Poet to read. The Poet's reading, however, is interrupted by the arrival of the Stranger, who calls herself Mariia. The Young Man and his friend recognize her and the former quietly slip out, making excuses as he leaves. The Hostess then asks the Poet to continue with his reading, but he declines. Instead, he rises and paces the room, trying to remember something. While he does this, an argument about cheese can be heard in the background. It then appears that the Poet has finally remembered; but as he begins to walk toward the Stranger, the Astronomer gets in his way. The Host and Hostess invite everyone to go into the dining room. As the other guests file out of the drawing room, the Astronomer tells the Poet of a paper he has delivered on the falling star Mariia. The Poet, according to the stage directions, "has forgotten everything." The Hostess urges them along from the threshold, but then notices that Mariia is nowhere to found. Outside the window, where Mariia had been standing, a star now shines. And there falls a "blue snow, just as blue as the dress coat of the Astronomer, who has vanished." With these disappearances, the play ends.

II

Stagings and Receptions

Despite its non-linear plot and structure, *The Stranger* encountered a warm reception, at least in Blok's own circle when Blok finally let the play out into the world. He read it to his family and friends on November 17, 1906 and received an enthusiastic response. Evgenii Ivanov, for example, was even more ardent in his response to *The Stranger* than he had been when he had first heard *The King on the*

Square read aloud. As he put it succinctly in his diary, "I was at Blok's and listened to the play *The Stranger.* Astonishing!" (Ivanov, 415). Others close to Blok also held the play in high regard. His mother was later to remark, "I love *The Stranger* more than all of Sasha's other dramas, more even than *The Rose and the Cross*" (Kotrelev and Timenchik, 3: 431).

As the play made its way to a wider audience, however, it encountered first indifference and then criticism. On January 12, 1907, Blok read *The Stranger* to a slightly larger group of friends and literary associates, including, among others, his wife, Georgii Chulkov, Sergei Gorodetskii, Fedor Sologub, Vladimir Piast, and Viacheslav Ivanov. Blok was pleased with the reception. He told his mother, "I read all the poems and *The Stranger* and had success" (8: 173). However, Aleksandr Kondrat'ev, who was also there, appears to have been somewhat indifferent. In his description of Blok's reading, Kondrat'ev sticks to the bare facts. He will only tell Sergei Sokolov, who as the editor of the publishing house Griffin [Grif] and an acquaintance of Blok's would surely have been interested in the play's contents, "Yesterday I listened to a reading of *The Stranger*" (Kotrelev and Timenchik, 3: 268). Kondrat'ev does promise to tell another correspondent, Boris Ber, about the reading, but, as one commentator wryly puts it, "We do not know the story which was promised to Ber" (Kotrelev and Timenchik, 3: 268).

Kondrat'ev's indifference foreshadowed the ambivalent reaction Blok encountered when he read *The Stranger* on February 1, 1907 at a meeting of the literary-artistic "Circle of the Young" at Petersburg University (Dolgopolov, 4: 576). Vil'gel'm Zorgenfrei gave a lively account of the proceedings. He wrote, "For the first time, it seems, in Petersburg the representatives of the new poetry met face to face with the public, which was inclined to be, in part, passively expectant and, in part, watchful. I remember the whispering back and forth, the separate perplexed and ironic exclamations; but I also remember the anxious watchfulness of the listeners." Although Zorgenfrei concludes, "That evening the new poetry gained victory over the inert elements of the crowd," the audience's mixed reaction renders such a conclusion questionable (cited by Dolgopolov, 4: 576).

The play, to be sure, attracted admirers, many of whom proved to be passionate and loyal. This is also true of most of the critics who have examined the play. As one critic has remarked, "In A. Blok's lyrical dramaturgy, the third drama, *The Stranger*, which concludes the trilogy, has received the highest appraisal from specialists" (Lenchik 1971, 159). Much the same can be said of Meyerhold, who immediately decided to stage it in Vera Kommissarzhevskaia's theater. At the end of November, 1906, in fact, Blok told his mother that he was planning to give the manuscript to Meyerhold (Blok 1927-32, 1: 159-60).[2] Two months later, Blok remarked in a letter to his friend Aleksandr Gippius that *The Stranger* would be staged the following season (8: 176). The following November, Blok wrote to his mother and announced that he, Meyerhold, and actors from the Komissarzhevskaia theater were to give an actors' reading of the play (8: 218). Ironically, an event which took place one day after Blok wrote this letter dashed any hope of staging *The Stranger* that season.

---

[2] Beketova dates the letter 29 November, 1906 in her notes to the correspondence (Blok 1927-32, 1: 333). Her opinion appears highly probable inasmuch as this letter comes between a letter dated 27 November and one dated 30 November.

On November 28, 1907, a censor issued his report on the play. He wrote, "This play represents such a decadent muddle that I will not undertake to examine its content. The circumstance, however, that, judging by several allusions, the author depicted the mother of God in the character of the 'stranger,' should be recognized as sufficient grounds for the prohibition of this play" (cited by Dolgopolov, 4: 576). Even five years later, when an attempt to stage *The Stranger* was again undertaken, the play failed to pass the censor, receiving the censor's stamp, "Considered unsuitable for presentation" (cited by Dolgopolov, 4: 576-7).

The Stranger, unlike *The King on the Square*, did eventually play before an audience. Over six years after Blok completed it, the play was performed on February 3, 1913 (Dolgopolov, 4: 577). The young actors who played in the production came from the classes of Sof'ia Khaliutina, an actress from the Moscow Art Theater (Poliakova, 236 and Fel'dman, 331). Sergei Sokolov, or Krechetov as he was known in the theater, directed the play. Although hardly a household name, Sokolov was an experienced director, who together with Briusov and Meyerhold had attempted but failed to establish the "Lighthouse" theater in Moscow in 1905 (Fel'dman, 326). Little is known about his staging of *The Stranger*, other than what can be garnered from the lone notice about the play that appeared in the *Moscow Register*. This notice sets the tone for the generally negative reaction of the press to this and later stagings of the play. The correspondent from the *Moscow Register* argued that the play belonged to the "most extreme tendencies of modernism" (cited by Dolgopolov, 4: 577). Also apparent from this review is the fact that *The Stranger*, like *A Puppet Show*, created a great deal of consternation amongst its first audience. The correspondent goes on to say, "The change of the author's moods and experiences is embodied in capricious, whimsical images, similar to sleeping dreams" (cited by Dolgopolov, 4: 577). Like the censor, the correspondent abandons any attempt to sort out the play's contents, saying that the work "leaves the impression of some kind of rebus, for which you vainly seek an interpretation" (cited by Dolgopolov, 4: 577). The correspondent goes on to pick the production apart.

The next production of *The Stranger* came in April, 1914 under Meyerhold's direction. Like Meyerhold's work on *A Puppet Show* at the Komissarzhevskaia Theater, this staging would prove to be a pivotal event in the history of Russian and of modern drama generally, despite a negative response from the press. Meyerhold had been and remained passionately interested in putting on the play. As Valentina Verigina recalls in her memoirs, "The idea to stage *The Stranger* had long ago and, it seems, not just once entered Meyerhold's head, and one fine day, or more precisely, evening at our place on Aleksandrovskii Prospect, he expressed his desire especially insistently" (Verigina 1974, 205). At the time, Meyerhold was co-editing the journal *Love for the Three Oranges* [*Liubov' k trem apel'sinam*]. He persuaded his partners to sponsor a staging of both *The Stranger* and *A Puppet Show*. In this way, Meyerhold put *The Stranger* on stage under the auspices of the editorial board of *Love for the Three Oranges*, using actors primarily from his Meyerhold Studio. The editorial board would later go to great lengths to clarify this point in print. In particular, the board wished to dispell the notion that the performance was either a student production or a forum to showcase the techniques of the *commedia dell'arte* (See Volkov 1929, 2: 323).

The performance of the two plays sparked a great deal of excitement. Verigina recalls, "At the first performance, there were a lot of people, and not an empty seat remained" (Verigina 1974, 208). The performance was not, however, what Meyerhold and company had hoped for. Verigina, who herself took part in the first play, *A Puppet Show*, admits, "The performance on the whole did not enjoy success" (Verigina 1974, 208). Blok's mother was considerably harsher in her appraisal of the performance. She wrote, "... it seems to me that this was all done badly at Meyerhold's. They played beneath any criticism. And all of his inventions were no good" (Kotrelev and Timenchik, 3: 431). Kuzmin, whose music for *A Puppet Show* from 1906 again accompanied the play for the April, 1914 performances of both *A Puppet Show* and *The Stranger*, goes even further: "It was a nightmare, Blok himself worst of all. Unbelievable nonsense" (Kuzmin, 2: 162).

The reviews share these impressions. Neither *A Puppet Show* nor *The Stranger* fared well. As Meyerhold's biographer, Nikolai Volkov noted, "The plays elicited a negative reaction from the majority, although from different points of view and with various reservations. For example, Evgenii Znosko-Borovskii considered that the puppet-theater devices which were applied to the performance suffocated the soul of Blok's dramas, that in the fulfillment of what was conceived there was much that was raw and weak" (see Volkov 1929, 318). Another reviewer felt that it was enough to poke fun at the costumes and makeup (see Volkov 1929, 320.) Other reviews echoed these sentiments. The poet Vladimir Iunger summarized the unfavorable newspapers responses for a friend, referring to the "downfall" of the production (Kotrelev and Timenchik, 3: 431).

The response was not entirely negative, especially among the writers who saw the performance of both plays. True, there were those, like Kuzmin, who hated the production. On the other hand, the plays also garnered staunch support. In fact, right after one of the performances, the poet Nikolai Gumilev got into an argument with Kuzmin, who accused Gumilev of merely pretending to like the plays. Gumilev insisted on his sincerity. He then turned to the group of poets who accompanied them, a group that included Anna Akhmatova, Osip Mandel'shtam, and Georgii Ivanov, and asked who agreed with him. According to Georgii Adamovich, who recounted the incident years later in Paris, everyone but Kuzmin expressed at least tacit agreement (Kotrelev and Timenchik, 3: 431). Some from the theatrical world also reacted positively. According to Volkov, for instance, the director Evgenii Vakhtangov was quite taken with the performance of both plays, particularly with the staging of *The Stranger*, which "left, in his own words, an uncommon impression on Vakhtangov" (Volkov 1929, 2: 322). Aleksei Gripich, one of Meyerhold's students and later a director, does Gumilev and Vakhtangov one better. "The Blok plays were the event of the theatrical season. They were received by the spectators in an extremely stormy fashion. Half of the spectators insistently applauded, the other half — no less insistently — whistled and hissed" (Gripich, 136).

Blok's own response reflects this general bifurcation of reaction to *The Stranger*. In the years following the staging of *A Puppet Show* at the Komissarzhevskaia Theater, Blok had cooled toward Meyerhold. Particularly after working on *The Rose and the Cross*, Blok began to distrust Meyerhold's approach to theater. This distrust grew to the point that, upon hearing the news that Meyerhold planned to stage *A Puppet Show* and *The Stranger*, Blok became extremely aggravated. He writes in his notebook the day after hearing the news, "Again everything that concerns Meyerholdism is painful to me. Irresistibly I like 'healthy realism,' Stanislavskii, and Musical drama. Everything I get out of theater, I get *from there* , but in Meyerholdism I strain and wither. Why do they love me? For the past and for the present, I fear, but not for the future, not for what I want" (Blok 1965, 209; italics in original).

A month before the first performance, though, Blok once again warmed toward Meyerhold. In his notebook, Blok jots down his impressions of a meeting with Meyerhold. "At four o'clock, V.È. Meyerhold — beautiful. For the first time in my life I understood (he explained) his essence". In the same entry, however, he sets down everything he dislikes in Meyerhold's work. He then goes on to say, "Contemporary naturalism is harmless because it is *outside of art*.... Modernism is poisonous because it is *with art*. *A puppet theater*, transferred to the Mariinskii stage, is *wildness*, barbarity, not creation. ... I love *psychology* in theater very much. And generally so that it is nourishing" (Blok 1965, 213-4; italics in original). Yet, Blok ends the same entry with the admission that, "After I had written this down, Meyerhold came to see me, and, after a tedious argument, he was suddenly able to tell me about himself and his own work, so that for the first time in my life, I felt a living, feeling, loving person in him" (Blok 1965, 214).

A thaw in their relations was under way, but it did not lead to a complete rapprochement. Blok's reaction to the performance of the two plays themselves was tepid. His impression of the opening night was particularly bad. Although Blok himself never wrote about it, friends and acquaintances recall a very morose figure. Verigina writes, "The performance on the whole did not enjoy a success. Nevertheless, they called Blok out. He forced himself to go out, with eyes lowered. Aleksandr Aleksandrovich went home gloomy and did not come to the performances for two or three days" (Verigina 1974, 208). One of Blok's acquaintances, Lidiia Segal' even felt the urge to leave town after the performance. As she wrote to Blok, "It was difficult to remain in Petersburg after I saw how your face turned to stone and I heard the voice of a lawn-tennis player, instead of shouting 'out' and 'ready,' utter the words of a tender neurasthenic — your Pierrot" (Kotrelev and Timenchik, 432). She was referring, of course, to the highly cadenced speech that Meyerhold was employing during this period.

However, according to Verigina, when Blok returned again several days later, he looked on the plays with different eyes. She writes, "He sat on the steps between the rows together with Iurii Bondi [an artist and Meyerhold's co-director for this production — TW], and this time he suddenly liked the performance. The poet said this to Iurii Mikhailovich. After this, Blok did not miss a single performance. He even regretted that he had interrupted his attendance after the first" (Verigina 1974, 208).

Because Blok never wrote about these performances, the reasons for his initial reservations and subsequent change of heart can only be surmised. His ambivalence most probably stemmed from his continuing predilection for "healthy realism." Meyerhold's daring innovations, in contrast, were at odds with the realist theater. Meyerhold introduced elements of many different theatrical traditions into the performance. For instance, "After *The Stranger* was finished, onto the stage came juggling Chinese children, who in the capacity of an interlude, did a series of simple tricks, and the participants in the plays tossed real oranges out to the audience" (Volkov 1929, 2: 321). According to Znosko-Borovskii, elements of the eastern theater predominated. "Individual moments of various theaters found expression in these performances, and if one were to single out one of these, then quite likely one would have to make an exception for the theater of the East, to which alluded so distinctly various details, such as: the Chinese jugglers in the capacity of an interlude, the oranges thrown out for the public, and much else" (cited by Volkov, 2: 323-24).

Nevertheless, Blok must have realized the demands *The Stranger* made on the theater. Moreover, Blok's return to the theater after an absence of two days suggests that even on the first night, Meyerhold did not fail entirely to engage these new demands. As the performances developed, everyone involved sensed the importance of this production. Not that everyone agreed on what was important about it. Blok's biographer, Avril Pyman, writes, "There was one moment which made theatrical history, when the grey figures knelt down with lighted candles forming a line of living footlights reminiscent of the theatre of the eighteenth century" (Pyman, 2: 200). Meyerhold himself, though, put the emphasis elsewhere. "The erection of the bridge for the second part of Blok's *The Stranger* in Petrograd in 1914 (the collaborative work of V. Meyerhold and Iu. M. Bondi) on the platform of the 'Tenishevskii auditorium,' which was free from theatrical elements, was the first attempt at the mounting of a stage area under the badge of constructivism" (Meierkhol'd 1968c, 18). These innovations, however, do not just reveal the importance of this production in Meyerhold's career. They also reflect certain aspects of *The Stranger* itself.

III

Parallelism

Meyerhold did not introduce these innovations for the sake of novelty. *The Stranger* required a new approach to theater, an approach which fell outside the domain of the realist theater. Andrei Fedorov, for instance, accurately describes the difficulties inherent in approaching the plot from the standpoint of a realist aesthetic: "The transitions from the everyday plane to the fantastic, the various possibilities of combination, and the union of them, by means of which one plane superimposes itself on the other and appears through it, are given in sharply underlined form, without plot motivation" (Fedorov 1972, 69). Moreover, the realist theater could hardly countenance either the transformation of a falling star into a woman, as happens in the second vision, or a woman's transformation back into a star, as happens in the third. The sudden appearance of the Blue one in the second vision poses similar problems, as do the disappearances of the Stranger and the Astronomer at the end of the play. Moreover, the stage directions go far beyond the parameters of realistic drama. The divisions between individual visions, for instance, remain indistinct. The "segues" between the three visions of the play appear better suited to film than theater. The stage directions which link the first vision to the second read as follows:

> It is as if the entire tavern dives somewhere. The walls part. The ceiling, which has bent once and for all, reveals the sky — wintry, blue, cold. In the blue evening snow opens —

> THE SECOND VISION
>
> The same evening. The end of a street at the edge of town. The last houses, breaking off suddenly, reveal a wide perspective: a black, empty bridge across a large river. On both sides of the river nod quiet ships with signal lights. Beyond the bridge stretches an endless, straight-as-an-arrow alley, which is framed by chains of street lights and trees white from frost. In the air the snow flutters like stars. (4: 81-2).

The segue between the second and third visions presents the director just as great a challenge:

> ... And the snow is melancholy. It has already dusted both the bridge and the ships. It has built white walls on the canvas of trees, along the wall of houses, on the telegraph lines. And the earthly distance and the river's distance rise up like white walls, so that everything is white, except for the signal lights on the boats and the illuminated windows of the houses. The snowy walls thicken. They seem close to one another. Little by little opens up —
>
> THE THIRD VISION
>
> A big guest room with white walls, on which electric lamps burn brightly (4: 93-4).

Taken together, these elements suggest that Blok, as playwright, continued to develop the non-realist dramatic innovations he had begun in *A Puppet Show*. At least at the time he wrote *The Stranger*, Blok was still consciously playing with the conventions of drama. Meyerhold's own theatrical innovations arose in response to and reflect directly the innovative structural elements of *The Stranger* itself. These innovations necessitated a break with the realist and naturalistic theater and, in so doing, allowed for the elaboration of Meyerhold's own theatrical poetics.

In much the same way, Blok elaborated a new language. In *The Stranger* Blok continued the parody of the language of his "Beautiful Lady" poems that he had begun in *A Puppet Show*. Where that language remained deeply monologic in his early poems, it now stood juxtaposed to other, competing languages. In *The Stranger*, Blok seeks to broaden the dramatic norms of his day and, in the process, undertakes a dialogue with dramatic tradition. The chief conduit of this dialogue, just as in *A Puppet Show* and *The King on the Square*, is carnival. *The Stranger* is saturated with carnivalistic overturnings and upendings and shows all the earmarks of extensive carnivalization. What results is not only a renewal of the dramatic tradition, but, in its most radical aspect, the renewal, the dialogizing of Blok's language.

The Stranger, like the plays that preceded it, belongs to the realm of the serio-comical, observing the three basic tenets of all serio-comical works. First, in *The Stranger*, " ... the starting point for understanding, evaluating, and shaping reality, is the living *present* ... " (Bakhtin 1984b, 108; italics in original). Commentators all agree on this aspect of the play. As Medvedev puts it, "It has been pointed out repeatedly in the literature about Al. Blok that the place and surroundings in which the action of his dramas take place were usually taken by the poet from his real impressions or memories and were written 'from nature'" (Medvedev, 54). Comparing *The Stranger* to *The King on the Square*, Leonid Dolgopolov says, "With much greater strength the impressions of real life make themselves felt in the third 'lyric drama' — *The Stranger* " (Dolgopolov, 4: 558).

The memoiristic literature also supports this point. For instance, his aunt, Mariia Beketova, writes, "The play *The Stranger*, which was permeated with his wanderings through the remote corners of the Petersburg side, was written in the first half of this same winter [1906-07 — TW]. The bar in the first vision was located on the corner of Geslerovskii Lane and Zelenina Street. The entire set, starting from the ships on the wallpaper and ending with the dramatis personae, are taken from nature: The 'spitting images' of Hauptmann and Verlaine, the gentleman who fingers through the crayfish, the girl in the kerchief, the curio seller — all of these people were seen by the poet during his visits to the tavern with the ships" (Beketova 1922, 103). As if to allay any remaining doubt about how "real" the setting is, Andrei Fedorov points out that Geslerovskii Lane is now Chkalovskii Prospect (Fedorov 1980, 94). Concerning the bridge in the second vision, Medvedev tells us, "This is the bridge and lane to Krestovskii Island from B. Zelenina Street" (Medvedev, 55).[3] As in so many of his poems of the same period, Blok's immediate surroundings left a clear imprint on *The Stranger.* It should be noted, however, that because Blok's method is not realistic, even natives of Petersburg sometimes disagree about the location of the action of *The Stranger* and the region Blok intended. For example, in their plans for a never realized staging of the play at Lugny-Poe's Théatre de l'Œuvre, Sergei Sudeikin and Samuil Vermel' set the action in the vicinity of the Potseluev Bridge over the Moika (Bezrodnyi, 228-31 passim).

The second characteristic of serio-comical genres consists in that they "... do not rely on *legend* and do not sanctify themselves through it, they *consciously* rely on *experience* (to be sure, as yet insufficiently mature) and on *free invention* ; their relationship to legend is in most cases deeply critical, and at times even resembles a cynical exposé" (Bakhtin 1984b, 108; italics in original). All of *The Stranger* borders on cynical exposé as the response from Blok's contemporaries demonstrates. Here, the poet of the *Verses about the Beautiful Lady* parodied himself and the beautiful. Like *A Puppet Show* before it, *The Stranger* elicited accusations of heresy against Blok.

The play's parodic tendencies took a number of particular forms. Through an extensive use of parallelism, the upper-class gathering of the third vision is set in parodic juxtaposition to the lower-class bar of the first vision, a circumstance to which we will return momentarily. The Poet, at one point the singer of the pure and divine Beautiful Lady, proves also to be a drunk who gets thrown out on his ear by bouncers. Nor are other poets immune to the ravages of alcohol. Hauptmann and Verlaine turn out to be just two more drunks. Even the Poet's poems take on parodic overtones. When he reads at the request of the Hostess in

[3] Medvedev apparently has in mind the Grand Krestovskii Bridge [Bol'shoi Krestovskii Most].

the third vision, the Poet and his high-minded verse appear as comically out of place in the refined vulgarity of the upper class as they did in the undistilled vulgarity of the bar. Parody in *The Stranger* thus turns out to be both self-parody and social satire.

The third characteristic of the serio-comical genres, their "deliberate multi-styled and hetero-voiced nature," also finds expression in *The Stranger* (Bakhtin 1984b, 108). The first and third versions are primarily in prose, while the second is dominated by verse. Moreover, the play fails to observe lines of demarcation between verse and prose even within a single character's speech. The Poet speaks in prose in the first and third visions, but in verse in the second. Likewise, the Astronomer and the Stranger-Mariia speak in verse in the second, but in prose in the third. This rejection of stylistic unity within the speech of individual characters has wide-ranging implications for their identity. Not only does the speech of one character blur into that of another, but this very blurring suggests that a single consciousness may stand behind the speech of two or more characters. In this way, similarities arise between the speech and poetry of the Poet and the Blue one to such an extent that the two have no existence apart from one another. Much the same is true of the star, the Stranger, and Mariia.

Besides these general traits that it shares with all serio-comical works, *The Stranger* also displays characteracteristics unique to carnivalized works. Of these characteristics, doubling proves to be perhaps the pivotal element of carnival in *The Stranger*. Blok's extensive use of it, in fact, assumes structural importance. It also paradoxically accounts both for the critical praise *The Stranger* has received and for the failure of critics to apprehend Blok's non-realist technique. Despite the gap between the expectations of realist critics and the play's actual structure, *The Stranger* has enjoyed great popularity amongst critics, greater than the other two plays of the trilogy, precisely because of its structure. For instance, Volkov argues that Blok "displays complex dramatic technique" when he first introduces the Stranger indirectly, through a cameo in the first vision (Volkov 1926, 56). Rubtsov writes in a similar vein, "The play is original in its compositional aspect: its three visions are linked together, forming a triptych about the Poet, who is stuffering from his own duality, and about the Stranger, a falling star" (Rubtsov, 56). Pavel Gromov goes one step further: "The construction of the whole, in relation to the intent, is in its own way perfect, masterly" (Gromov 1961c, 457).

Time and again critics point to the mastery of the play's structure and composition. Understanding the play's structure ultimately depends on elucidating Blok's use of doubles. Like *A Puppet Show*, *The Stranger* is polyphonic. As one critic has suggested, "However, it seems justified to us, taking into account the variability of the lyrical consciousness which is revealed through a system of doubles, to speak of the polyphonic principle of construction of the composition of A. Blok's lyrical drama [*The Stranger* — TW] as the development of a system of equal leitmotifs" (Karpova, 60). Critics stop just short of calling the play unequivocally polyphonic. This hesitation stems at least in part from Bakhtin's comments about drama, which were cited in relation to *A Puppet Show*. Bakhtin's stricture against polyphony in drama certainly applies to realist and neo-classical plays, but it is inadequate in regard to much modernist drama. It is here that Blok most actively and polemically engages tradition, and his use of doubles breaks down the traditional monologic parameters of drama and creates polyphony.

Any understanding of Blok's use of doubles, however, demands rigorous definition, inasmuch as he expands on the traditional uses of this technique. Doubling may be generally understood as the repetition, or parallelism of key elements, coupled with isolated oppositions. It belongs, in this sense, to what Gerard Manley Hopkins described as "the marked or abrupt kind of parallelism," in which "the effect is sought in likeness of things, and antithesis, contrast, and so on, where it is sought in unlikeness" (Hopkins, 85). The reason behind the favorable reception of *The Stranger* by critics — again, in the face of the play's patently unrealistic technique — surely finds its explanation in Hopkins's assertion that "... (t)he structure of poetry is that of continuous parallelism" (Hopkins, 84). Parallelism, in this sense, functions as a structuring device in *The Stranger*.

Many have pointed to parallelism in the play; yet, few have pursued the implications of this parallelism beyond the level of social satire. As a result, critics have not perceived that doubling, a particular kind of parallelism, unites every level of the play's structure. Even such a careful critic as Konstantin Mochulsky fails to assign any importance to Blok's use of parallelism as a structural device. In comparing the first and third visions, Mochulsky limits the importance of the parallels between the two to the depiction of the "vulgarity" of the worlds of the bar and the drawing room. Otherwise, in Mochulsky's opinion, "The author plays with the device of enigmatic correspondences, rather arbitrary and artificial" (Mochulsky, 152). Rubtsov puts forth a similar arugment. According to him, the parallelism between the first and third visions underscores the similarities between the world of the bar and the world of high society, in particular their banality. In Rubtsov's view, "All of A. Blok's passionate hatred for the petty bourgeoisie, for banality is expressed with the utmost clarity in this sharp grotesque, in these satirical sketches of *The Stranger*" (Rubtsov, 58). This interpretation of the play's parallelism as narrowly satirical resounds throughout most of the criticism on the play. Because of this failure to understand Blok's use of parallelism as a formal, organizing principle, critics must resort to the inappropriate category of "psychology" in order to define the structure of the play.

This psychology inevitably arises out of attempts to elucidate *The Stranger* as either Blok's own vision or as the vision of the drunken Poet. The question of whether or not the fantastical elements in *The Stranger* can be realistically motivated has assumed paramount importance for most critics. Even an insightful critic suggests, "Personifying various sides of this soul in a system of completed and apparently (but only 'apparently') independent images-characters, Blok does not simply half open for us the inner being of his soul (individual consciousness), but shows the tense battle, which its heroes — the masks of different sides of the soul or consciousness — wage in it (Lenchik 1971, 163-4). Another critic's useful analysis of the tempo of dialogue in *The Stranger* is hampered by similar assumptions. She writes, "The three visions reveal the emotional life of the play's lyrical subject" (Karpova, 62). The contention that the play's reality "is nothing other than the theatricalization of the inner world of an 'individual soul'" proves to be highly troublesome (Lenchik 1971, 163). Such a conception borders on psychologism. If the characters of *The Stranger* represent "different sides of the soul or consciousness," the reader is all but invited by Lenchik and other critics to guess which characters represent which parts of Blok's psyche. In such a reading, the drama itself degenerates into an allegory of Blok's mind.

Such psychologism, of course, contains an element of truth. Clearly some relationship exists between the work produced and the psyche that produces it. A one-to-one correspondence between character and psychical element, however, fails to provide a satisfactory explanation for either the biographical question of what *The Stranger* meant in terms of Blok's life or the literary question of which principles Blok chose to build the play upon. In the case of the former, such psychologism oversimplifies the complexity of the relationship between the writer and the work; while in the case of the latter, such an explanation reduces a drama which involves a number of independent characters into a monodrama which emanates from a single character. Blok's does not follow Evreinov's practice of the monodrama, and the application of the norms of that genre to *The Stranger* diminishes the independence of its form.

On the literary plane, this reduction leads to a serious misinterpretation of the forces at work in the play. While such characters as the Blue one are incomprehensible apart from the Poet, other characters are independent. Lenchik, for instance, provides no motivation for subordinating the Astronomer to the Poet. Rather, Lenchik argues, "The movement of the hero's thoughts, the real life of his soul ... define its [the play's — TW] composition" (Lenchik 1971, 164). With equal validity and equal inaccuracy, Lenchik could have said that the play emanates from the Astronomer. To assert that the entire play emanates from the psyche of any one character, in any case, is to do violence to the structure of the play itself.

Moreover, the play unfolds in such a way that what a character is, his psychological makeup, is less important than what he says. Not the inner relationship between what a character says and his psychological motivation for saying it, but rather the outward correspondence of a single remark uttered by two different characters — that is, the leitmotif associated with both — constitutes structural significance in *The Stranger*. The play consequently stands in polemical contrast to the psychology of the realist tradition. This contrast, of course, guarantees a clash with the realist tradition, especially in terms of structure. As one critic puts it, "The first act, from the point of view of traditional dramatic structures, is very strange" (Gromov 1961c, 457). Another suggests much the same thing, when she notes, "The originality of the play's composition is that the departure point of the action is not at the beginning, but in the middle of the drama" (Rodina, 158). Thus, if the action *per se* — that is, the action around which the psychological dilemma arrays itself — does not begin until the second vision, it cannot be the fulcrum on which the play rests. Some other principle has replaced plot as action. That principle is parallelism. Understood in its broadest terms, this parallelism at the level of device is of a piece with doubling, parallelism at the level of character. Perhaps the most striking instance of doubling, or parallelism, at the level of device in the play manifests itself in the structures of the first and third visions.

Were this not the case, the first vision would consist of merely random snatches of barroom dialogue. However, as the third vision unfolds, the structure of the first vision ceases to be random. The first vision opens with two men, who are discussing a fur coat, being interrupted by a third:

> ONE: I bought this fur coat for twenty-five rubles. And to you Sashka, I won't let it go for any reason for less than thirty.

ANOTHER [persuasively and with resentment]: Yeah, you're lying! ... Just you give it here ... I'll (give) you ...
THIRD [moustached, yells]: Be quiet! Don't fight! Another bottle, my friend.
(4: 73-4)

The same conversation, now transposed into the speech of the upper class, reappears at the beginning of the third vision:

HOST OF THE HOUSE [in the foyer]: A-a-ah! Well, haven't you wrapped yourself up, my good man!
VOICE OF THE GUEST: And the cold, I'll report to you! In a fur coat and I still almost froze.
...

HOST: And where was it sewn?
GUEST: At Chevalier's.
...

HOST: And how much did you pay?
GUEST: A thousand.
...

HOSTESS: Cher Ivan Pavlovich! Come in, come in! We've been waiting just for you! Here, Arkadii Romanovich promised us to sing today!
(4: 94-5).

We should also note that at the end of both of these segments, another character approaches the group. In the first vision, a waiter runs up [podbegat'] when another bottle is called for, while in the second, Arkadii Romanovich makes various gestures as he walks up to the hostess [podxodia k xoziaike].

In a similar manner, the second conversation in the first vision sets forth the theme of the second conversation of the third vision. In the first vision, a young seminarian goes into raptures over a dancer, only to be laughed at by his cohorts. This situation repeats itself in the third vision. When Misha sings the praises of the dancer Serpantini, his friend Georges tells him, "To dance as she did yesterday means to have no shame" (4: 95). The interference of a character, who is not directly involved, interrupts both of these conversations, just as the end of the conversations that preceded them are marked by the appearance of a character, who does not participate in the conversation. In the first vision, a drunken Verlaine mutters loudly, "To each his own. To each his own. ..." (4: 75). In the third, an old man interrupts the conversation with the exclamation, "Whorehouse" (4: 96). The old man goes on to embarrass the Hostess by telling her that her dress has come undone in the back.

The next parallel motif is linked to the entrance of a man and a woman. In both instances, the woman relates an anecdote, which she herself interrupts in order to ask her companion for something. The man then tells the woman to be quiet. In the first vision, "A girl in a kerchief enters and excitedly tells her companion how a guest of the night wanted to rob her and how they dragged him to the police station" (Mochulsky, 149). The woman, who is identified simply as a Girl, then asks her companion, who likewise is simply a Man, for a twenty-kopeck piece. The Man gives it to her, and she asks if he is not sad about something (4: 75). The Man replies, "Drink and shut your trap" (4: 75). The same motifs unfold in the third vision in the interactions of the Lady and the Red-haired Gentleman. When they enter, they greet the Hostess, and the Lady immediately sets about relating an anecdote to her. The Lady, however, interrupts herself to ask the Red-haired Gentleman for her kerchief. When he hands it to her, the Lady asks, "Are you miserable, perhaps?" (4: 97). The Lady receives the same answer the Girl in the first vision got: "Drink and shut your trap" (4: 98).

Once these conversations end, two men, who are discussing a woman, become the focus of the audience's attention. The first tells the second that a woman is waiting for him. In the first vision, a Young Man makes the announcement to an inebriated Hauptmann. Likewise in the third vision, it is a Young Man who heralds the news, but this time he gives it to a friend, who is identified only as Kostia but who can easily be recognized as the one who led the Stranger away. The replies of Hauptmann and Kostia to the news that a woman awaits them differ, but bear witness to one and the same motive. Hauptmann replies that the woman can wait and invites his companion to drink some more. Kostia makes no reply during this first exchange, but moments later he responds to the news by hiding behind the Young Man. In both instances, the man endeavors to avoid the woman.

At this point in both visions, the Poet enters. The same utterances that accompany his entrance in the first vision accompany it in the third, although in a slightly different order. For instance, the Poet's entrance in the first vision is heralded by more of Verlaine's nonsensical mumbling. The Poet then enters and exchanges a few words with the Waiter. In contrast, when the Poet enters the drawing room in the third vision, it is the Hostess who greets him. In the midst of greeting the Poet, she is interrupted by the nonsensical sputterings of the Old Man. Though the exact order changes, the basic components of the parallelism remain the same. At this point in both visions, the Poet and his interlocutor exchange a few more words.

Next come segments which parallel one another in terms of their respective positions, but not in terms of the characters who are involved. The Seminarian and one of his fellow drinkers return at this point in the first vision to continue their argument about the dancer. In the third vision, on the other hand, the Host interrupts the Poet's reading to greet the Stranger at the front door. Not recognizing her, he calls the Hostess to the door. Once this brief segment ends, the two visions return to their former, strict parallelism.

In the first vision, the Young Man returns to tell Hauptmann again that the woman is still waiting for him. Hauptmann again tells the Young Man to let her wait. In the third vision, the Young Man recognizes the woman at the door as one of Kostia's consorts. It is at this point, as mentioned above, that Kostia tries to hide behind the Young Man. Blok emphatically ties these two incidents together by having the Young Man in the first vision address Hauptmann not by the writer's real name, Gerhart, but as "brother Kostia", the name of the Young Man's friend in the third vision (4: 77).

Perhaps the most important parallel in the entire play arises at this juncture. In the first vision, the Man in the Coat enters and tries to sell a cameo, on which is depicted the Woman who Rules the World. At this same juncture in the third vision, the Stranger enters. The Hostess asks her what her name is. She gives herself the name Mariia at the point where the Poet refers to the cameo as the Woman who Rules the World in the first vision.

Having established this parallel, Blok abandons the strict parallelism that has predominated up to this point. True, numerous similarities arise in the exchanges between the Man in the Coat and his Interlocutor in the first vision and the Poet and the Astronomer in the third, but the reins are slack. The end of the first vision serves as a recapitulation of the vision's main themes. Thus, the Seminarian, Verlaine, Hauptmann, and Poet all return one more time to sound the motifs already associated with them.

No such recapitulation, however, occurs at the end of the third vision. Instead, Blok draws attention to the artifice of the parallelism between the first and third visions by means of several direct references to motifs from the first vision. References to the Seminarian's motifs occupy an especially prominent place. Out of the din arise his exclamations, "No, how she danced" and "And you won't get it" (4: 100). The Man in the Coat's references to the Russian intelligentsia recur here as well. Finally, a "stout man" leaps out into the middle of the room with a cry of "Brie!" which takes the audience back to the conversation between the Man in the Coat and his Interlocutor about cheese in the first vision (4: 100-1). The Poet seems on the verge of remembering the first vision as he starts towards the Stranger-Mariia. The Astronomer cuts him off, however, and he fails to remember. They exchange a few remarks in a room now abandoned by the other characters. The Hostess returns to inquire about the whereabouts of the Stranger-Mariia only to find that she and the others have disappeared.

The fact that Blok abandons strict parallelism lends particular emphasis to the last parallel, the association between the cameo of the Woman who Rules the World and the Stranger. Once this association is established, Blok uses the end of the third vision to recapitulate themes from the first vision, as we have seen, as well as from the second vision. At the end of the third vision, the Poet and the Astronomer conclude the conversation they began in the second vision.

Yet, even the extensive parallels that arise between the first and third visions do not exhaust Blok's use of parallelism. Even the second vision, which seemingly stands by itself, reveals a consistent parallelism. It falls into four parallel parts, which are arranged in such a way that the first two parts mirror the second two. The second vision opens and ends with the Poet and the Astonomer on stage. In both instances, the Astronomer appears on the stage first and is only later joined by the Poet. The two middle segments of the vision, on the other hand, concern the Stranger. In the second segment, she meets the Blue one, whose relation to her is platonic. In the third, she encounters a character, known only as a Gentleman, whose relation to her is physical. In this way, the second vision divides evenly into two parts, which reflect one another parodically.

This pervasive parallelism serves to delineate for both the reader and the audience which motifs, characters, and scenes correspond to one another. They serve, in other words, as doubles for one another. In consequence, a critic like Gromov can justifiably argue, "It is as if entire social strata, which are linked by the unity of a certain vital and heart-felt problem, turn out to be 'doubles'" (Gromov

1961c, 462). Rodina also refers to the two visions as doubles (Rodina, 158). More accurately, however, social strata do not turn out to be doubles. Rather, it is certain structures within the play that double one another.

Blok highlights this use of parallelism as a means of demarcation by setting it against the background of the very indistinct boundaries, the almost impossible segues between the visions mentioned earlier. If dramatic structure — the conventional stops at the end of scenes and acts — is understood as a concretized boundary which facilitates the staging of a work, then Blok, as author, engages this traditional conception of dramatic structure polemically. (His decision to call the three parts of *The Stranger* "visions" and not acts or scenes is telling.) In its stead, he places an all-encompassing parallelism, which provides a different, but equivalent structure. Inasmuch as Blok turns traditional structures inside out and creates "new modes of interrelationship" between characters and formal elements, the structure of *The Stranger* may be profitably understood as carnivalized (Bakhtin 1984b, 123). Blok dons, as it were, the mask of the fool and acts the part of the ingenue playwright. Pretending not to understand traditional dramatic structures, he creates his own and thereby calls those traditional structures into question.

IV

Doubles and Parallelism

Doubling, again understood as parallelism, also serves as an organizing principle at the level of character. In terms of the minor characters, we have already seen how every character in the first vision plays off of a double in the third vision. Doubling also accounts for the alignment of the main characters. Blok's use of doubles in *The Stranger*, however, becomes much more intricate and extensive than in his two previous plays. The very magnitude of this problem has led to considerable disagreement in the literature on the play about which characters are, in fact, doubles. On the one hand, Mochulsky can identify the Blue one as "the poet's soul" (Mochulsky, 151), while on the other, Gromov can assert, "The Blue one and the Gentleman in the bowler are inwardly linked between themselves, just as Pierrot and Harlequin are" (Gromov 1961c, 459). The search for a criterion by which to delineate just what a double is thus assumes paramount importance.

In point of fact, defining what a double is does not involve a new definition of the term, but rather just refining the traditional definition. Both Mochulsky and Gromov are, to a certain extent, correct. Doubling does account for both the relationship between the Poet and the Blue one and that between the Blue one and the Gentleman; however, these relationships represent opposed doubling processes. In Bakhtin's view, the double creates parody, which is inseparable from a carnival sense of the world. "Parodying is the creation of a *decrowning double*; it is that same 'world turned inside out'" (Bakhtin 1984b, 127). Consequently, doubling is a process that simultaneously likens the double and the parodied object and contrasts them. As such, it belongs fundamentally to the realm of metaphorical processes. Consider, in this regard, Roman Jakobson's assertion, "Metaphor works through creative association by similarity and contrast" (Jakobson 1987b,

306). Doubling thus constitutes a particular kind of parallelism, in which certain similarities between characters are underscored in order to emphasize certain other contrasts and oppositions.

Yet, as Roman Jakobson has argued, an artistic text is not a neutral background for the processes of language, in particular for those of metaphor. In Jakobson's words, "*The poetic function projects the principle of equivalence from the axis of selection into the axis of combination*" (Jakobson 1987a, 71; italics in original). One consequence that issues from this principle is that those processes associated with the axis of selection, such as metaphor, become superimposed on those processes associated with the axis of combination, such as metonymy. As a result, Jakobson says, "In poetry, where similarity is superinduced upon contiguity, any metonymy is slightly metaphoric and any metaphor has a metonymic tint" (Jakobson 1987a, 85). While metaphoric processes are more apparent, metonymic processes provide a constant substratum, upon which metaphors are grounded.

In regard to the question of doubling, the key becomes to determine which of these processes, the metaphoric or the metonymic, predominates. If it is the former, what results is a double, who is either like or unlike the character being doubled. If the latter, what results is a double, whose relation to the character being doubled depends more on contiguity, more on spatial or temporal proximity than on likeness. Classic examples of the former abound in the works of Dostoevskii: Raskol'nikov and Svidrigailov, Luzhin, and Lebeziatnikov; Ivan Karamazov and Smerdiakov, the devil, and the Grand Inquisitor. For examples of the latter, we turn to doubles generally associated with comic literature, such as Gogol's Kovalev and his nose, and Kafka's Gregor Samsa and the dung beetle. Significantly, the preeminent characteristic that distinguishes metaphoric doubles from metonymic ones is a function of the manner in which the double is derived. Metaphoric doubles take on a life of their own. While they are like the characters they double, they exist apart from them. Metonymic doubles, on the other hand, are intimately tied to the character they double. In fact, they cease to have any meaning whatsoever if cut off from that other character.

If applied to *The Stranger*, this standard reveals the symmetry of Blok's use of doubles. For instance, the Poet has a number of doubles. The most important of these is the Astronomer, who doubles the Poet metaphorically and not metonymically. Though they both believe in the same thing, namely the being that manifests itself variously as a star, the Stranger, and Mariia, they completely fail to understand one another, despite their common bond. The Astronomer's sober, analytical, scientific method parodies the Poet's drunken, intuitive, quasi-mystical belief. In Rodina's words, the Astronomer is " ... a man, who decomposes 'mysticism' with mathematics, who loves to see the stars in their place, in the sky" (Rodina, 162). Nowhere does this contrast become clearer than at the end of the second vision, when the Astronomer bemoans the disappearance of a "beautiful star" and the Poet, after awaking from a drunken sleep, laments the departure of a "tall woman in black." The Astronomer does not know that the "beautiful star" fell to earth to become the Poet's "tall woman in black," nor does the Poet know that his beloved was once the Astronomer's star. Though they lament the same thing, they fail to recognize that they have this sorrow in common. This failure thus assumes parodic overtones, especially at the end of the third vision. In giving an account of their findings, the Poet and the Astronomer each state their findings in the other's language. The Astronomer, in language more fitting to a writer than a scientist, announces, "I have entered a new paragraph into my lists: 'The star Mariia has fallen!'" (4: 101). The Poet, on the other hand, states dispassionately, "My search was without result" (4: 102).

Besides the Astronomer, other doubles also shadow the Poet, though in different ways. If the Astonomer is related to the Poet in terms of likeness and dissimilarity, others are related by mere contiguity. The most important of the latter sort is the Blue one who is separated from the Poet only in time and space. He appears, significantly, after bouncers have thrown the Poet into a snowdrift. The Poet falls into a drunken sleep, and the Blue one appears. Moreover, once the Blue one disappears, the Poet eventually makes his way out the snowdrift back to the bridge. Thus, Mochulsky's characterization of the Blue one as "the poet's soul" falls very near the mark. As a double, the Blue one is related to the Poet metonymically, just as the Poet's own soul might be said to stand in metonymic relation to the Poet.

Other doubles, both metaphoric and metonymic, abound in *The Stranger*. In his attitude towards the Stranger, the Poet echoes both the Seminarian of the first vision and the young man Misha in the third. The question of how these three are related to one another has often eluded commentators. For instance, Rodina claims, on the one hand, "The Seminarian is a folk, elemental poet ," but, on the other, "The Seminarian is not the Poet's double, but his analogue on the level of folk existence ..." (Rodina, 160). Rodina correctly identifies the hierarchy that exists between the two, that in fact the Seminarian is in some way modeled after the Poet. However, she is mistaken in not perceiving them as doubles, since they stand in parodic counterpoint to each other. For instance, the Poet, while perusing the cameo he has bought from the Curio-seller, remarks, "This is — She is — the Woman who Rules the World. ... We are all enchanted by Her" (4: 78). His myth, however, elicits parody. In their worldly obsessions, both the Seminarian and Misha, his double from the third vision, reduce the Poet's myth. The Seminarian parodies the religious overtones of the Poet's myth when he says, "And she danced, I'll tell you, my dear friend you, like a heavenly creation" (4: 74). Misha also parodies the Poet's conception of poetry, the Symbolist understanding of poetry as music, when he says of the dancer, "Serpantini herself is the embodiment of music" (4: 96).

Two other doubles continue this parody of the Poet as a poet. Verlaine, the embodiment of banality itself, mumbles to himself, "To each his own. To each his own..." (4: 75). Or, as he puts it more elaborately later, "And everything passes. And to each his own worry." (4: 77). Hauptmann also parodies the Poet, in particular the Poet's metonymical double, the Blue one. The Blue one remains pure in his idealization of the Stranger, saying, "I do not dare to touch you" (4: 87). Hauptmann, on the other hand, has grown cynical. When the young man runs in to tell him that a woman is waiting at the door for him, Hauptmann replies, "Okay. She'll hang around some more" (4: 75). Just how deep this cynicism runs becomes clear later when the young man tells Hauptmann that the woman is freezing outside. Hauptmann replies, "Stop it. If you indulge the feminine temper, nothing will remain of a man — you can just spit in his ugly mug. Let her hang around, and we'll sit here for a while longer" (4: 78).

And just as doubles trail after the Poet, doubles also shadow the Stranger. Again, they are of two sorts, metaphoric and metonymic. Out of her earthly passion, the Stranger begets metaphoric doubles. The first, the Girl in the bar, parodies the Stranger because she appears to be a prostitute. Mochulsky describes the Girl this way: "A girl in a kerchief enters and excitedly tells her companion how a guest of the night wanted to rob her and how they dragged him to the police station" (Mochulsky, 149). Gromov suggests that the veiled references to her profession were more pronounced in the rough drafts. He points out that in the rough draft, the Man in the coat asks twenty kopecks for the cameo of the Woman who Rules the World. Gromov continues, "The Girl in the kerchief, who demands a 'twenty-kopeck piece' in the final redaction, in this text [rough draft — TW] also asks for 'twenty kopecks.' Considering the constant play between the two plans (and) the mirror-like quality of the stylistic construction of the play, the similar parallelism signifies that the Woman who Rules the World is sold for the same price as a street prostitute" (Gromov 1961c, 486). The Stranger's other double, the Lady in the third vision, who is also a double of the Girl in the kerchief, parodies the spiritual bankruptcy of these earthly passions. Upon entering the drawing room, the Lady tells the Hostess a piece of gossip, about which they both giggle. This complete lack of seriousness reflects another side of the Stranger's earthly desires.

On the other hand, not all of the Stranger's doubles reflect likeness primarily. Other of her doubles stand primarily in a temporal or spatial relation to her. At the beginning of the second vision, before the Stranger appears, the stage directions depict a star. "Describing a slow arc, a bright and heavy star rolls across the sky" (4: 84). This star turns into the Stranger in the next sentence. "A moment later along the bridge walks a beautiful woman ..." (4: 84). Just as the Poet disappears before the Blue one appears, so too the star falls before the Stranger materializes. In much the same way, the Stranger's exit marks a transition back to the star. When the Hostess searches the drawing room for Mariia, or Mary as she calls the Stranger, the stage directions reveal, "Beyond the window shines a bright star" (4: 102). Thus, in this case, the temporal relationship between the Stranger and the star reigns supreme, since they can only appear consecutively.

The Astonomer too has his doubles. We have already seen that he and the Poet metaphorically double one another. Metonymic doubles follow him as well. The most important of these is the Gentleman who persuades the Stranger to spend the night with him in the second vision. Both the Gentleman, a sensualist, and the Astronomer, a scientist, share a faith in the senses as opposed to faith in the spirit, which distinguishes the Poet and the Blue one. Rodina's characterization of the Astronomer as "a man, who decomposes 'mysticism' with mathematics" is particularly apt in this regard. Metonymic associations further clarify the relationship. Again the temporal sequence assumes a vital role. The Stranger is twice conjured to appear and twice met. The Poet is the first to conjure her when, at the end of the first vision, he says, "Appear! Appear!" (4: 81). At the end of the first segment of the second vision, the Astronomer conjures her to appear. This time, however, the Astronomer conjures a falling star to fall toward him. "Fly here! Here! Here!" (4: 84). The Stranger is met in the same order by the metonymic doubles of those who conjure her to appear. First, the Blue one and then the Gentleman meet her and talk with her.

This last observation points to an important implication that Blok's use of doubles has for the play's structure. In this particular case, the Poet metaphorically doubles not only the Astronomer, but the latter's metonymic double, the Gentleman, as well. The Astonomer likewise metaphorically doubles the Poet and the Poet's metonymic double, the Blue one. Put in more general terms, the metonymic doubles of a given character are at one and the same time metaphoric doubles of any other character that is a metaphoric double of the first character and vice versa.

V

Carnival Masks

Doubling, then, is extensive in *The Stranger.* It is so extensive and so complex, in fact, that it would seem to border on the chaotic, did it not serve a straightforward purpose: each double is a polemical reflection of its referrent. The ethereal quality of the Blue one, for example, serves as counterweight to the Poet's drunken stupor. The double destabilizes the single, unitary language of its referrent and, in so doing, calls into question the ideology of the referrent. The double effects this process by donning the traditional masks of the fool, the rogue, and the clown. The mask of the fool, in particular, takes on special importance. Most of the main characters — the Poet, the Astronomer, the Stranger, Mariia — are, to varying degrees, fools. We have already referred to the Poet's failure to understand that he and the Astronomer grieve over the same thing at the end of the second vision. His metonymic double also demonstrates the fool's polemical and "naive incomprehension" (Bakhtin 1981a, 405). When the Stranger asks the Blue one, "Do you know passion?," he replies, "My blood is silent" (4: 87). While this denial of earthly passions is seemingly passive, it contains within it the seed of active renunciation. The Blue one actively refuses to acknowledge his own sexual and earthly desires. The failure to synthesize the earthly and spiritual leads to the bifurcation of one consciousness into two characters — the Poet and the Blue one.

The other important mask in The Stranger is that of the clown. The clown "... is a rogue who dons the mask of a fool in order to motivate distortions and shufflings of languages and labels, thus unmasking them by not understanding them" (Bakhtin 1981a, 404-5). In *The Stranger* the most important clown appears under the guise of the Gentleman. The Gentleman parodies the high-flown language of the poet, while ostensibly giving credence to it. For instance, when the Stranger tells him that the man she was with was a poet, the Gentleman cries, "I too am a poet! I too am a poet!" (4: 88). And to prove it, he devotes a one-line couplet (!) to her, "Aah, how fine you are!" (4: 88). Later he claims to quote Shakespeare, but his "quotation" begets only parody: "'Your every wish is my command', / As old man Shakespeare said ... / You see now that I / Am no stranger to poetry" (4: 88). The Gentleman's unabashed guile manifests itself in other ways as well. For example, when the Stranger asks him, "Do you want to love me?," he replies, "O, yes! I am very much not against it" (4: 88). Or again, when she asks, "Can you embrace me?," the Gentleman responds, "I would like to know why / I can't embrace you?" (4: 88). By thus pretending to be a poet, the Gentleman exposes the failure of the Poet and Blue one to integrate his earthly and spiritual desires.

We should also note in passing that the Gentleman's metonymic double, the Astonomer, also exhibits the traits of the clown. Although he claims to be interested only in the stars, his sincerity comes into question at the end of the play. The Poet seems on the verge of remembering the first vision and takes a few, tentative steps toward the Stranger. It is the Astronomer, however, who prevents him from remembering and from reaching the Stranger. The stage directions tell us, "For a moment it seems that he [the Poet — TW] remembered everything. He makes several quick strides toward the Stranger. But he is cut off by the Astronomer [who is] in a blue coat and who enters from the anteroom" (4: 101). Given the special attention Blok pays to structure in *The Stranger*, this event assumes greater importance than mere coincidence and again suggests the importance of doubling throughout the play.

All of these characteristics — from the doubles to the presence of the masks of the fool, rogue, and clown — stem from more deeply rooted elements of carnival. In *The Stranger*, as in other works of carnivalized literature, the most deeply rooted carnival elements concern the carnival king. "The primary carnivalistic act," as Bakhtin has argued, "is the *mock crowning and subsequent decrowning of the carnival king*" (Bakhtin 1984b, 124; italics in original). The primary arena for the ritual crowning and decrowning of the carnival king is the carnival square. Each of the play's three settings — the tavern, the bridge, and the living room — represents a carnival square. As Bakhtin argues, "(T)he central arena could only be the square, for by its very idea carnival *belongs to the whole people*, it is *universal*, *everyone* must participate in its familiar contact" (Bakhtin 1984b, 128). As literature transforms the carnival square, any place that fosters free contact between people may serve as a carnival square. In Bakhtin's own words, "Other places of action as well (provided they are realistically motivated by the plot, of course) can, if they become meeting- and contact-points for heterogeneous people — streets, taverns, roads, bathhouses, decks of ships, and so on — take on this additional carnival-square significance (for all the naturalistic qualities of the representation, the universal symbol-system of carnival is in no danger of naturalism)" (Bakhtin 1984b, 128-9). From this perspective, the tavern serves to bring together a diverse group of people, ranging from the Poet himself to a seminarian to a prostitute to the "spitting images" of Hauptmann and Verlaine. Similarly, the bridge provides a conduit for everyone who wishes to cross from one side of the river to the other. Finally, the drawing room too, though less obviously than the tavern and the bridge, provides a meeting place for a wide array of people. At first glance, it appears more restricted than the other two settings. However, because the drawing room is a variant — or to again adopt terminology ordinarily restricted to the typology of characters, the carnival double — of the tavern, the carnival function of each setting depends on the other.

In *The Stranger*, the carnival king's fall occupies what is structurally the middle of the play. As noted above, the play divides neatly into three visions, the first and third of which frame the second. The second, in its turn, contains four distinct episodes, of which the first and the fourth — both of which center around the Astronomer and the Poet — frame the second and third. The second and the third contrast with one another, the only constant being the carnival king, the Stranger. In the second, the Blue one pays homage to the Stranger as to a deity.

She parodies his intentions through her persistent questions about earthly passions. In effect, she debunks the Blue one's "official" language. The next episode brings the fall of the Stranger to its culmination, as she goes off with the Gentleman.

Abuse constitutes a pervasive part of decrowning, and the Stranger receives a great deal of it. Besides the obvious implications of her encounter with the Gentleman, various other slights and insults arise throughout the remainder of the play. When the Stranger, as Mariia, enters the drawing room in the third vision, two of the guests begin to talk amongst themselves. The first, identified only the Young man, tells his friend, "Kostia, she is waiting by the doors ..." (4: 98). His friend replies, "But it can't be ..." (4: 99). He then proceeds to slip out the door, excusing himself by saying, "I'm not entirely well" (4: 100). His unwillingness to see Mariia clearly implies that she is not only not a woman he would worship, but a woman of questionable morals who could embarrass him.

The position of this incident within the structure of the play lends further credence to this assertion. Mariia appears in the third vision at precisely the same juncture that the cameo of the Woman who Rules the World appears in the first. Gromov's remarks about the drafts of the play take on particular relevance here. Since, in the first vision, the Girl, who is clearly a prostitute, asks for a "twenty-kopeck piece" and since the cameo also costs twenty kopecks, Gromov argues that "... the similar parallelism signifies that the Woman who Rules the World is sold for the same price as a street prostitute" (Gromov 1961c, 486). The fact that Mariia and the cameo appear at the same juncture in parallel visions suggests not only a tie between them, but that what is true of the cameo is by extension true of Mariia as well.

The decrowning of the Stranger thus becomes complete. Critics have generally not understood this process, but they have intuited it. Their understanding of it, however, has been strictly negative. This has given rise, as in the critical treatment of *A Puppet Show*, to the commonly held belief that Blok renounced Vladimir Solov'ev and mysticism altogether in the trilogy of lyrical dramas. The problem with such an interpretation lies in its misapprehension of the decrowning process. Decrowning is never merely negative. In Bakhtin's words, "All the symbolic aspects of this ceremonial of decrowning acquire a second and positive level of meaning — it is not naked, absolute negation and destruction (absolute negation, like absolute affirmation, is unknown to carnival)" (Bakhtin 1984b, 125).

In *The Stranger* Blok does not renounce the Beautiful Lady. Rather, he sets the monologic language of mysticism, in which he had formerly enshrouded her, in dialogic opposition to those languages formerly renounced by mysticism, principally that of sensuality. What Blok aspires to in *The Stranger* is a language that encompasses not only the language of the Beautiful Lady and the world beyond, but also the language of sensual love and this world. Blok's polemic with dramatic convention in *The Stranger* should be understood as a consequence of his attempt to elaborate this language. His radically innovative approach to drama arose out of demands created by his language. Nowhere does this become more apparent than in the relationships between his main characters.

At the heart of these relationships, lies the theme of desire. The Stranger's fall — her decision to fulfill her earthly desires — occupies the highest point in the dramatic action of this "tragedy." However, her fall fails to become a resolution: she shines as a star again at the end of the play. This lack of resolution, in fact, finds expression in the appellation Blok uses for her name. She is the Stranger not only because no one knows who she is, but also because no one knows what she is. For the Poet she is an ideal woman; for the Astronomer she is a star; for the Gentleman she is a woman of questionable virtue. The carnivalistic underpinnings of her character reveal themselves precisely in this amalgam of mutually exclusive potentialities. This quality is much more pronounced in the dialogizing context of the drama *The Stranger* than in the poem of the same title. As one critic points out, "The heroine of the poem, for all of her mysteriousness and aloofness from banal reality, to which she is contrasted, is all the same placed precisely in the concrete situation of a suburban restaurant, (while) in the drama she is an astral being, and her appearance at night on the bridge immediately follows the falling of a star" (Fedorov 1980, 93). Such potentialities thus exceed the bounds of realistic motivation and, consequently, call forth new forms. The largely positive appraisal *The Stranger* has garnered stems, in no small part, from this organic fusion of form and theme. Gromov is surely right when he writes, "*The Stranger*, which brings the trilogy of lyrical dramas of 1906 to a close, represents one of the most important works in Blok's ideational-artistic development" (Gromov 1961c, 454).

CHAPTER FOUR

THE TRILOGY AS TRILOGY: THE CARNIVAL-GROTESQUE AND THE DESTRUCTIVE STATUE MYTH

I

Lyric, Drama, and Lyric Drama

The problem of *A Puppet Show*, *The King on the Square*, and *The Stranger* as a trilogy is at once one of the most difficult and, at the same time, one of the least examined questions in the critical literature on the three plays. Problems of terminology reflect the failure of this question to penetrate into the criticism on Blok's dramas. On one hand, Gromov (1961c), Rodina, Rubtsov, and Volkov (1926) all refer to the three plays as a trilogy. On the other, Fedorov (1972, 41; 1980, 54) refers to them as a "cycle of lyrical dramas," which echoes Dolgopolov's phrase, the "dramatic cycle of 1906" (4: 559). Other critics do not dwell on the plays as a trilogy at all and opt for the generic term "lyric dramas" (Medvedev, 11-15 passim).

The problems that attend the use of the term trilogy are obvious: The traditional characteristics of a trilogy are absent. For example, Blok does not develop the same subject matter through the course of his three plays. The chronological and historical development that Aleksei Tolstoi explores in *The Death of Ivan the Terrible*, *Tsar Fedor*, and *Tsar Boris* is alien to Blok's plays. Similarly, Blok does not introduce characters from one play into the next. Sukhovo-Kobylin's method of following Lidochka from *Krechinsky's Wedding* to *The Case* and Tarelkin from *The Case* to *Tarelkin's Death* has no parallel in Blok's dramas. As a result, Blok's trilogy, if it can be called that at all, seems to be nothing more than a collection of three plays.

Yet, critics persist in referring to them as a trilogy. To a certain extent, Blok himself is responsible for egging them on. In the introduction to the first collection of the lyrical dramas, Blok provided an explanation that critics have been all too willing to accept at face value. "All three dramas," wrote Blok, "are linked among themselves by the unity of the fundamental character type and its strivings" (4: 434). On the basis of this assertion, critics have understood Pierrot and the two Poets as this fundamental type that makes the plays cohere. Seen from this vantage point, these characters are so similar that they may be treated, if not as a single, recurring character, then as the focal points of the trilogy.

The merits of this argument are hard won, and problems abound. For instance, these characters, even if they do belong to a fundamental type, are quite distinct from one another. It would be pedantic to conflate Pierrot's naiveté with either the amorality of the Poet in *The King on the Square* or the dissoluteness of the Poet in *The Stranger*. Moreover, the subordinate position that this fundamental type occupies suggests that Pierrot and the two Poets are not as central to Blok's plays as Hamlet, for example, is to Shakespeare's tragedy. On the contrary, from the foregoing analyses, Columbine in *A Puppet Show*, the King in *The King on the Square*, and the Stranger in *The Stranger* prove to be much more central in terms of organization. In each case, the "fundamental character type" plays a structurally subordinate role.

Blok's understanding of the "fundamental character type" and its ability to unify the trilogy hinges on how he defined, or more to the point, did not define the term "lyric drama." While he provides the reader with a fascinating definition of "lyric," Blok surprisingly never states what a lyric drama is. The lyric, for Blok, represents the realm of the subjective. He wrote, "The experiences of the soul, in our time solitary by necessity, are consolidated in the lyric. ... These experiences are usually chaotic, complex" (4: 433). As a result, "The ideal lyric poet is a complex instrument, which reproduces equally the most contradictory experiences" (4: 433-4). Such a definition betrays, of course, Blok's bias as a lyric poet. While he suggests something of the experience of the poet himself, Blok reveals little about the work such a poet produces.

In fact, Blok's definition of lyric very nearly contradicts the only evidence by which such a definition could be judged, namely the work itself. If the poet's own experiences are "chaotic", the form of lyric poetry rarely is. Of all literary forms, the lyric is the most structured and unified, since a single voice underlies it. Yet, whatever the shortcomings of his definition generally, Blok paradoxically arrives at a very precise definition of what he sought to achieve in his own poetry during this period.

Blok's emphasis on the "fundamental character type" must be understood in light of the latter's failure to assume predominance in these plays. In other words, since Columbine and Harlequin, for example, are not subordinate to Pierrot, Pierrot's voice, the voice of the "fundamental type", ceases to occupy a privileged position, such as that enjoyed by the voice of Blok's persona in his first volume of poems, *Verses about the Beautiful Lady*. The consequent result is the breakdown of a strictly monologic authorial point of view. This breakdown rarely becomes absolute; nonetheless, it extends through the fabric of Blok's work and alters it radically.

Blok himself appears well aware of this breakdown of a single and unified voice. When he describes what Pierrot and the two Poets share, he suggests that they all seek the one, monologic truth even in the face of its breakdown: "They all seek a beautiful, free, and radiant *life*, which alone can knock off their weak shoulders the unbearable burden of *lyrical* doubts and contradictions and drive away troublesome and spectral doubles. For all three the beautiful life is the incarnation of the image of the Eternal Feminine" (4: 434; italics in original). As monologic belief breaks down under the pressure of lyric doubt, the voice of a given character ceases to be unified. The fundamental type finds himself pursued by doubles. In this sense, as monologic truth itself breaks down, the image of its bearer becomes non-coincident with itself. For instance, where the Beautiful Lady belonged without question to another world, Columbine and the Unknown Woman become part of both this and that, other world.

What unites these plays then is not merely Pierrot and the two Poets, but rather the dialogic orchestration of their voices with those of the other main characters. In each play, the voice of the "fundamental type" is answered and complicated by a metaphoric double. Pierrot and Harlequin are a paradigmatic example. The voices of these two become differentiated in their relation to the lead female character, or in the case of *The King on the Square*, in relation to her dream. The lead female character serves as a polemical voice, which forces the fundamental type and his metaphorical double to define themselves. This process of truth-in-the-making sets these plays off from Blok's earlier work and unites them as a trilogy. The failure of these three plays to truly resolve their dramatic conflicts, so often cited as a shortcoming by critics, flows as a logical consequence out of this process and points to their very real structural integrity.

The carnival underpinnings of this process inform a new approach in Blok's artistic method. Every aspect of his work renews itself. Blok pits old themes against their opposites. Solov'evian mysticism encounters sensual blasphemy in *A Puppet Show*, the monarchy of the select faces popular revolution in *The King on the Square*, and platonic love mingles with Eros in *The Stranger*. What had been unquestioned is turned upside down. The distinguishing characteristic of this upending lies in its complete failure to reach new, unitary truths. Nothing is resolved, and everything remains potential.

As the unquestioned authority of the monologic, lyric voice breaks down, every voice in these dramas becomes independent and viable on its own. Privilege and hierarchy are undermined. As a result, every voice, including the author's, enters into dialogue with every other voice. The ramifications for the authorial voice and its position are profound. The authorial voice even finds itself confronted by its doubles. The Author in *A Puppet Show* and the Fool in *The King on the Square* reveal the artifice of the authorial voice and show its relation to their own voices. The author thus becomes an explicit presence in his own creation. Of course, the author is always a presence in the creation, but traditionally that presence becomes manifest only when the work is seen in its totality. Blok, on the other hand, reveals his participation to the reader or spectator as the work unfolds. He emphasizes process, rather than product.

As a consequence, the relation of author and character is reconfigured. This relation always proves problematic in drama. As Veltrusky has observed, "The distinction between the sense put into the speech by the character and that which the author puts into it is uncertain. The language of the characters is, basically, the author's language as well. It is true that the degree of the sameness varies from one dramatic structure to another. It ranges from complete identity, as in Mæterlinck's plays, to extreme differentiation, such as is found in certain realistic plays" (Veltrusky, 44). At first glance, it would appear that Blok's plays, as symbolist dramas, should be similar to Mæterlinck's. However, Blok parodies not only Mæterlinck's themes, but his devices as well. The breakdown of authorial hierarchies that defines Blok's plays is alien to Mæterlinck's dramaturgy. A single, undifferentiated voice makes Mæterlinck's work cohere from start to finish.

However, the difference between Blok's plays and Mæterlinck's does not mean that Blok's are therefore realistic. What Blok's trilogy of lyric dramas shares with realistic plays is the "extreme differentiation" between the voices of author and character that Veltrusky observes. The difference between Blok and the realists lies in the relation between these voices. In the best realist plays, the author's voice does not intrude on the characters and is apparent only in the totality of the work. Hierarchically, the authorial voice is predominant, even though its presence remains implicit. In lesser realist plays, the author's voice may come through in the speeches of a spokesman. Even in weaker plays, though, the authorial voice prevails over all others. Consequently, if the author's spokesman is too strident, the authorial voice drowns out all others, and the piece deteriorates into the exposition of the author's views.

Blok's plays, on the other hand, do away with the privileged position of the authorial voice while maintaining extreme differentiation between it and the voices of the characters. The position of Blok's voice in his plays parallels the position Bakhtin ascribes to Dostoevsky's in the latter's novels. Blok and Dostoevsky are ideologists in their own work, and the validity of their positions is constantly tested against the truths of their characters. The unique position of the authorial voice in Blok's plays sets them off from other plays. By itself, it cannot justify the application of the term trilogy to the plays. When coupled with the principal types, their doubles, the orchestration of the authorial voice with other voices, and elements of the carnival-grotesque, however, the position of the authorial voice becomes one piece of evidence among many that supports the use of the term.

II

The Destructive Statue Myth

Such affinities in form are buttressed by recurrent patterns of imagery, which assume a stable configuration in all three plays, a configuration that proves to be an important element of their unity as a trilogy. Other works of carnivalized literature exert a powerful influence. In particular, Pushkin's influence, or more precisely the influence of what Roman Jakobson has defined as "the myth of the destructive statue" in Pushkin's work, plays a decisive role (Jakobson 1987c, 329).

Pushkin's destructive statue myth exerts its influence most clearly in *The King on the Square*. The other two plays also reveal its influence, but in muted form. The modifications of the Pushkinian myth in these plays become more apparent when compared with the more or less canonical treatment of the myth in *The King on the Square*. For the sake of clarity, I will disrupt chronological order and begin with Blok's second play. Jakobson identifies three pivotal characteristics of Pushkin's destructive statue myth, all of which Blok observes in *The King on the Square*. Jakobson describes the first as follows: "*A man is weary, he settles down, he longs for rest, and this motif is intertwined with desire for a woman*" (Jakobson 1987c, 321; italics in original). In Blok's play, the Poet complains of being tired, weary, and depressed. The first time he appears on stage, in fact, he asks the Architect, "Teach me to fight with melancholy" (4: 37). In the course of the same exchange, he goes on to tell the Architect, "There's nothing for me to strive for — I am doomed to melancholy" (4: 37). He goes on, "Consciousness prevents me from living" (4: 37). The Architect agrees, "You're sick" (4: 38).

This melancholy, however, does not interfere with his desire for the Architect's Daughter. He tells her, "Be with me! My wings grow! / ... / (My) heart is open only to you" (4: 41-2). He further emphasizes this by addressing her as "princess." The Architect's Daughter herself recognizes the fact that the Poet desires her, which she acknowledges by addressing him as "You, who are enchanted by me" (4: 43). When it becomes apparent that the Architect's Daughter will leave to realize her dream, the Poet begs her, "I breathe your fairytale — / Don't go away from me" (4: 43). This statement reveals the Poet's passivity and dependence on the Architect's Daughter. It is this dependence that intertwines the motif of the Poet's weariness with that of his desire for the Architect's Daughter. As he himself admits, "I am weak when the crowd rages, / I am weak when your father speaks, / (My) heart is open only to you" (4: 41). He implicitly ties his feelings of weakness and weariness to his desire for her.

The second characteristic of the destructive statue myth centers around the relationship between the desired woman and the statue. Jakobson defines it this way: "*The statue, more precisely the being which is inseparably connected with the statue, has a supernatural, unfathomable power over this desired woman*"(Jakobson 1987, 322; italics in original). In *The King on the Square*, the power which the statue of the King exercises over the Architect's Daughter becomes most apparent in her decision to leave the living, flesh-and-blood Poet for the statue of the King. Significantly, this decision hinges on her belief in the supernatural rebirth of the King.

In passing we should also note that part of the power the statue exerts on the Architect's Daughter derives from unresolved and unconscious sexual energies. Though attracted to the Poet, she ultimately leaves him for a statue built by her father, a circumstance the reader or spectator discovers only late in the play. As the Architect tells the crowd after his daughter, the Poet, and the statue have perished, "I hewed hard marble — and everyday you admired the beauty of these ancient curls, which came out from under my chisel. You broke apart my creation" (4: 60). Moreover, Blok underscores the relationship between the creator and the creation in his description of the Architect in the dramatis personae. There the Architect appears as "an old man in wide and dark clothes. In the features of his face and his gray hair he resembles the King" (4: 22). Elsewhere in the text, the First man in the first act refers to the Architect as a "titan" (4: 30). Thus, the statue's power over the Architect's Daughter exists on the psychological level as well as the supernatural. Despite her apparent rebellion against her father, the Architect's Daughter vouchsafes her loyalty and remains obedient to him by sacrificing herself to his creation.

The third characteristic of the destructive statue myth concerns the inevitable denouement of the tragedy. Jakobson writes, "*After a vain resistance the man perishes through the intervention of the statue, which has miraculously set itself into motion, and the woman vanishes*" (Jakobson 1987, 325). In *The King on the Square*, the Poet perishes as result of his desire for the Architect's Daughter. As he begins his fateful ascent up the stairs before the terrace collapses, the Poet tells her, "I am coming to you!" (4: 59). Once he reaches her, the terrace collapses, and he, the statue of the King, and the Architect's Daughter disappear.

What is seemingly absent from Blok's version of the destructive statue myth is the statue's active participation in the demise of the Poet. This absence, however, proves illusory.[1] As noted above, the Architect and the King are, in fact, doubles. As creator and creation, they are the active and passive aspects respectively of the same principle. From this vantage point, the Architect's otherwise enigmatic remarks at the end of the play find resolution. For instance, he says to the crowd, "I sent you my beloved son, and you killed him" (4: 60). The monologic intent of the Architect becomes apparent in this paraphrase of God's words about Christ in the New Testament. The Architect makes a conscious decision to sacrifice the Poet. Moreover, in light of the sexual tensions at work between father, daughter, and suitor, parallels between *The King on the Square* and Pushkin's *The Stone Guest* become apparent. If the statue of the commander kills Don Juan for his advances on Doña Anna, the statue of the King, in its function as a double for the Architect, likewise destroys the Poet because of his desire for the Architect's Daughter.

The presence of the destructive statue myth in *The King on the Square* does not merely demonstrate Pushkin's influence; it also provides an interpretation of a number of details that otherwise appear disconnected. These details all fit into the general carnivalized texture of the work because they are based on carnivalistic contrasts and upendings, but appear through the specific influence of Pushkin and the statue myth. One of the play's most important motifs is the theme of rigidification.[2] In his study, Jakobson traces the same theme through the three Pushkin texts named above, *The Stone Guest*, *The Bronze Horseman*, and *The Folktale about the Golden Cockerel.* He writes, "In the drama, in the the epic poem, and in the fairytale the image of the animated statue evokes the opposite image of rigidified people, whether it involves a mere comparison of them to a statue, an accidental situation, or actual dying and death" (Jakobson 1987, 326). This motif clearly reveals a carnivalistic basis. On the one hand, the oxymoronic contrast of the "living dead" and the "dead living" embodies the sharp, grotesque juxtaposition of dissimilar entities so typical of carnival; while, on the other, the intermingling of life and death imagery suggests a symbiotic relation between the two, death in the act of regeneration and life in the process of degeneration.

In *The King on the Square*, this motif is particularly strong. In the first act, the First remarks, "In the whole city I know two living people" (4: 30). This motif, in fact, dominates the exchanges between him and his interlocutors. When the First says they will wait another day, the Second says, "Another whole day! Empty and light! It's better to die" (4: 31). The First responds, "I swear to you: We will all die towards nightfall!" (4: 31). Still in the first act, the Seller of Roses remarks, "I

[1] The crowd endows with the King with animacy. A voice in the crowd says, "The King nodded his head today" (4: 44). Later, after the terrace has collapsed, they are surprised not to find the body of the King. "Cries of horror are heard: "A statue! — A stone idol! — Where is the king?" (4: 59).

[2] Another example of this process is Blok's bird imagery. At the end of the second act, the Poet refers to the Golden one as a "golden bird," an epithet that brings to mind Pushkin's golden cockerel. The apparent difference between Blok's man and Pushkin's bird proves to be illusory: both are tied to the statue motif. Pushkin's bird is a statue, and Blok's Golden one, "a loyal servant of the King," serves a statue. Metonymically, he is related to the statue motif.

am dying from the hot sun, from the dust, from fatigue, from hunger" (4: 33). In the beginning of the third act, the first of the two men who are leaning on the railing simply dies. Toward the very end of the play, a beggar in the crowd cries out, "Help! I am dying..." (4: 58). The theme of rigidification gives rise to a number of even more specialized motifs. The motif of dead or dying children, in particular, recurs numerous times. In the second act, the Architect explains the Poet's melancholy, saying, "Perhaps, many children have died, and the mothers cry too loudly" (4: 39). After the monologue of the Architect's Daughter at the feet of the statue, a beggarwoman cries out, "My child is dying" (4: 58). Rigidification takes still other forms. The Poet remarks to the Architect, "The sea seems to me glass, and people dolls" (4: 37).

The pervasiveness of these motifs makes *The King on the Square* the clearest example of Pushkin's destructive statue myth influenced Blok. Pushkin's myth is also apparent in Blok's two other lyric dramas, but in a more attenuated form. In *The Stranger*, as in *The King on the Square*, and the reader encounters an older, professional man, who has dedicated himself to an ideal; a young woman, who is associated either by herself or others with an ideal; and a young man, who desires the young woman. With several qualifications, much the same pattern becomes evident in *A Puppet Show*.

In *The Stranger*, the theme and many of the motifs of the destructive statue arise, but their coherence is not as readily apparent as in *The King on the Square*. When the star becomes the Stranger near the beginning of the second vision, the stage directions state, "She waits like a statue" (4: 84). Other evidence, however, suggests that this remark is not so off-handed as it appears. Blok himself explicitly acknowledged a debt to one of the great manifestations of the myth, Pushkin's *The Stone Guest*. Evgenii Ivanov notes in a diary entry made just days after Blok had finished *The Stranger*, "A. Blok was at my place. Pushkin's *The Stone Guest* is an automaton. Through him fate knocks at the door. The bond of *The Stranger* with *The Stone Guest* is through its cardboardness. Sasha Blok says that he would not be terrified if he came and took him by the hand, like Don Juan" (Ivanov, 415).[3] Such an explicit statement of the relationship between the *The Stranger* and *The Stone Guest*, unexpected as it is, emphasizes the importance of at the destructive statue myth to Blok's play. Critics have sometimes seen links between *The Stranger* and the other two works by Pushkin that the destructive statue myth figures into, but have never examined the destructive statue myth in relation to them (see Volkov 1926, 57).

In fact, if we examine *The Stranger* from this standpoint, we find that it exhibits all of the characteristics of the statue myth, except one — the statue. Yet even the statue, in a reduced form, appears. In all other respects, the manifestations of the myth in the play are very orthodox, and all three characteristics of the myth noted by Jakobson are observed. The Poet, for example, provides a good example of a man who is weary, but who at the same time desires a woman. Unable to realize his desire for the ideal woman he writes about, he takes refuge in bars and alcohol. His retreat from the idealism of his verse suggests moral weariness.

---

[3] Ivanov refers to the play and not the poem as may be deduced not only from the fact that the diary entry follows fast on the heels of a reading of the play at which Ivanov was present, but also from other remarks about the play which surround the entry.

Nonetheless, he does not give up all hope of seeing his ideal. At the end of the first vision, he summons her, "Appear! Appear!" (4: 81).

The second characteristic of the myth, the statue and its inexplicable power over the desired woman, also manifests itself in *The Stranger*. At first glance, the absence of a statue in *The Stranger* would seemingly argue against the presence of the statue myth. However, analysis of the play's structure reveals a clear connection between the Stranger (Mariia) and the cameo of the Woman who Rules the World. In *The Stranger* the cameo occupies the same totemic space a statue occupies in more canonical versions of the statue myth.

Moreover, other considerations reinforce this interpretation. For example, the first epigraph from the *Idiot* points to other modes of representation that fulfill a similar purpose. Like the cameo in the play, the photograph mentioned in the epigraph is a repesentation of a woman. Thus, the function of statue, cameo, and photograph is the same.[4] In this sense, it is no accident that the Poet emphasizes precisely this representation in his verses about the Stranger: "And from an icon in tender roses / She slowly descended..." (4: 99). Nor is it coincidental that critics have pointed to the influence of Mæterlinck's *Sister Beatrice*, in which a statue comes to life.[5]

Jakobson also stipulates that it is the being who is associated with the statue, not the statue itself, that exercises power over the desired woman. From this point of view, the interactions between the Astronomer and the Poet in the last vision assume greater significance than is generally granted them. When the Poet sees Mariia, everything begins to come back to him. "For a moment, it seems that he has remembered everything" (4: 101). However, as soon as he has begun to remember and has started toward Mariia, the Astronomer stops him in his tracks. After talking with the Astronomer, the Poet "has forgotten everything" (4: 102). And once he has forgotten everything, Mariia disappears and becomes a star. Thus, even if there is no statue in the play, the Astronomer is connected to the power normally allocated to a statue in this myth. Then too, the Astronomer's interest in stars suggests a powerful, if unstated bond between him and the Stranger.

The third and perhaps most obvious characteristic of the myth, the destruction of the man who desires the woman, also finds expression in *The Stranger*. Here again, first impressions play down the importance of the statue myth. However, several elements of this last characteristic manifest themselves clearly, and the ambiguity of the stage directions suggests the other elements that are not noted explicitly. For instance, at the end of the third vision, the stage directions explicitly mark out the disappearance of the Stranger-Mariia. To the Hostess's cry, "Where is Mary? Where is Mary?," the stage directions provide the answer, "Beyond the window burns a bright star" (4: 102). The Stranger's disappearance thus falls squarely within the parameters of the statue myth.

[4] Volkov was the first to emphasize the importance of Nastas'ia Filippovna's portrait. He insists, "Reflecting further on the meaning of Nastas'ia Filippovna's portrait, we see that it exerted an influence not only on the image of the Stranger, but also on the drama's architectonics" (Volkov 1926, 61).

[5] This has been pointed out by, among others, M.V. Bezrodnyi. While Bezrodnyi does not mention the destructive statue myth, several of his points are germane to our discussion (Bezrodnyi 1987, 143-9 passim).

At least on the surface, however, the second part of Jakobson's definition — that the man perishes — appears to be unrealized. On closer examination, though, the stage directions that follow the Hostess's question prove to be ambiguous. In their entirety, they read, "There is no longer anyone by the dark curtain. Beyond the window burns a bright star. A blue snow, as blue as the cloak of the Astronomer who has vanished, is falling" (4: 102). Not a word is said about the Poet. Perhaps he is still in the room, perhaps not. The expression, "There is no longer anyone by the dark curtain", certainly applies to the Stranger, who had been standing by the curtain moments before, but it may equally apply to the other two people who remained in the room with her, the Poet and the Astronomer. The latter possibility gains credence in light of the fact that the stage directions speak of the "Astronomer, who has vanished". Moreover, since it is not just any snow that falls, but a blue one, and since that snow is as blue as the Astronomer's cloak, the thematic matrix of Poet-blue-coat-Astronomer comes to play a critical role. If it is not the Poet who has disappeared, it is that blue part of him — his soul, as Mochulsky would have it — that has. The Poet's vision of the Stranger perishes, and with it vanishes Mariia.

In this way, all three of the distinguishing characteristics of the destructive statue myth manifest themselves in *The Stranger*. It should be noted, however, that the myth assumes a more attenuated, reduced character in *The Stranger* if compared to its role in *The King on the Square*. While *The Stranger* observes the myth's inner correlations, it abandons the outer manifestations of the myth, most importantly the statue. The very existence of these inner correlations, however, points to the importance of the statue myth.

The myth is a subtextual constant in all three dramas. It is present even in *A Puppet Show*, where its manifestations are least apparent. Evgenii Ivanov provides the key in the diary entry cited earlier. Of paramount interest is the observation that "The bond of *The Stranger* with *The Stone Guest* is through its cardboardness" (Ivanov, 415). The word "cardboardness" suggests the figure of Columbine, whom Pierrot describes as his "cardboard girlfriend" (4: 15). The association proves to be of vital significance.

A Puppet Show observes, again in attenuated form, the three main characteristics of the statue myth. First, Pierrot displays a great weariness and certainly desires Columbine.[6] Secondly, Harlequin exerts a mysterious power over Columbine. He has only to snap his fingers, and she follows him, though she still professes her love for Pierrot. And finally, Columbine vanishes not once, but twice.

Qualifications must be made, of course. First, there is no statue. However, the significance of this absence abates in light of Evgenii Ivanov's diary entry about the ties between *The Stone Guest* and *The Stranger*. Blok's comments, as rendered by Ivanov, suggest that "cardboardness" serves the same totemic function in Blok's variations on the statue myth that statues and statue-like qualities occupy in Pushkin's orthodox version of the myth.

Another peculiarity of Blok's version of the myth centers around Harlequin, who instead of Pierrot, disappears at the end of the play. More importantly perhaps, Harlequin does not perish because of the intervention of a statue. In fact,

---

[6] Concerning the former, we should recall Lidiia Segal"s description of Pierrot as a "neurasthenic" (Kotrelev and Timenchik, 3: 432).

since he exerts a mysterious power over Columbine, we might expect him to be associated with a statue or something that bears the statue's destructive powers. In this way his disappearance has much in common with the disappearance of the Astronomer at the end of *The Stranger* and the statue of the king at the end of *The King on the Square*. This similarity — the way in which the figure, who would be associated with a statue in a more canonical version of the myth, turns his powers on himself and causes himself to perish — points to Blok's distinctly personal variation on the Pushkin myth.

The question of why the myth of the destructive statue had such an influence on the dramas naturally arises. The answer lies in the extensive influence the myth exerted on all of Blok's work throughout this period. Jakobson himself recognized the importance of Pushkin's destructive statue myth in Blok's work, and although he did not name the lyric dramas explicitly, he did remark on the presence of the myth in Blok's lyric poetry of these years. Jakobson wrote, "In the poem 'The Steps of the Commander' Aleksandr Blok resumes the Pushkinian conception of an adoring Don Juan, a Doña Anna who tantalizingly vanishes and the heavy steps 'of old fate,' and in the poems of the cycle *The City* he evokes the eternal life of a metallic Peter who vibrates between arrested sleep and dreadful activity ('Petr,' 'The Rally')" (Jakobson 1987, 363).[7] Of the poems Jakobson singles out, the earliest, "Petr", was written in February, 1904 and the latest, "The Steps of the Commander" was written first in September, 1910 and rewritten in February, 1912. Blok wrote the third poem, "The Rally", in October, 1905, the fall before he began work on his dramas. The presence of the myth in the plays then coincides with the period when the Pushkinian myth was most important for Blok.

The myth attracted Blok for the same reason other carnivalized themes and forms attracted him: it allowed him to dismantle the monologic structure of his early work. The statue myth allowed for the upending and renewal of the themes of love and sex. In the early poetry, the treatment of love is platonic. Not so, in the plays. The possibilities are already evident in the canonic Pushkin texts, especially *The Stone Guest* and *The Folktale about the Golden Cockerel*,[8] where sexual desire and expectations are upended in carnivalistic decrownings. Thus, Don Juan, who is renowned for his sexual conquests, desires Doña Anna, only to discover that this desire leads to his destruction. Similarly, Tsar Dadon's sexual desire appears unnatural, "eccentric" in the face of the death of his sons. Again his desire leads to his destruction. To take the *The Stranger* as typical example from Blok's work, the carnivalistic overturnings are even more pronounced. The Beautiful Lady, the source of spiritual yearning, appears, but frustrates the Poet's spiritual desires. Instead of an ideal, she turns out to be a woman of easy virtue. The oblique

[7] For the sake of consistency, I have taken the liberty of bringing Jakobson's transliteration into accord with that used throughout this chapter.

[8] We should note in this regard that a character referred to as an astronomer appears in both *The Stranger* and *The Folktale about the Golden Cockerel.* Volkov implicitly argues for a parallel between the two when he suggests that the monologue of Blok's Astronomer at the end of second vision echoes the ending of *The Folktale about the Golden Cockerel.* Volkov does not, however, develop this suggestion beyond a mere mention (Volkov, 57).

references to prostitution further underscore this upending. A new, if sometimes farcical, understanding becomes possible.

The presence of the myth, in readily recognizable variations, in Pushkin and Blok suggests the vital importance of carnivalized literature as a conduit for influence. The general laws of carnivalization become embodied in more particular forms, such as the myth of the destructive statue, and through these more particular forms, one poet influences another. As a result, the influence of one poet on another may be very pronounced, yet difficult to pin down, especially at the level of device.

If we now return to the question of whether or not Blok's three lyric dramas constitute a trilogy, we see that what they share is significant: a fundamental type who is part of a triangle, doubles, masks, a reconfigured authorial voice, and the destructive statue myth. Blok eschews the more common characteristics of trilogy and instead composes variations on a theme. Whether such variations can bear the burden of thematic unity usually associated with a trilogy remains in doubt. Yet, the fabric of the three plays is quite consistent, and if it is not possible to speak of the three plays as a trilogy, it is possible to speak of their common poetics.

Aleksandr Blok in 1886–7. Photo courtesy of the Union of Theater Workers' Library, Moscow.

Aleksandr Blok in Kiev, 1907. Photo courtesy of the Union of Theater Workers' Library, Moscow.

Sofiia Mendeleeva as Gertrude and Aleksandr Blok as Hamlet, August 1, 1898. Photo courtesy of the Union of Theater Workers' Library, Moscow.

Aleksandr Blok as Hamlet, 1898. Photo courtesy of the Union of Theater Workers' Library, Moscow.

Aleksandr Blok and his dog, 1909. Photo courtesy of the Union of Theater Workers' Library, Moscow.

Aleksandr Blok and his wife Liubov Mendeleeva. Photo courtesy of the Union of Theater Workers' Library, Moscow.

Aleksandr Blok in 1907. Photo courtesy of the Union of Theater Workers' Library, Moscow.

Olga Forsh's drawing of Blok and Dante. Photo courtesy of the Union of Theater Workers' Library, Moscow.

A poster for a production of *The Stranger* at the Khaliutina Studio in Moscow, 1913. Photo courtesy of the Union of Theater Workers' Library, Moscow.

Lidiia Iliashenko as The Stranger in Meyerhold's production of the play at the Tenishev school auditorium, 1914. Photo courtesy of the Union of Theater Workers' Library, Moscow.

The cover of *The Rose and The Cross*, a manuscript book designed by Nikolai Kupreianov, 1915. Photo courtesy of the Union of Theater Workers' Library, Moscow.

First page of the manuscript book of *The Rose and The Cross* designed by Nikolai Kupreianov in 1915. Photo courtesy of the Union of Theater Workers' Library, Moscow.

CHAPTER FIVE

TOWARDS "HEALTHY REALISM": *THE SONG OF FATE*

> Do not forget duty — This is the only music. There is no life or passion without duty.
>
> -Blok (1978, 224)

I

Beyond Lyric Drama

The composition of his trilogy of lyric dramas occupied Blok throughout most of 1906, and only after finishing *The Stranger* in November, 1906 did Blok take a break from writing plays. The exact duration of this break can only be approximated since the dates on the extant manuscripts are contradicted by evidence in Blok's letters. According to the manuscripts, Blok began work on his next play, *The Song of Fate*, in April, 1907 and finished it on January 29, 1908. However, in January of 1908 Blok told Valerii Briusov that he had been tormenting himself over the play for a year, and that suggests that his work on the play may have commenced as early as January, 1907 (Blok and Briusov, 1: 511).

In any case, the break was short, lasting between two and five months, but this interval marks an important change in Blok's attitude toward his material. This attitude necessitated new dramatic means and resulted in halting progress on the play. Whereas *The Stranger* came more easily to Blok than even *A Puppet Show*, his work on *The Song of Fate* turned out to be even more labored than that on *The King on the Square*. In part, Blok's impeded progress on *The Song of Fate* stemmed from the same circumstance that complicated his work on *The King on the Square*: In contrast to *A Puppet Show* and *The Stranger*, neither *The King on the Square* nor *The Song of Fate* grew out of a poem. In his first and third plays, Blok had extrapolated a coherent constellation of themes and images from poem to play. His method was somewhat different in his second and fourth plays. Neither had coherence *a priori*, but rather attained such coherence, if at all, only gradually. Both plays share motifs with and draw on various of Blok's poems, but these never serve to unify either play and, in fact, sometimes contribute to the centrifugal forces that threaten their coherence. His search for unity and his attempt to strengthen such centripetal forces as would lend coherence prolonged Blok's work on both plays.

It was certainly not for want of concentration and labor that the writing and rewriting of the first draft went on for well over a year, in fact, until April 1908. Already by January 1908, the play seemed to be taking shape. Blok wrote to his mother early that month, "I have already drafted three acts, i.e. I have made it to a turning point: the most difficult is done, and now there remains only a final concentration of all my powers and much menial and persistent work." Moreover, Blok showed no fastidiousness or sentimentality where the material was concerned. In the same letter, he tells his mother, "Here I am not idle (in its entirety, for example, I am getting rid of the well written, but ideologically unsatisfactory fifth act)" (8: 224. For more on this question, see Medvedev, 81-90 passim). To much the same effect, he wrote to his mother a little more than a week later, "The drama is moving along; I am now writing the fourth act. This is an entire sphere of life, in which I build, break, and arrange in my own way" (8: 225). Despite this open attitude toward his materials, the problems Blok encountered did not lend themselves to easy resolution.

Without a doubt, personal problems complicated Blok's work. His romantic feelings for the actress Natal'ia Volokhova, after a summer's hiatus, seemed to deepen through the autumn and winter of 1907. The very tone in which Blok writes about *The Song of Fate* suggests, in fact, how great the strain had become. For instance, in turning down Anastasiia Chebotarevskaia's invitation to organize a literary evening, Blok wrote, "I am going through a very difficult crisis and am writing agonizingly a large piece..." (8: 226). The strain left an indelible mark on Blok's attitude toward his work on the play. Even when it was all done, Blok associated suffering with it. He wrote to Andrei Belyi, "I have finally finished my drama almost completely, have suffered through it, and perhaps something better has come out of it than its predecessors. I would very much like for you to know it" (8: 233).

The labored progress of his work gave rise to doubt. Blok swung back and forth between great enthusiasm and great disdain for the play. He wrote to his mother, "*The Song of Fate* is very important to me; I am afraid for it. This is my favorite child" (Blok 1927-32, 1: 210-1). Perhaps because of this worry, Blok sought others' opinions, a behavior that was quite uncharacteristic of him. Whenever he found a willing audience, he read the play aloud. For instance, in January of 1908 he went in search of his friend, Evgenii Ivanov. Not finding him at home, Blok refused to let an opportunity go to waste and proceeded to read the play to Ivanov's sister. Ivanov himself was not off the hook, however. Blok wrote to say, "When I have written some more, I will ask you too to listen to it" (8: 228). In point of fact, Ivanov would have any number of opportunities to hear the play read aloud in the course of the next year.

At about the same time, Blok read the play to his aunt, Mariia Beketova. Her response, while not hostile, elicited a certain anxiety from Blok. He wrote to his mother to ask, "Did aunt write to you about my drama? I read it to her because it is hard to find a person who would tell me the truth: writers will treat it one-sidedly, and the people near to me are the dramatis personae themselves. Aunt made several practical observations, which I took to heart. The curse of abstractedness pursues me in this play too, though perhaps to a lesser extent than in the rest" (8: 226-7). Blok took his aunt's observations quite seriously and went back to work.

Blok labored intensively on the play throughout the first four months of 1908; and almost immediately after finishing the first complete version, he invited friends and fellow writers to a series of readings. (See, for instance, 8: 236 and 239). The first took place on May 1, 1908. As is apparent from his invitation to the writer Aleksei Remizov and his wife Serafima, Blok remained concerned for his "favorite child": "I very much want for you and Serafima Pavlovna to read the play, which at last I have finished. I would be happy if you and Serafima Pavlovna were to come to my place on Galernaia street on Thursday, 1 May, about nine o'clock. If a long reading does not frighten you, come, please, I will be waiting at nine o'clock in the evening. It is called *The Song of Fate*, I am very afraid for it" (Blok and Remizov, 2: 85).

Despite these initial fears, the reading went well generally. Nagging doubts, however, were expressed by some of those closest to Blok, especially his aunt. As he wrote to his mother afterwards, "I am living by *The Song of Fate*, which I read a few days ago to a small circle (about ten people) and remained very satisfied with the impression and individual criticisms (as before, aunt regards it more hopelessly than anyone. She somehow inwardly does not acknowledge it, and I do not at all trust her in regard to this, my favorite child)." Undaunted, Blok had already made preparations for the next reading of the play at the home of Georgii Chulkov. Besides the Chulkovs, Blok had invited Leonid Andreev, Fedor Sologub, Viacheslav Ivanov, Mikhail Kuzmin, and Maksimilian Voloshin. In relation to the reading, Blok told his mother, "I am gathering and painstakingly listening to all opinions of both writers and also non-writers. This time it is very important to me how they regard it. This is my first piece, in which I am finding ground that is not shaky and is not only lyrical. So I am defining for myself the meaning of *The Song of Fate* and accordingly I love it more than all that I have written. I very much want to read it to you in its new, finished form" (8: 240). The second reading, like the first, met with a generally positive reception. Vera Komissarzhevskaia sought it for her theater (8: 224), and Leonid Andreev asked Blok to place the play in the almanac "Sweetbrier" (Blok 1927-32, 1: 197). He added that he hoped to read it to Stanislavskii and the Moscow Art Theater soon after the second reading. Perhaps the only shadow on the proceedings was cast by the absence of the poet Mikhail Kuzmin.[1] Given Kuzmin's negative reaction to Meyerhold's staging of *A Puppet Show* and *The Stranger* in 1914, his absence from the reading may have already expressed his disenchantment with Blok's dramas.

[1] Vera Shvarsalon, Viacheslav Ivanov's stepdaughter, commented in her diary, "We ... were at N.G.'s [Chulkova's] at Blok's reading — K[uzmin] did not go, though I very much hoped he would and at the same time almost knew that he would not come" (Kotrelev and Timenchik, 3: 326).

II

Unrealized Stagings: The Moscow Art Theater and Others

Otherwise encouraged by the responses to his readings, Blok politely declined Komissarzhevskaia's offer and, instead, moved quickly to acquaint Konstantin Stanislavskii and Vladimir Nemirovich-Danchenko with the play.[2] Gradually, Blok had become disenchanted with non-realist theater and longed to see his play on the stage of the Moscow Art Theater. A growing predilection for "healthy realism" turned Blok away from Meyerhold and towards Stanislavskii (Blok 1965, 209). At first, the decision to read the play to Stanislavskii seemed a good one. Blok wrote to his father to say that Stanislavskii "was captivated" by the play and that "maybe he will stage it, but I still have to work on it" (Blok 1927-32, 1: 212-3). Several years later, he would write in a similar vein that Stanislavskii had praised *The Song of Fate* "to the sky" and that Nemirovich-Danchenko had also "praised it excessively, but in his own somewhat banal way" (7: 187). No doubt Nemirovich-Danchenko's exclamation, "Goodness gracious, what a talented boy," was still ringing in Blok's ears. (See also Beketova 1922, 112). Others who knew the director echoed Blok's appraisal of Stanislavskii's reaction. The actor and director, Kazimir Bravich, who belonged to Vera Komissarzhevskaia's theater at the time, told Fedor Komissarzhevskii that Stanislavskii, Nemirovich-Danchenko, and the "Areopagus of the Moscow theater" gave the play high praise. "I have not read it," said Bravich, "because Blok, in accordance with their directions, is redoing it, but I talked with him about the play since apparently there can be no discussion of him giving the play to us" (Kotrelev and Timenchik, 3: 326).

Blok was elated and set right to work on revisions. It could be said, in fact, that with the completion of a manuscript version of *The Song of Fate* in April, 1908, Blok's work on the play was only just beginning. The play, as it was then constituted, fell into five segments, which Blok called tableaux. By the autumn of that year, the structure of *The Song of Fate* had altered considerably. As before, Blok saw the play as a pivotal work in his career, but harbored no sentimental feeling for any of its parts. In June, Blok wrote to his wife, "*The Song of Fate* is still as important for me. But now in a new way, as if I experienced it still more, and I look at it more objectively and freely" (8: 244). Blok, in fact, freely jettisoned whole acts. Less than a week later, Blok writes again to his wife, this time to say, "I have devised the third act" (Blok 1978, 237). Only days later the new version was finished. (8: 245).

July saw new readings, which engendered doubt. As he wrote to his mother, "I read *The Song of Fate* to the Gorodetskiis and Meyerhold. Meyerhold said quite a lot that was valuable — strongly criticized it. Again I doubt the play. Let it lie for a while yet" (8: 247). In the same letter, he also remarked that his

[2] In a letter, dated 14 May, 1908, to Fedor Komisarzhevskii, Kazimir Vikent'evich Bravich [pseudonym of Kazimir Baranovich] suggests that Stanislavskii and Nemirovich-Danchenko had already heard the play (Kotrelev and Timenchik, 3: 326). On this basis, the reading apparently took place between the second reading on 4 May and 14 May.

friend Evgenii Ivanov continued to regard the play negatively. Blok's mother saw her son's interest in other people's opinions in a positive light: "It is good that he is listening this way to all opinions about his play and accepts them this way" (Kotrelev and Timenchik, 3: 331). Perhaps the one deleterious effect of listening to others so intently, however, was that Blok never attained total confidence in the work. As he prepared to send the revised version to Stanislavskii, Blok confided to his wife, "I looked through *The Song of Fate* again. I will give it out to be copied and, it seems, I will send it finally to the Art Theater. Let be what will be" (8: 250).

Blok's own doubts were exacerbated by the increasingly negative reaction the play encountered. The opinions of his aunt and Evgenii Ivanov had long been clear, but now others close to Blok echoed their sentiments, sometimes in vitriolic terms. Perhaps nowhere is this so apparent as in the case of Anna Gorodetskaia, the wife of the poet Sergei Gorodetskii. About a year after Blok finished the second version of the play, Gorodetskaia wrote to him in response to a negative review Blok had written of her husband's book *Rus'*. In that letter, Gorodetskaia tells Blok that *The Song of Fate* was "beneath even the most condescending criticism as much in the artistic as in the social sense — it is simply pathetic in its impotence" (Blok, Gorodetskaia, and Gorodetskii, 2: 39). Although her anger grew out of Blok's criticism of her husband and although she later apologized for her remarks, the very fact that Gorodetskaia, out of all of Blok's works, focused on *The Song of Fate* is significant. Blok's favorite child was fast proving to be his Achilles' heel.

Such opinions, whether expressed openly or privately at the time as in Gorodetskaia's case, did nothing to promote Blok's confidence in the play. Nor did Stanislavskii's agonizingly slow reply. After Stanislavskii acknowledged receipt of the revised manuscript on 11 September, Blok would hear nothing else from the director until November (Stanislavskii, 7: 412). Blok, in general, always tried to put Stanislavskii's motives in the best possible light. For instance, he excused Stanislavskii's slow reply by saying, "Mæterlinck is at Stanislavskii's, so he still has not written to me a decisive answer about *The Song of Fate*" (8: 254). Not every playwright was so forgiving. Like Blok, Bulgakov in his time would be alternately encouraged and then rebuffed by Stanislavskii. Unlike Blok, he detected caprice in the great director's actions and portrayed it caustically in his novel *A Theatrical Romance*.

When Blok did finally receive a telegram from the Moscow Art Theater in the middle of November, Stanislavskii replied in response to a rather desperate letter that Blok had sent on November 7. In the interim, Blok had received an offer to publish the play. He wrote to Stanislavskii,

> Forgive me for pressing you for an answer in regard to my play: the problem is that I have gotten an offer to print it, and indeed it should be printed just out of financial considerations, but I feel dependent on your decision in this regard.
>
> If you have read through my revision, please write to me, whether or not you find it acceptable for the theater and whether or not you want to stage it. If the answer is yes, might it nonetheless be published now, or do you want it to remain unprinted until its staging?
>
> For all sorts of reasons, both internal and external, your answer is very important for me.

> Right now I do not know if I need to work some more on *The Song of Fate*. At least I do not know how to approach it now; it is still too close. And it seems there are shortcomings, and some big ones. But are these just shortcomings, or is the whole thing defective? (8: 260).

Despite such pitiless honesty, the director did little to assuage Blok's misgivings. As Blok told his mother, "Stanislavskii telegraphed: 'This season will not succeed staging play. Details by letter in a week. Necessary to advise publishing play.' I was not counting on this season, but can I count on next?" (8: 261). It is perhaps symptomatic that Stanislavskii signed this, the most curt and perfunctory of his correspondence with Blok with his theatrical pseudonym (Stanislavskii), while he signed other, more encouraging letters with his given name (Alekseev).

Stanislavskii's telegram, it would seem, intensified Blok's doubts. To make matters worse, the "details by letter" failed to materialize "in a week." Blok waited patiently for two weeks before he finally broke down and wrote once more to Stanislavskii. In this letter, Blok suggested that he would be willing to postpone publication of the play until it could be performed, provided that Stanislavskii could make assurances that the play would in fact be staged the following season. Nonetheless, Blok tone is apologetic: "Forgive me for pestering you so with the play, but its fate worries me very much." As becomes apparent, the play retained its former significance for Blok. He writes,

> If anything in the play does not satisfy you, please write to me. Are you disappointed in it after the revision? Or does it present difficulties for the theater that are too large? After all here I myself am no judge at all. Nonetheless, for this play my soul asks for the stage — in contrast to all the others I have written before it.
>
> You understand, my deeply esteemed Konstantin Sergeevich, how unpleasant it is to remain in an indefinite position in a matter so important for me; for that reason do not judge me harshly, I beg you (8: 263-4).

It was this letter that finally elicited the long since promised response from Stanislavskii. After excusing himself for his tardy reply, Stanislavskii explained some of the difficulties he had encountered and went on to say that it was as yet premature to talk about the repertoire for the following season. He then set forth his misgivings about *The Song of Fate*:

> I read your play about four times.
>
> As before I love the first tableaux. I fell in love with the new ones too for their poetry and temperament, but I did not fall in love with the characters and the play itself. I realized that my enthusiasm concerns the talent of the author and not his composition. I am not a critic; I am not a literary man; and so I refuse to criticize.
>
> I have not come to any conclusion and so can only write what I felt and thought about you and your play.
>
> I am writing in any event since your ability to hear out others' opinions encourages me.
>
> If you tear up this letter, not having read it through, — I will also understand since I do not undertake to say anything weighty and important.

> In a word, do as you wish, only do not get angry at your sincere admirer.
>
> I always read individual acts of your play with enthusiasm; I grow excited and I catch myself on the fact that it is not the characters and their feelings that interest me, but the author of the play. I read the whole play, and again I grow excited, and again I think that you will soon write something very big. Quite probably I do not understand something that binds all the acts into one harmonious whole, and maybe there is no unity in the play.
>
> Almost every time the fact that the action takes place in Russia disquiets me. Why?[3]
>
> On other days it seems to me that this play is an important transitional step in your work, that you yourself are dissatisfied with it and rush about in an agonizing search.
>
> Sometimes — and often — I blame myself. It seems to me that I am an incorrigible realist, that I flirt with my quests in art; in point of fact, the path goes no further than Chekhov for me."

Stanislavskii then launches into a lengthy discussion of realism and its relation to his method. Out of these considerations, Stanislavskii explains, come his misgivings about the play: "When I approach your play with such thoughts, then it turns out that the places that captivate me are mathematically exact both in the sense of the physiology and the psychology of man; and there, where interest flags, there seem to me to be mistakes that contradict human nature." Stanislavskii ends by excusing himself for his "blunt letter." He includes, however, a postscript that is supercilious, if not insulting: "Forgive me for this hasty letter. I am writing it at a make-up table in the intermission between two acts" (Stanislavskii, 7: 415-6). In fairness, not every commentator attributes the same motives that I do to Stanislavskii. For example, the scholar who first published Blok's letters of November 7 and November 29 to Stanislavskii, suggested that the director refrained from answering earlier not only because of his busy schedule, but also because he "wanted to check thoroughly his impressions from the play before deciding its fate" (Lakshin, 191).

Despite the criticisms and such slights as the postscript, Blok took the letter well. Still, he felt the need to reply, and within a week, had sent Stanislavskii a long response. In it Blok thanks Stanislavskii for his letter: "It is important and dear to me; I take deeply into consideration all that you write; I take it to heart." Nonetheless, he insists that his theme is a "living, real theme; it is not only *bigger than me*, it is bigger than all of us; and it is our universal theme." This theme, as he tells Stanislavskii later in the same letter, is the "*theme of Russia* (the question of the intelligentsia and the people, in particular)." As for the expression of that theme, however, Blok offers only a tepid defense: "Now: As concerns, in particular, *The Song of Fate*, I myself know little about it; it is better to say it is alive for me personally up to now, so much so that I am not convinced to the end by your words. Maybe you are right that the characters are lifeless (with the

[3] Despite his sometimes harsh tone, Stanislavskii in fact held back. In a draft of this letter, he said, "... the fact that the action takes place in Russian bothers me — I do not feel it" (Stanislavskii, 7: 727).

exception of some). But I love all of them tenderly; the greater part I see clearly before me." Blok then takes up what Stanislavskii had referred to as the "mathematically exact," or as Blok paraphrases him, "the artist's striving toward 'mathematics'": "From this point of view, many mistakes were probably made in *The Song of Fate*. I want you to hear me, to know that ... I in no case want to forget 'form' for 'content,' to neglect the mathematical precision, the strictest polishing of a valuable stone. But *this stone*, which I perhaps have not known how to polish in *The Song of Fate* — it is valuable. I myself am a poor master, a blaspheming 'lyric poet,' — and it is not because of my good services that the stone fell into my hands. But once it is in my hands, I am struck by its radiance; I *repent* of my blasphemy; I *must* find in myself the strength, the patience, and the ability of a master to sacrifice." These last characteristics Blok finds in Stanislavskii: "In you I feel not only the strength, the patience, and the ability to sacrifice, but also the *right of strictest judgment*. I believe you profoundly; that is why, returning to the play, I am not at all anxious about its fate in essence; I know that if necessary, you will fall in love with it, and if not necessary, you will reject it, following the mathematics of art, the love for its severe truths. I see in you an artist, to whom *only* beauty and *only* utility are little, to whom the *Sublime* that covers and exhausts the one and the other is indispensable. And because of all of this, I believe in your *realism*." As he brings the letter to a close, Blok seems implicitly to accept Stanislavskii's condemnation of *The Song of Fate*: "in principle I want a staging of a play, if not *The Song of Fate*, then some other" (8: 265-7; Blok's italics throughout).

With these words, Blok appears to have surrendered all hope for staging *The Song of Fate*. If it was destined not run in the Moscow Art Theater, he would have it in no other. As he told his mother several days later, "Liuba [his wife, Liubov' — TW] and I have the impression that he will not stage the play, and I am not mourning about this because I believe in Stanislavskii. If there really are no reasons for getting by without the theater, he will stage it; if there is even one against the theater, it is not necessary" (8: 268).

His interest in *The Song of Fate* had not vanished altogether, however. On December 18, 1908 Blok read the revised play before a small gathering at his apartment. He is careful to warn at least one of the guests of the length of the reading (Blok and Piast, 2: 203). Blok's wife told his mother that the eight to ten people who attended the reading reacted generally in a positive manner: "It was very heterogeneous; maybe for that reason it seemed all the more to me after the reading and over tea that something was lacking in the sense of their joint appearance at our place, or else I have grown unused to gatherings. Everyone spoke one by one with Sasha about the play. Almost everyone was happy with it, attaches meaning to it, likes it, etc." (Kotrelev and Timenchik, 3: 343). The drama, in fact, continued to generate interest, and Blok tried to nurture that interest by giving more readings. Blok describes one particularly successful reading in this way: "There remains with me the most joyous impression: they listened very well and attentively, and for that reason I myself read better than usual" (8: 275).

Nor had interest in staging the play abated. Even as he turned his attention to the publication of the play and made arrangements with the publishing house "Sweetbrier," offers to stage the play continued to pour in. However, Blok rejected out of hand all offers other than the one Stanislavskii would never make. For example, when an offer to stage the play came from the Aleksandrinskii Theater, where Meyerhold had just begun directing, Blok reacted almost hostilely. He wrote to his mother, "Merezhkovskii proposes it for the Aleksandrinka, but I am asking him to wait; I do not want the Aleksandrinka very much; everything smells worse from it" (8: 268). Indeed, Blok would dissuade all other directors and politely turn down all other offers.

Leonid Andreev, for instance, approached Blok on behalf of the New Dramatic Theater (Andreev, 86). Although he must have known he was running out of opportunities to stage *The Song of Fate*, he turned Andreev down. The determining impact that Stanislavskii's opinion had on Blok's own becomes clear in the poet's reply to Andreev. He wrote:

> So I am informing you by letter of all my concerns about *The Song of Fate*.
>
> After many rereadings, revisions, conversations and correspondence with Stanislavskii, I have come to the conclusion that the play has still not been carried to that degree of clarity, when one can perform it on a stage. I am not speaking about even shortcomings that are clear now for me in entire dialogues (which, however, I still do not have the strength to correct); there is a certain incoherence in the whole. That I myself see all this all the more clearly comforts me, but along with that, it persuades me that it is not necessary to perform any further manipulations on the play, except printing. It is time to print it, even if later there were to arise new variants and revisions, because I want what has been said for the reader to be heard. But to present it in such a form to the spectator through the paws of an actor is all the same to rub salt in a not-yet-healed wound: it will only hurt worse.
>
> You, of course, will understand all this. For now I just want to thank you for the invitation ..." (8: 278-9).

Any hope for realizing the play on stage was gone at least until after publication of the play, and if he could not have Stanislavskii and the Moscow Art Theater, he wanted to wash his hands of the theater entirely. As Avril Pyman has aptly observed, "He refused them all, and those contacts with the theatre that he could not avoid filled him with spleen and boredom" (Pyman 1980, 2: 31). It is no coincidence that Blok became particularly fond of the cinema at this time.

In spite of Stanislavskii's negative opinion, Blok continued to harbor a fondness for his "favorite child." May and June of 1909 found Blok in Italy on a trip that would leave a profound impression. Even amidst the splendors of the Renaissance, however, Blok's thoughts occasionally returned to *The Song of Fate*, which had not yet appeared in print before his departure. From Florence, Blok wrote to his mother to ask, "Are they writing anything about *The Song of Fate*, and has it come out? Has anyone written anything good?" (8: 287).

It was only after his return from Italy and Germany that Blok seemed finally willing to let go of the play. He acquiesced to the views of those, such as his friend, Evgenii Ivanov, who retained as before his negative opinion of *The Song of Fate*. Ivanov, however, pointed out to Blok a key insight into the problems inherent in the work. He wrote to Blok in July, "One profound theme runs right through the play. That is the agonizing desire for incarnation: the words and dramatis personae are avid to take on flesh and blood, to become incarnate. In this there is a kind of reaching out on the part of the author himself to the first commandment of being, to the 'I am'" (cited by Pyman 1980, 2: 59). Blok replied, "I haven't written to you, and I haven't answered exclusively because of my own swinishness and laziness. Besides that I keep your letter about *The Song of Fate* in my soul. It is likely that your critique from the standpoint of 'mysticism' is exhaustive. I say 'yes' to all that you write; and in accordance with this, to *The Song of Fate* itself I say, after many reservations, 'no.' Well, God be with it" (8: 290). With these words Blok would have seemed to lay the play to rest.

However, neither Blok nor others were so easily persuaded. Interest in the play would continue to arise throughout the rest of Blok's life. Blok himself returned to the play at the end of May, 1912. In his notebook, he jotted down two lists, one of what he had accomplished in the first five months of 1912, the other of what remained to be done. In the latter, he included "a new edition of *Theater* (with *The Song of Fate*)" (7: 147). Although this edition never materialized, within several months, other, outside interest welled up. As Blok wrote in his diary in late October, "In the evening — at Meyerhold's, who talked about *The Song of Fate* at the Aleksandrinka (?!) and wants to see me" (7: 171). Meyerhold's desire to stage the play at the Aleksandrinskii Theater had remained undiminished after four years.

This episode bears particular importance because it forced Blok to review and reconsider not only the play, but also his relation to the theater in general and to Meyerhold in particular. He remained highly critical of modernism. "About the modernists," he wrote at the time, "I fear that they do not have a *pivot*, but only talented flourishes around emptiness" (7: 164). Quite apart from his growing predilection for "healthy realism," Blok's feelings about Meyerhold were complicated by personal problems. His wife had studied with Meyerhold and performed under his direction. In the course of her work with Meyerhold the previous summer, Mendeleeva-Blok had taken up with an actor, Konstantin Kuz'min-Karavaev. While Blok could certainly not blame Meyerhold for his wife's infidelity, this circumstance must have added to his impatience with anything connected to Meyerhold.

Nonetheless, Meyerhold's offer gave Blok pause. His diary gives some indication of just how carefully he reconsidered his relations with Meyerhold:

> *Meyerhold*: he talked a lot, said much that was significant, but the whole time this 'conforming' person, as A.M. Remizov says, sits in him. — Meyerhold said: I fell in love with the details of everyday life, but I approach it differently than Stanislavskii; I am closer to Stanislavskii than I was in the period of Komissarzhevskaia's theater (I had finished saying it before that). — He developed a long theory about how his worldview, in which there is much from Hoffman, from *A Puppet Show*, from Mæterlinck, — became blended together with the director's technical devices (doll-likeness), demonstrating that he is closer to Pushkin, i.e. humanity, than I and many think. This blending was elicited by a whole series of plays, which he had to stage in the period of Komissarzhevskaia's theater and which emphasized doll-likeness. Theater, — says Meyerhold, — is a play of masks; a "play of characters," as I objected, or 'experience,' as he called the same thing, — is, in essence, the same thing; this is only a squabble over words.
>
> Affirming the latter, Meyerhold once again confirmed that words are not important to him. I understand this; he is right in many respects. *But*, I

> think, behind words stand opinions, and behind opinions — the aspiration of the mind — the aspiration of the heart, and the heart is human. In this way, the question of two truths — Stanislavskii's and Meyerhold's —*for me remains* insoluble ("I am Stanislavskii's pupil," — said Meyerhold, by the way).
>
> The Aleksandrinka, — says Meyerhold, — was Rossi's creation and has to return to the spirit of the [18]30's, Mochalov. Today's actors (he does not know how they live) are far from this. He himself is a player, free in his choice of plays, the period of the staging, the choice of stage designer.
>
> *The Song of Fate*, he says (almost four years have already passed, — he has not reread it), it appears to him, it comes back to him, he feels that from this impression that remained with him, something of his own might grow in it, only I have to grant him a lot of freedom.

He then turns to the play itself. As he recounts its genesis and subsequent development, his own disillusionment becomes apparent:

> After his departure I began to think more and more about how I now regard this *Song of Fate*, which passed through so many stages both from without and from within me.
>
> *1908*: I read to many, dreamed about Volokhova-Faina, and she thought about this. Stanislavskii praised it terribly, ordered me to redo two tableaux, and I redid them that same summer into one (here 'Kulikovo Field' was born in Shakhmatovo).[4] Nemirovich-Danchenko also praised it excessively, but in his own somewhat banal way.
>
> When I sent the manuscript off, the Art Theater was silent for a long time. Finally, Stanislavskii sent a long letter about how it was impossible and unnecessary to stage the play. I believed this, otherwise — this put an end to it for me because I myself, moving away from the play, became disillusioned with it.
>
> *The spring of 1909*, before our departure for Italy, it was buried in the IX almanac of 'Sweetbrier' to the music of Kopel'man's reproofs,[5]... of conversations with L. Andreev (he too, I remember, proposed staging the play). [...] It was around this time (1910) I categorically already considered *The Song of Fate* an *idiotic* play and considered it such until the last few months when I began to reread it, having in mind a new edition of my *Theater* (in the beginning through Alcion, and now through Sirin).[6] Rereading it, I was moved by much in it.

[4] "Kulikovo Field" refers to one of Blok's most famous poetic cycles, "On the Field of Kulikovo" ['Na pole Kulikovom"]. Shakhmatovo was the country estate of Blok's family.

[5] Solomon Kopel'man was the owner of "Sweetbrier."

[6] Alcion [Al'tsion] was the musical division of the Moscow publishing house Musaget. Sirin was a Petersburg publishing house, named for the Old Russian mythic bird with the face and breast of a woman. Sirin was also be the pen name under which Vladimir Nabokov would achieve renown as a Russian novelist.

He was so moved, in fact, that he made plans for revisions:

> I will try to throw out from there (both for print and for a possible staging) everything banal, everything stupid, also anything like Leonid Andreev that sticks out of it. We will see what remains then of this doltish Herman. By the way — NB: The *Merezhkovskiis* always more or less sympathized with the play (7: 186-8).

External circumstances, however, would prevent these plans from reaching fruition.

Meyerhold did his best to realize *The Song of Fate* on stage. He set up a meeting between Blok and Vladimir Teliakovskii, the director of the Imperial Theaters, which included the Aleksandrinskii. Negotiations became serious. They centered not only on *The Song of Fate*, but also apparently on Blok's next play, *The Rose and the Cross*. A note of excitement is clearly perceptible in his diary when he records the invitation: "Telephones: Meyerhold — Teliakovskii has invited us to his place on 1 January at 5 o'clock. (*The Song of Fate*, new play (!), committee)" (7: 198). The meeting itself started well, although Blok was hardly impressed with Teliakovskii. Later he noted in his diary, "At five o'clock I arrived at Teliakovskii's, the director of the imperial theaters. We sat with Merezhkovskii and Golovin for an hour and a half.[7] The director is complacent, ignorant, naive, and weak." Perhaps because he still hoped to see *The Rose and the Cross* on the stage of the Moscow Art Theater, Blok was only half-hearted in his attempt to sway an audience he did not respect. In fact, he proved a poor advocate for his own cause. As he himself noted in his diary, "About *The Song of Fate* — I read excerpts — Merezhkovskii and I explained it. I said that, in the form in which the play exists, I am dissatisfied with it." Consequently, no matter auspiciously the meeting may have begun, it ended in disappointment: "The discussions about the committee and about *The Song of Fate* were left until next time" (7: 201-2). Ultimately, *The Song of Fate* would not be staged during Blok's lifetime.

The play then lay dormant until 1919, when an opportunity to reissue the dramas arose. Blok had no illusions about the play's weaknesses; and, in one sense, the decision to include the play in a new edition of his dramas flew in the face of his better artistic judgment. However, by 1919, Blok had long since abandoned any idea of art for art's sake. He stressed, instead, art that was true to life, a striving that he earlier called "healthy realism" and Evgenii Ivanov characterized as an "agonizing desire for incarnation." He no longer accepted the exaggerated claims for art made by such people as Mikhail Tereshchenko, the financier and owner of the Sirin publishing house, who played a pivotal role in the development of *The Rose and the Cross*. By publishing *The Song of Fate*, a work he considered truer to life than to art, together with the more purely aesthetic works of the trilogy of lyric dramas, Blok marked a final break with the very idea of art for art's sake: "In deciding to include *The Song of Fate*, from which I am trying to throw out everything that was very stupid (a work of a good and stupid time), in *Theater*, I am freeing myself once and for all from the will of M.I. Tereshchenko" (7: 355).

---

[7] Aleksandr Golovin was set designer at the Aleksandrinskii Theater.

III

Editions and Revisions

However, Blok remained a conscientious craftsman to the end of his days and saw all too clearly the play's defects. While he felt the need to include *The Song of Fate* with his other plays, he could not acquiesce to it as an accomplished work. As a result, Blok embarked on a major revision of the text. In the process, he elucidated a radically new structure. The play, as printed in the Sweetbrier almanac, fell into four acts. The first and fourth acts contained two scenes each, while the second and third each consisted of only one. By contrast, the final, and presumably authoritative, version consists of seven tableaux, which are not grouped into acts. The net difference then between the six scenes of the 1909 version and the seven tableaux of the 1919 version is a single tableau, a remnant from the drafts written before the 1908 revisions undertaken for Stanislavskii. Blok wrote nothing new, but returned to an earlier conception of the play. The passage in question, the scene in Faina's dressing room, would become the fourth tableau of the 1919 version.[8] Beyond this, Blok, in Medvedev's words, "thickens, condenses the verbal fabric, ... For this he rebuilds the construction of phrases, does away with a series of passing remarks, and shortens the characters' lyrical monologues" (Medvedev, 79). Along these lines, Blok sought to strengthen the dramatic action by eliminating much that was not essential.

What resulted was a "dramatic poem," born from the cocoon of the "dramatic prologue" of 1909. The 1919 version best represents Blok's intentions, both in terms of style and content. Two epigraphs, one from 1 John 4: 18 and the other from Gogol's *Dead Souls*, introduce the printed text. As in the earlier version, the first tableau of the 1919 play centers around the arrival of an ailing Monk, who has been brought up the winding path to Herman and Elena's remote home at the top of a hill. The Monk tells them that he mistook their house for the dwelling place of the mysterious Faina because he saw big white wings above it. He reveals a "vast world" to Herman, who has just dreamed about a swan: Beyond the hills, Herman sees a "big, white swan" not in a dream, but for real this time. Herman's erstwhile Friend, whose advances Elena rebuffs, dismisses Faina as just a "singer in a variety show" (4: 111). Herman decides that he must leave the comfort of his home behind and go out into the world. Herman and Elena swear their loyalty to one another, and the first tableau ends as Herman makes his way down the hill.

As the second begins, "it is as if the house, Elena, and the Monk had departed into the past" (4: 115). Elena, her head bent over her work, listens to the Monk tell about Faina, how every night she stood forlorn on a high precipice as if waiting for someone, how she eventually fled, and how he pursued her. Elena

[8] It is interesting to note that Blok did not use the other tableau abandoned during the summer, 1908 revisions. The so-called "Scene at the Station" came to light only after Blok's death when Medvedev published it (Medvedev, 81-91).

notices a light outside. Although she does not know it, the light comes from the lantern she gave to Herman, who has lost his way and is on the verge of returning until a vision of a woman, whose clothes and scarf are strewn with stars, appears before him and beckons him to follow. At this moment Elena tells the Monk that she feels as if a requiem had just been sung.

Herman, by the beginning of the third tableau, arrives in the city, where he attends the World Trade Exhibition, now in its seventy-seventh day. Everywhere playbills announce that Faina will sing "The Song of Fate" in the *Palace of Culture.* Herman's Friend finds him at the exhibition and warns against the pity Herman feels for the poverty-stricken and the suffering he has seen in the city. Herman decries the "doll-like people" who appear on stage (4: 125). An orator then asks that someone change places with a man sentenced to death. Herman hesitates, fails to act, and begins to doubt his own motives. He decides, however, that his conscience is clean. When Faina takes the stage to sing "The Song of Fate," Herman approaches, and Faina lashes him across the face with her whip.

The scene shifts in the fourth tableau to Faina's dressing room, where writers, reporters, artists, and poets await Faina and outdo one another in singing her praises. She refuses to admit them, chasing them out with her whip. The Old Woman who looks after Faina's needs tells her the story of a young hero who asks a beautiful swan to be his wife. Although the swan turns out to be Faina herself, she interrupts the Old Woman's tale and begins her own, which echoes much of what the Monk told Elena about Faina. She then proposes a game: She will look in the mirror, and whomever she sees will be her groom. In the mirror she sees Herman, who has fallen in love with her. Faina tells him to leave, but changes her mind. She kisses him on the lips and then summarily dismisses him.

Herman and Faina do not immediately meet again. Rather, the fifth tableau opens on the edge of the city in a wide, vacant lot illuminated by a full moon. To the right a swan dreamily rocks back and forth in a park pond. All is silent until a troika pulls up, and Faina and her Companion get out. Her relationship with the Companion turns out to be transitory in nature: She invokes the image of the swan and exhorts her Groom to appear. Soon after, Herman and his Friend arrive, Herman holding a red ribbon Faina has dropped. Herman delivers a long soliloquy. In the course of this meditation, he likens his waiting to that of the Russian warriors held in reserve during the battle of Kulikovo, the turning point in Russia's attempt to throw off the Tartar yoke. Faina returns and now recognizes in Herman the one she has waited for. Their departure in the troika ends the fifth tableau.

Another sharp change in locale marks the sixth tableau, in which the action is again set at Herman and Elena's house. Their Friend has returned to tell Elena of Herman's apparent infidelity. Elena pours out her grief to the Monk, who tells her to follow her own "white road" because nothing remains here for her: Herman's mother has died, and Herman, despite his promises, will not return. Elena, saddened but with resolve, leaves to follow her own "white, snowy road," at the end of which, the Monk says, she will find Herman's soul. As the tableau comes to a close, the Monk carefully closes the door and shutters and sits down on the steps to watch as Elena makes her down the hill. A candle burns on the porch.

The curtain opens on the seventh and final tableau and reveals a hill in an empty, snow-swept plain on a cold, gloomy day. Herman celebrates his break with the old world and his rebirth in a new one. Faina asks about his past. Herman claims to remember nothing before her whip, but Faina upbraids him for his "beautiful words" and tells him to abandon them and become human. Herman lapses into a sort of delirium, in which he sees Elena as an angel with wings. Faina despairs, but Herman has a vision of a hero. When he comes to, Faina "with hitherto absent melancholy and tenderness" asks Herman three questions. In reply, he says that he does not know her, but that he loves her and will find her. Faina kisses him three times and tells him that the time for their meeting has not yet come. She leaves, and a peddler comes upon Herman. Taking Herman for a vagrant, the peddler offers to lead him to a neighboring town. Confident that he will find his way from there, Herman tells the peddler to lead on. With their departure, the curtain falls.

IV

Genre: Drama and Epic

Even a synopsis demonstrates many of the play's idiosyncracies, and had the play been produced, no doubt the reviews would have been harsher than those for either *A Puppet Show* or *The Stranger*. Still, the failure of *The Song of Fate* is a complex question. In the opinion of one commentator, "To expect an exhaustive and indisputable answer to it [the question of the play's failure — TW] is, of course, naive. Even more naive is to propose it." Yet, as the same commentator admits, "But more or less well-grounded suppositions in this realm are not impossible" (Medvedev, 58). Agreeing on what constitutes "well-grounded suppositions" is, of course, another matter. Still, almost everyone who has written about the play reiterates several points. In Medvedev's words, "*The Song of Fate* first and foremost suffers from a weak pulsation of the dramatic nerve" (Medvedev, 57). Volkov adds, "As a work of theater, *The Song of Fate* is vulnerable, first and foremost, from the standpoint of the content of its action. In it is lacking that which constitutes a prerequisite of genuine drama of high quality — a growth of action, a tempo of action that quickens apace. Together with this the shortcomings typical of lyric dramaturgy are not compensated for with purely lyrical virtues. The lyric of *The Song of Fate*, in the majority of cases, is either stylized prose or rhetoric. Neither the one nor the other, of course, is capable of replacing genuine pathos and genuine feeling" (Volkov 1926, 93). Later commentators have echoed the sentiments of these first commentators.

If critics have seen any strength at all in the play, they see it in "Blok's attempt to comprehend Russia in his consciousness, as a landmark in his subsequent development" (Volkov 1926, 93). Without a doubt, this view has merit. The years 1908 and 1909 found Blok consumed with Russia as a theme. Significantly, many of the poems that would eventually go into *Homeland* date from this period. It is a matter of no small importance that the crowning achievement of *Homeland*, the cycle *On the Field of Kulikovo*, grew out of his work on *The Song of Fate*.[9] Given the importance of this theme not only in and of itself but also in terms of its significance for Blok's later work, especially for *Retribution* and *The Twelve*, Stanislavskii was undoubtedly correct in calling *The Song of Fate* "an important transitional step" (Stanislavskii, 7: 415-6).

In their attempts to elucidate the ideational content of the theme of Russia, commentators often have had recourse to Blok's prose. Many of the themes of his creative work recur in his non-fiction. The problem inherent in this approach rests in the deformation of the theme in question. As Jan Mukařovsky once observed, "Even when the poet sometimes expresses himself in a different genre from the one which is basic for him, this expression bears traces of his dominant genre" (Mukařovsky, 152). These "traces" are especially apparent when Blok turns to prose. Yet, critics have typically reversed the polarity of this generic deformation. For instance, when Pavel Gromov attempts to explicate Blok's theme as the collision of a national-historical principle with a lyric one, he writes, "It is for this reason that Blok's publicism has such a particular character: this is 'lyric prose' which has an independent meaning, but which at the same time prepares material for Blok, the poet" (Gromov 1961b, 491).

Without a doubt, the explicit dichotomies explored in his articles "The People and the Intelligentsia" and "The Elements and Culture" echo many of the motifs found in *The Song of Fate*. However, such a thematic approach masks important synchronic features in the play. Indeed, theme by itself explains little. The very fact that Blok successfully formulated the theme of Russia in his lyric poetry and, to a lesser extent, in his prose means that the problems in *The Song of Fate* stem not from a premature attempt to express this theme as some critics have argued, but from considerations of genre. In fact, it is precisely in its genre that Blok's fourth play differs from the three that preceded it. Whereas the first three are, without caveat, lyric dramas, *The Song of Fate* renders that term problematic. Volkov is surely right in insisting that the lyric in *The Song of Fate* is "either stylized prose or rhetoric." The oscillation in Blok's choice of subtitle clearly demonstrates just how perplexing *The Song of Fate* was. What began as a "dramatic prologue" in 1909 evolved into a "dramatic poem" in 1919. Blok's decision to use the adjective "dramatic" and not the noun "drama" suggests that he himself was aware that he had not succeeded in the end in tailoring a drama. The term "prologue" proved similarly unsatisfactory since the question of what *The Song of Fate* might be a prologue to remains in doubt.

As with Blok's other plays, critics have accorded relatively little question to the question of the play's genre. What attempts have been made have centered on melodrama. One critic, for example, explains the play's genre in terms of Romantic dramaturgy (Kipnis, esp. 76). Another accurately depicts the influence of Wagner and Nietzsche on Blok and concludes from this that *The Song of Fate* is a melodrama (Wörn, 496-505 passim). In both cases, the theme of music and the structure of Romantic melodrama are conflated. The temptation of such an explanation is clear: Music was generally regarded as the highest form of art during

[9] In calling both *Homeland* and *On the Field of Kulikovo* cycles, I use the term advisedly. *Homeland* is a cycle that consists of poems written between 1907 and 1916. In contrast, Blok wrote *On the Field of Kulikovo* in a relatively short interval of time, between 7 June and 23 December, 1908. As it stands in Blok's *Collected Works*, *On the Field of Kulikovo* is best understood as a cycle within a cycle.

the Symbolist era, and in Blok's play this conception is encoded in the title. However, these considerations are thematic, not generic. Although Herman is a descendant of the Romantic hero and although Wagner and Nietzsche's ideas about music influenced Blok, these insights fail to clarify the question of genre.

What then is *The Song of Fate*? The key lies in the term "dramatic poem." Blok's choice of poem, or *poèma* in Russian, is loaded. Far more than just a lyric poem, the *poèma* in the Russian tradition describes a long, and in the nineteenth century, narrative poem typically on a theme of broad historical or legendary import. Blok clearly alluded to this tradition by drawing on one the most famous for the second of the two epigraphs to *The Song of Fate*. For that second epigraph, Blok quotes *Dead Souls*, which Gogol called a *poèma*. The *poèma* in Gogol's hands outgrew its former bounds to become synonymous with epic, the national epic in particular. Blok explicitly draws attention to this aspect of the Gogolian tradition by choosing a quotation that deals with Russia. In its entirety the epigraph runs as follows:

> Rus'! Rus'! Everything in you is open, empty, and flat; — nothing seduces or charms the gaze. But what incomprehensible, mysterious force draws me to you? And why is your melancholy song, unreal along your whole length and breadth, from sea to sea, audible and why does it resound incessantly in my ears? What is in it, in this song? What calls, and sobs, and grabs me by the heart? — Rus'! What is it you want from me? What incomprehensible bond is concealed between us? Isn't it here, in you won't a boundless thought be born, when you yourself are without end? Is it possible not to be a hero here, when there is space for him to show himself and walk around? (4: 103; compare to Gogol, 231-2).

The call to the epic and the heroic sets the tone for the play. Whatever the play's final form, Blok's intentions were nothing short of epic.

Epic though Blok's intentions may have been, to call *The Song of Fate* an epic would be a mistake. From the standpoint of genre, the admixture of epic and drama is jarring, if not incongruous. Their union, as in Brecht's epic drama, was still years off. Moreover, the term "prologue," Blok's first choice as a subtitle, turns out to be apt, even for the revised 1919 version of the play. *The Song of Fate* fails to become more than a prelude to an epic journey because it deals with only the birth of Herman as a hero and with the very beginning of his journey. This becomes clear in the first line of the play when Elena tells her husband, "Wake up, Herman!" Although he has awakened by the end of the play, Herman has only just set out on his journey. There will be no return in *The Song of Fate*. The closure usually associated with the epic form is entirely lacking here.

Still, elements of the epic form appear in full force. The very fact that Herman embarks on a journey points to epic intention on Blok's part. This intention is mitigated by the apparent aimlessness of Herman's journey. Heroic action, at first glance at least, is absent. Not until the fifth tableau, in fact, does Herman's heroic intent become evident. Even here, however, it is not Herman's heroic action; it is referred heroism. As he tells his Friend,

> Everthing that has been, everything that will be surrounded me: it is exactly as if these last few days I have lived the life of all times, I have lived by the

> torments of my homeland. I remember the horrible day of battle on the Kulikovo field.— The prince arose with the troops on the hill; the earth trembled from the creaking of the Tatar carts; the eagle's cry threatened with adversity. Then crept in ill-boding night, and the Nepriadva adorned itself with mist like a bride with a veil. The prince and the voivode arose at the foot of the hill and listened to the earth: the swans and geese restlessly splashed; a widow sobbed; a mother beat against her son's stirrup. Above the Russian camp there stood only silence, and distant summer lightning blazed. But the wind chased away the mist, and there dawned just such an autumn morning, and also, I recall, it smelled of burning. And the prince's gleaming banner advanced from the knoll. When the first monk and Tatar fell dead, the hosts collided, and all day they fought, hacked, gnawed each other ... And the fresh troops all day had to lie in wait, only to watch, and lament, and strain to be in action ... And the voivode kept repeating, warning: it's still early, our hour has not struck. — O Lord! I know, like any warrior of that host in ambush, how the heart begs for work, and how it is still early, early! ... But there it is — morning! Again the solemn music of the sun, like war trumpets, like a distant battle ... but I am here, like a warrior in ambush. I do not dare to fight; I do not know what to do; I must not; my hour has not struck! — That is why I do not sleep at night: I await with my whole heart the one who will come and say: 'Your hour has struck! It is time!'" (4: 149).

Many of these motifs are sounded in the first draft by the Monk, who tells Elena that, before he becoming a star, he had been a warrior who died on the field of battle. (See in this regard Gromov 1961b, 513). By the end of the play, such grandiloquent lyricism deteriorates into rhetoric because Herman's actions, few and far between as they are, fail to support it. As Faina tells Herman in the seventh tableau, "It is all words! Beautiful words" (4: 160). In the end, it is this discrepancy between word and deed that undermines *The Song of Fate* as an independent work. Nonetheless, such "beautiful words" might serve as a prologue to true heroic action.

Yet, even if such heroic action as Herman dreams of were to unfold in *The Song of Fate*, it would be fundamentally unlike that in Homer. What Bowra once wrote in regard to Virgil applies to Blok: "Virgil abandons the scheme of life by which the hero lives and dies for his own glory, and replaces a personal by a social ideal. The old concept of a man's honour is merged in a scheme of morality where duties are laid down with precision and must be fulfilled if the gods' will is to be done" (Bowra, 13). Herman's speech about his thirst for action clearly sets the parameters of his heroic action: he will be a Russian hero or none at all. The example of the national epic resounds through much of *The Song of Fate*. In this sense, Virgil's struggle against the anarchic and anti-social individualism of the Homeric hero finds resonance in Blok's attempt to break free of lyricism, especially as the expression of the exclusively individual. Again, Bowra's assessment of Virgil's efforts applies forcefully to Blok's: "Because he wished to write a poem about something much larger than the destinies of individual heroes, he created a type of epic in which the characters represent something outside themselves, and the events displayed have other interests than their immediate excitement in the context" (Bowra, 15).

Stripped of such excitement, the play finds its structural center somewhere other than in plot. Moreover, since Blok is not interested in Herman as a man, but as an emblem of Russia, the play's structural center cannot rest in realistic psychology. In Bowra's words, "The writers of literary epic are almost forced to point a moral. Their heroes are examples of what men ought to be or types of human destiny whose very mistakes must be marked and remembered. In themselves they may be misty and even characterless, but they are not meant to be characters so much as examples" (Bowra, 16). Much of the criticism levelled against *The Song of Fate*, if viewed from this perspective, falls apart. Nearly every commentator who has written about the play has remarked on Herman's weakness and lack of character. Typical, in this regard, is Andrei Fedorov, who said of Herman, "By an irony of fate Blok's own words about Mæterlinck's characters as 'weak-willed, feeble people who are drawn by a small fate' turn out to be applicable to him" (Fedorov 1980, 122). Yet, as is clear from the speech of the Man in Glasses about Faina's connection to the soul of the people, Herman's example is to be emulated since he has intuited the path to the people. The ending especially helps to clarify this point. Herman is, for all intents and purposes, saved by peddler. As has been pointed out many times, the fact that a peddler leads Herman to safety suggests an allusion to Nekrasov's *The Peddlers* and the tradition of Russian civic poetry. The allusion to the civic tradition, with its emphasis on the plight of the people, underscores the didactic element in *The Song of Fate*.

Other elements of the national epic also arise in *The Song of Fate*. For instance, the divine ordination of the heroic act assumes the same prominent place here that it does in earlier epics. Thomas Greene, in his study of the epic, writes, "The heroic act assumes its highest prestige by its divine authorization, the authorization which became symbolized with increasing frequency in the Renaissance by the literal descent of the angelic messenger to the hero" (Greene, 18). In this regard, motifs from Tolstoi's "What People Live By" play a pivotal role here. In large part, these motifs have gone unnoticed because critics have taken their cue from Pavel Medvedev, who argued that the central image at issue here, a recurring identification of the Monk as an angel, derived from a source other than Tolstoi. According to Medvedev, Blok's wife pointed out that the image appeared in a reproduction of a picture by the Finnish artist Simberg in the journal *World of Art* (Medvedev, 65). Particularly as this view originated with Blok's wife, it seems authoritative. However, one source should not obscure others.

Although the angel imagery occurs more often in the first two versions of the play, it occurs with great frequency even in the final redaction. Elena, in describing the Monk for Herman, says, "He's just like an angel with a broken wing" (4: 105). Her description echoes Herman's dream of the white swan. Elena underscores this image by repeating it in her next line, another description of the Monk, but this time for the Friend: "He is very much like an angel; it even seemed to me that he had big white wings" (4: 106). Perhaps the most striking example arises in the 1909 version of the play when Elena and the Monk part. Elena tells him, "Well, farewell ... Angel of God" (Blok 1909, 244). Taken by itself, such imagery might constitute, as Medvedev held, "a typical story of a fallen angel" (Medvedev, 65).

However, Gromov has demonstrated that this imagery derives from the fallen star imagery of *The Stranger*. He points out that in the first draft, the Monk tells Elena that he was warrior who died in battle. After his death, a "white maiden" turned him into an angel or a wandering star, a comet. The association of the fallen angel and the fallen star imagery becomes critical to understanding how the characters are related. The monk as fallen star, Gromov argues, grows out of the Stranger as fallen star and ultimately depends on the same motif in Apollon Grigor'ev's poetry. Gromov goes on to show that Faina is also associated with this imagery in the first draft. In the scene in Faina's dressing room, Herman likens Faina to a star (Gromov 1961b, 507-8). Gromov does not exhaust this image, however. Particularly in the final version of the play, this complex of images depends heavily on Elena. The Friend, for instance, associates this imagery with Elena: "Already from that hill I saw your white dress, and it was as if you had big white wings behind your shoulders" (4: 106). The ambiguity of this image is critical. Since it is unclear whether the Friend likens Elena to an angel or a swan, both are summoned up. The angel imagery points to the topic under discussion, namely Herman's calling. The swan imagery figures prominently in "On the Field of Kulikovo," where it signals the heroic theme. The same association arises in Herman's delirious visions in the seventh tableau. Describing what he sees to Faina, Herman affirms the Friend's vision of Elena: "Who is this? An angel in white clothes! Golden locks of hair! Wings behind the shoulders! How she shines! In her hands is a lily… a lily or a candle? A wedding candle! Elena! O Lord! Elena!" (4: 164).

The very complexity of this imagery suggests that the image of the fallen star by itself is not enough to explain the Monk's role. Moreover, other considerations point to Tolstoi's "What Men Live by." Throughout *The Song of Fate*, Blok has recourse to several of Tolstoi's motifs. The angel imagery is, of course, the most striking. Besides angels, the two works also share the motif of a sick or injured person who is brought to the house of the protagonist. In "What Men Live By" a bootmaker finds a man by the road and, after some initial hesitation, takes him home. In *The Song of Fate* the motif shows up twice: In the first instance, the Monk is brought to Herman's house from the road, despite Elena's misgivings. In the second, a peddler finds Herman in a field in the middle of a blizzard and leads him to safety, despite his conviction that Herman is a vagrant. From this point of view, it is not insignificant that initially the peddler was a muzhik, a common peasant, since a muzhik figures into "What Men Live by" as well. Tolstoi's bootmaker does not own his own home, but rents from a muzhik.

Quite apart from elements of plot, the image of light emanating from the angelic figure is common to "What Men Live By" and *The Song of Fate*, at least in drafts and in its 1909 incarnation. In Tolstoi's story light marks the moment when the fallen angel attains the last of the three pieces of wisdom and becomes once again an angel: "The masters saw that light was coming from Mikhail" (Tolstoi, 25: 22). The light grows gradually stronger. As departure of the angel nears, "all of him was arrayed with light so that it was impossible for the eye to look at him" (Tolstoi, 25: 24). In *The Song of Fate* similar imagery surrounds the figure that would become the Monk. That figure, which actually is an angel in the drafts, tells Elena, "When the white maiden lifted me up, I began to appear to people as a large star" (Medvedev, 65). Blok eliminated this passage from the published versions, but the image did not disappear entirely from the 1909 version. There Elena does not, as she does in the 1919 version, simply say, "He is exactly like an angel with a broken wing." Rather, the image was initially more detailed: "He is exactly like an angel with a broken wing and a radiant visage" (Blok 1909, 200). Although this motif disappears almost entirely in the final version, its presence in drafts and in the 1909 version adds heft to the similarities between "What Men Live By" and *The Song of Fate*.

Perhaps the most convincing piece of evidence pointing to Tolstoi's story, however, is Blok's choice of epigraph. Tolstoi begins his story with a massive epigraph, which in part is composed of verses seven, eight, twelve, sixteen, and twenty from 1 John 4. Blok chose one of the intervening verses, verse eighteen, from 1 John 4 for his epigraph. From this standpoint, the fact that Blok wrote an article about Tolstoi just as he was readying the manuscript of the play for Stanislavskii in August, 1908 seems hardly coincidental. That he equates the "birthday of Lev Nikolaevich Tolstoi" with the "day of not only my angel but also that of thousands of other people" at the very least points to the saint and not the soldier, to Tolstoi in his last period, to the author of "What Men Live By" (5: 302).

The allusion to Tolstoi's story emphasizes that Herman's fate is divinely ordained. Without these references to "What Men Live By," the opposite might appear to be true, at least at first glance. Herman, after all, abandons his devoted wife for, to quote his Friend, a "variety show singer with a very questionable reputation" (4: 111).[10] Throughout the play, however, Herman insists that his conscience must remain clean. Before he even sets out, he prays, "Preserve for me only the ardor of my youthful soul and a living conscience, O Lord" (4: 116). Once he has set out on his journey, he stops to examine his conscience. After he fails to take the place of the condemned in the Palace of Culture, he decides that it remains clean (4: 126). Or again, at the end of the play after Faina's departure, he reflects, "One thing remains: that for which I asked you, O Lord: a clean conscience" (4: 166). These declamations would be sheer hypocrisy, were his fate not divinely ordained, were he not compelled in some sense to leave Elena. The 1909 version bolsters the Tolstoi allusions with more direct reference to a summons from on high. In the third act he echoes Faina when he says, "Someone has called me" (Blok 1909, 234).

With this divine summons, Herman's epic fate reveals itself to be Christian, and it is little surprise that *The Song of Fate* contains, albeit in parodic form, direct reference and allusions to the preeminent Christian epic, Dante's *Divine Comedy.* Nor was this the first time that Dante's work had informed Blok's. In fact, Blok's first book of poetry, *Verses about the Beautiful Lady*, owes a debt to Dante's *Vita Nuova*. Yet, if Blok approached Dante's work solemnly in that early work, he betrays a different orientation in *The Song of Fate*. In stark contrast to the persona of Dante's poem, a seeker who becomes lost in the middle of his days, Herman is a complacent day-dreamer who has to be quite literally awakened as the play begins. His journey, in fact, reverses the topos of the traditional epic. For Dante's hero, the way to the mount of virtuous joy is blocked by beasts, and he must descend into Hell before ascending up the mountain of Purgatory to the Garden above. As A. Bartlett Giamatti has suggested, "The movement of the poem is the movement of Christianity itself, from a wilderness to a City" (Giamatti, 94). For Herman, the path is the opposite. He leaves the idyllic setting of his home and descends into the

[10] Prikhod'ko regards Herman's departure from home as the "character's renunciation of his egoism" and likens Herman to a medieval knight (Prikhod'ko 1993, 40). Although the comparison is forced, Prikhod'ko's understanding of Herman's self-renunciation is insightful.

Hell of the City and the World Trade Exhibition, only to ascend to the wilderness of a snowy hill at the end of the play. The point of departure in *The Song of Fate* is strikingly akin to the destination in *The Divine Comedy.* Giamatti argues that in the *Paradiso* "the twin images of Garden and City are married in the final, luminous vision" (Giamatti, 118). Much the same could be said of Herman and Elena's home. If allowances are made for its private and secular character, their home synthesizes a life of cultivation with a wild setting. In this sense, Elena's preoccupation with the lily, which she fears will not come up in Herman's absence, reflects not only the ideal of a cultivated garden, but also a mystical ideal in the face of the pandemonium that Herman will confront in the city.[11]

Other parodic parallels between the two works become apparent along the way. Herman's guide through the nether regions of the city is not an enlightened Virgil, but his cynical Friend. It is the Friend, in fact, who makes the associations with the *Divine Comedy* explicit:

> Yes, we are in the walls of the Palace of Culture. The inscription,
> Patterned like the inscription of the gates
> Of Dante's enigmatic Hell,
> Tells of this. We will go into the crowd,
> Observing man's stupidity
> (4: 122).

Indeed, the axes on which this technological hell rests are not good and evil, but backwardness and progress.

Similarly, the woman Herman seeks could hardly be more unlike Dante's angelic Beatrice. Where the latter's character is monolithic in its virtue, Faina's is elusive, non-coincident. According to the Friend, she is a woman of "questionable reputation." The Man in Glasses maintains, to the contrary, that "she has brought us part of the people's soul" (4: 134). For the Monk, she is different still, a melancholy woman who would leave her village's dance around a fire to look out over a precipice as if she were waiting for someone (4: 116). Whoever she is, Faina is the woman toward whom Herman ascends. In fact, his pursuit of Faina is quixotic inasmuch as he abandons Elena, who embodies much of Beatrice's virtue.

This bifurcation of the feminine image marks the waning of Dante's influence and the ascendance of that of the national epic. Elena and Faina follow in a long tradition of paired and opposed female epic heroines. Typically, "the first wife represents a national identity which must be abandoned" (Griffiths and Rabinowitz, 72. See also Clowes). Elena, in this sense, represents an idyllic, perhaps aristocratic, domestic identity, one that takes shape away from other people, in comparative comfort and safety. As Herman says to Elena, "I understood that we are alone on a blessed island, cut off from the whole world. Is it really possible to live so alone and so happily?" (4: 110). He decides that is not possible and abandons Elena. His journey takes him to Faina, who represents an identity that is not tied to the domestic. As she herself tells Herman in the last tableau, "There, you are all like that... Exactly like dead people... but I am alive! I never had a home, or relatives, or friends! Wherever I want to go, I go!" (4: 161).

---

[11] Blok's immediate source for the image of the lily is Vladimir Solov'ev, mystic, poet and philosopher.

To a certain extent, this opposition of Elena and Faina organizes space in the play.[12] Where the scenes that involve Elena take place indoors or on the porch, those that involve Faina take place most often outdoors. The two exceptions of this are the third and fourth tableaux, which take place in the World Trade Exhibition and Faina's dressing room repectively. The first is so large as to mimic an open space, while the second is truly an exception. This opposition, in turn, affects spatial relationships and explains their seemingly paradoxical arrangment. Although country scenes are usually associated with open spaces and city scenes with enclosed, these usual associations are reversed in *The Song of Fate*. The rural scenes, because they include Elena and thus the domestic, take place inside, while the scenes in the city, because of Faina, take place outside.

V

Old World and New

As an element of a national epic, the opposition of Elena and Faina buttresses a more generalized opposition of the domestic, the domain of the hearth, and what might best be described as the elemental, an opposition which first found expression somewhat earlier in "Hard Times" ["Bezvremen'e"]. This article, which Blok published in 1906, provides important insights into *The Song of Fate*. In "Hard Times," Blok discusses, amongst other topics, "the Golden Age, the highest point of that feeling, which is now on the wane, the feeling of the domestic hearth" (5: 70).[13] To the tranquility and peace usually associated with the bygone era of the hearth Blok contrasts the world contemporary to him: "What can be done? What can be done? The domestic hearth is no more. ... The pure morals, the tranquil smiles, the quiet evenings — everything is covered with cobwebs, and time itself has stopped. Happiness has grown cold, the hearths have gone out. Doors are open to the blizzard-swept square" (5: 70). The rhetorical question, "What can be done?" echoes the titles of works by Chernyshevskii and Lenin and, like the allusions in *The Song of Fate* to Nekrasov, invokes the civic tradition in Russian literature.

This opposition of hearth to the elemental world outside provides the framework of Herman's dilemma, and much of the imagery and vocabulary of "Hard Times" finds a place in *The Song of Fate*. Herman's home, for example, is clearly associated with the world of the hearth. It is twice described as "tranquil," first by the Monk and the second time by Elena (4: 108 and 4: 158, respectively). Situated high on a hill, the little white house is isolated and quiet, nearly free from incursions by the outside world. By contrast, the scenes involving Faina take place

[12] Wörn's contention that time and space have a mythic character in *The Song of Fate* seems apt in this regard. (See Wörn, 519-22.)

[13] The phrase Blok employs here, "domestic hearth" [domashnii ochag], can figuratively also mean a "home." However, because he entitles the first part of the article simply "Hearth" [ochag], the more literal rendering is perhaps truer to Blok's intent.

either in public, in such venues as the Palace of Culture, or out in the elements. The seventh tableau, which takes place on a snow-covered hill in the middle of a snowstorm, is typical in this regard. It is true, however, that in describing the snowstorm, Blok uses the word *metel'*, and not the word *v'iuga*, the adjectival form of which appears in "Hard Times." Nonetheless, the two are often given as synonyms; and this variation in vocabulary should not cloud the consistency in Blok's treatment of the theme. Consistency in this theme appears to have been at the heart of Blok's revisions. Perhaps the clearest example arises in the stage directions that describe Herman's departure. In the 1909 version, "Elena sobs, throws her arms on Herman's shoulders, all of her trembling, like the true, hot, and infinitely long hidden elements" (Blok 1909, 209). Blok, however, systematically eliminated any and all association between Elena and the elements. In the 1919 version, Elena's reaction is toned down: "Elena, sobbing, throws her arms on Herman's shoulders." Blok soft-pedals the violent, elemental emotion of the earlier version: "Elena quietly walks to the house" (4: 114).

Moreover, explicit references to the domain of the hearth and the domestic occur in the play. The most powerful comes in Herman's monologue at the beginning of the seventh tableau. Here, as in several other passages, Herman insists on the fundamental unreality of his past:

> Everything has passed. The past is a dream. ...
> Grown accustomed to domestic comfort,
> To the warmth and light of family hearths,
> The wretched soul would not endure
> Such freedom and such happiness
> (4: 159).

Herman explicitly links the new world with freedom and happiness, thereby implying that the world of the hearth should be associated with enslavement. This association becomes clearer later in the same monologue:

> I'm as if christened with a second christening
> In a different font — of cold and snow.
> No need for stunted life — three are too few for me!
> No need for hearth and quiet —
> I need the world with the wind singing its songs!
> No need for slavish death — let
> Life and death be a united blizzard!
> (4: 159-60).

Here references to Blok's cycle *The Snow Mask*, which loosely traces the development of a passionate affair, come to the fore. The image of the second christening in a baptismal font of snow, for example, first appeared in a poem from that cycle entitled "Second Christening" ["Vtoroe kreshchen'e"]: "And in a new font of snow / I am christened with a second christening" (2: 216). Such quotations underscore the erotic nature of Herman's rebirth. Yet, this new life, born as it is of a cold passion, is brutal and elemental. Nurture and warmth, the hallmarks of the hearth, are relics of the past. Yet even this passion must be overcome in order not to impede Herman's moral growth. Bowra's remarks about the passion between

Aeneas and Dido apply to Herman and Faina's passion as well: "[T]he one great love episode of the *Aeneid*, Dido's passion for Aeneas, is treated in a tragic spirit and takes its place in the poem as a fearful obstacle which the hero has to overcome in his moral progress and the prelude of disasters to come in the relations of Rome and Carthage" (Bowra, 25). Likewise, at the end of *The Song of Fate*, Faina is called away; their time has not yet come.

This overarching theme, the passing of the world of the hearth, finds manifold expression in *The Song of Fate*. Aside from the obvious example of Herman's decision to leave home in search of Faina, other, more subtle statements of the theme occur, especially in the form of allusion. The most striking instance alludes to Chekhov's work, to *The Cherry Orchard* in particular. The allusion appears in the sixth tableau, just after Elena insists that, contrary to the Monk's assertions, Herman will return: "There — he is coming now." Herman, however, does not appear. Instead, as the reader discovers in the stage directions, "At this moment a certain sound can be heard from the plains: tender, soft, musical: as if a raven had cawed, or someone had touched a taut string" (4: 157).

Blok, of course, refers here to the image of the breaking string that figures so prominently in the second and fourth acts of *The Cherry Orchard*. Chekhov's second act takes place in a field, to which very nearly the whole group has gone on an outing. As the sun sets and everyone has fallen silent, the stage directions indicate, "Suddenly there can be heard a distant sound, as if from the sky, the sound of a broken string, dying away, sad" (Chekhov, 13: 224). The repetition of this image in the fourth act is almost exact: the verb *razdavat'sia* is replaced by the verb *slyshat'sia*, and the adverb "suddenly" is eliminated (Chekhov, 13: 254). Despite the apparent differences between Blok's string and Chekhov's, several similarities become apparent. First, in all three instances, reflexive verbs convey auditory perception. Blok uses the verb *donosit'sia*, while Chekhov uses *razdavat'sia* in the second act and *slyshat'sia* in the fourth. Secondly, the direction from which the sound emanates is oriented vertically. In *The Song of Fate* the sound comes *up* the hill "from the plain," while it comes *down* "as if from the sky" in Chekhov. Finally, even the comparison of the sound to the cry of a bird occurs in both. Blok makes the comparison explicitly in his stage directions. Chekhov, however, leaves the comparison to one of his characters. It is Gaev, who says, "And maybe, it was some kind of bird ... like a heron" (Chekhov, 13: 224).

As in *The Song of Fate*, the image of the string in *The Cherry Orchard* is associated with the theme of the passing of the world of the hearth. Chekhov contrasts Ranevskaia's sentimental attachment to the cherry orchard with Lopakhin's pragmatic plan to save the estate by levelling the trees and parcelling the land into lots. In broad terms Blok's distinction between the world of the hearth and a new world in which the hearth has grown cold could be applied to *The Cherry Orchard*. Ranevskaia, for instance, certainly views the orchard through the prism of her own warm and sentimental affections and memories, the death of her son foremost among them. In act one, she barely makes it into the house before she is overcome with emotion: "The nursery, my dear, wonderful room ... I slept here when I was little ... (Weeps.) And now I am like a little one" (Chekhov, 13: 199). In one sense, the play becomes a record of her inability to move beyond this sentiment. Her brother too seems trapped by sentiment, which forms the basis of his rhapsodic and maudlin monologues. Such sentiment is understandable in the happy children of the old regime; however, quite surprisingly even Firs, one of those who suffered under the old regime, reminisces about the good old days.

By contrast, Trofimov and Ania make a clean break with the past. As Trofimov describes their generation to Ania, "We are about two hundred years behind. We still have absolutely nothing; we do not have a definite relation to the past. We only philosophize, complain about melancholy, or drink vodka. Afterall it so clear that in order to begin to live in the present, it is necessary first to expiate our past, to have done with it, but to expiate it is possible only by suffering, only by extraordinary, constant labor." Ania replies, "The home in which we live has not been ours for a long time already, and I will leave. I give you my word" (Chekhov, 13: 227-8). At the end of the play, their departure is the least hindered, the most joyous, for they perceive it as a new beginning.

Lopakhin and Varia represent a third and different relation to the world of the hearth. Both have heartfelt attachments to the orchard, yet both recognize that the world has changed and that they must, however reluctantly, move on. Out of affection, Varia does everything in her power to make her mother comfortable; yet, her mother's impractical nature at times drives her to distraction. Her very status as an adopted child subtly underlines her provisional relation to the orchard and the old regime. Lopakhin too, while bound by affection for Ranevskaia, cannot save the orchard for her. Forced to fend for himself early in life, he is nothing if not pragmatic. The opportunity to save the estate, or at least to salvage from it some financial gain, by felling the orchard seems to Lopakhin a not ignoble compromise. In the end, the romance between Lopakhin and Varia, though failed, is founded on a past they hold partly in common.

Similar attitudes to the world of the hearth become apparent in *The Song of Fate*. Elena and Herman's mother are bound by the hearth and cannot see beyond it. Herman's mother, unable to change, dies there. Elena, on the other hand, accepts the necessity of leaving the hearth behind only after the death of her mother-in-law. Herman's Friend, by way of contrast, seems cynically detached from the world of the hearth and perhaps never had any attachment to it. Faina too, born outside of the hearth, harbors no affection for it. Perhaps only Herman bridges the two worlds. Still, his attachment to the world of the hearth is weaker than Lopakhin's. For instance, after he leaves Elena, he never looks back, even when Faina reminds him of the wife who waits for him patiently.

Despite such similarities, Blok represents the world of the hearth as more certainly a part of the past than does Chekhov. Perhaps the best evidence of this tendency arises in the conduct of those characters who do not belong to the world of the hearth and who have only momentary dealings with those who do. For instance, the beggar who asks directions in Act Two of *The Cherry Orchard* serves to remind those gathered of the suffering in the world beyond the orchard. By contrast, Blok portrays such figures as heralds of the future, not just reminders of the present. After all it is the peddler who stumbles upon Herman at the end of *The Song of Fate* who shows him the road.

The road to the future, which is understood as the realm of the elemental that will replace the world of the hearth, is intricately associated with the notion of fate. Herman's kinship to certain literary antecedents, particularly Hermann, the hero of Pushkin's "The Queen of Spades," underscores this point. As one commentator has remarked, "The name of the drama's hero, Herman, by dint of its very rarity and unexpectedness could not have been chosen by Blok without consideration of Hermann, the hero of Pushkin's 'Queen of Spades'" (Rodina, 177). However, even those commentators who have recognized this correlation have failed to demonstrate convincingly how Blok incorporated it into the play. Rodina, for instance, argues that by invoking the name of Hermann, Blok brought a "revolutionary theme" to the foreground (Rodina, 178). While plausible, Rodina's contention concerns a theme that is tangential to both works. Rodina concedes as much by turning to other of Pushkin's works, such as "The Captain's Daughter," for illustration. More importantly, this argument ignores many of the other ties between "The Queen of Spades" and *The Song of Fate*.

Perhaps the most important is the role of numbers in the two works. Numbers, of course, occupy a privileged place in the scholarship on "The Queen of Spades" and represent too large a topic to be dealt with exhaustively here. (For a detailed account of numbers and their role in "The Queen of Spades" in English, see Debreczeny, 219-22.) However, a brief overview will suffice to show that similar patterns arise in both Pushkin's story and Blok's play. The numbers three, seven, and eleven predominate in "The Queen of Spades." They and their multiples appear to be ubiquitous, infiltrating almost every aspect of the story. Three, seven, and eleven, for example, are the numerical values of the cards the ghost of the Countess reveals to Hermann. In his quest for a fortune, Hermann appears at Chekalinskii's gaming table on three consecutive evenings. The story itself falls into seven parts. Such examples could be and have been developed far more extensively; however, even this brief sampling provides the proper orientation of the role of numbers in *The Song of Fate*.

As in "The Queen of Spades," three, seven, eleven, and their multiples arise at key junctures. For example, Herman arrives at the World Trade Exhibition on the seventy-seventh day of festivities, which proves also to be the occasion of Faina's seventy-seventh appearance.[14] When they part at the end of the play, Faina tells Herman, "I kiss you three times" (4: 166). Nor is it insignificant that the play itself falls into seven tableaux, especially since Blok did not settle on this structure until the last revision in 1919 and since, to achieve it, he abandoned the more conventional four-act structure of the 1909 version. Even in his choice of interpolated material, Blok used only what was consistent with this constellation of numbers. Thus, the thirty-three ships that set sail in the Old Woman's folktale in the fourth tableau observe not only the trebling so common in folktales, but also, as the product of three and eleven, the particular role of numbers in *The Song of Fate*.

This correspondence between Blok's and Pushkin's use of numbers points to broader thematic similarities. When Blok first conceived the play, the theme of numbers intersected, as it does in "The Queen of Spades," with the theme of gambling. Unfortunately, the material that would have clarified this point has not come down to us. A note Blok made on the last page of the drafts of *The Song of Fate* constitutes the sum total of the evidence that remains: "Besides this, there were sketches of a scene of *great talent* between Elena, the Friend, Faina, and Herman in a gambling house. It was destroyed by me, as were all other sketches" (Medvedev, 61). While Blok's motives for destroying these sketches are unclear, the gambling theme, if we are to judge by the considerable space he initially allotted to it, was one of the play's more important themes. Although stripped away in the

[14] At least one critic sees in the repetition of the number seventy-seven an apocalyptic sign (Prikhod'ko 1993, 41).

course of further revision, the gambling theme, coupled with the theme of numbers, reinforced the allusions to "The Queen of Spades."

In Pushkin's story, the use of numbers and gambling renders causality ambiguous. Hermann, who is teased for his rational and cautious nature, seems to act out of free will. From this standpoint, his madness would seem to compensate for the guilt about the death of the countess he does not acknowledge. Other episodes suggest, on the contrary, that Hermann is but a pawn of fate. The ghost of the countess appears to Hermann quite against her will to impart the secret of the three cards. Moreover, the similarity between Hermann's name and that of St. Germain, with whom the secret of the cards originated, suggests that they are somehow connected and that the secret of the three cards must inevitably be revealed to Hermann. That higher powers conspire to determine the fate of man is a plausible interpretation of the epilogue, in which Lizaveta marries and takes on a ward of her own and; thus, though the cast has changed, the story plays itself out all over again. It could even be argued that the greatest strength of "The Queen of Spades" is Pushkin's seemingly effortless tightrope walk between the ideas of free will and fate. Because good arguments for both ideas present themselves, the reader delves back into the story in search of resolution.

Blok, however, did not seek ambiguity. Fate, unequivocal and inescapable, pursues the epic hero at every step. Portraying Herman's fate as a matter of free will would thus have undermined him as an epic hero. Thus, Blok systematically cut out any material that hindered Herman as an epic hero. Since gambling can be ambiguous in this regard — and clearly Blok looked at the example of "The Queen of Spades" carefully — the scene at the gambling house was one of the first to go. The theme of numbers, on the other hand, remained because it reinforced the seeming inevitability of events. In other words, if the numbers three, seven, eleven, and their multiples occur often enough, a pattern becomes apparent. Patterns, being planned, imply a patterning consciousness, which is consistent with the theme of fate. Consequently, Blok retained the theme of numbers, although his use of it is far less extensive than Pushkin's. Blok's allusion to "The Queen of Spades" then is complex and selective: although Hermann and Herman may be near namesakes, the one letter that differentiates their names signals difference as well as similarity.

VI

Carnival and Epic

However, even as Blok carefully prepares the theme of Herman's fate, he undermines it. Given that Blok embarked on *The Song of Fate* hard on the heels of the trilogy of lyric dramas, the extent to which elements of carnival penetrate his fourth play should come as no surprise. Here, however, carnival in no way organizes the work as in the first three plays. *The Song of Fate* lacks their technical consistency, whether the non-coincidence in characterization of *A Puppet Show*, the ideological tension and clear crowning and decrowning of *The King on the Square*, or the carefully wrought parallelism of *The Stranger*. In it, none of the techniques that tear at the monologic framework are developed beyond an embryonic form. What carnival does arise, though, is enough to interfere with *The Song of Fate* as an epic work.

This shift towards carnival makes itself felt in Blok's parodic treatment of Dante's hell, in the city that hosts the World Trade Exhibition. The city to which Herman travels is never named, but it might be described in these terms: "A city with its millions and its world-wide trade, its crystal palace, its world exhibition ...." Although accurate, this description comes not from *The Song of Fate*, but from Dostoevskii's *Winter Notes on Summer Impressions.*[15] In fact, much of what is said about the World Trade Exhibition and the Palace of Culture bears strong resemblance to the crystal palace Dostoevskii describes. "Yes, the exhibition is striking," writes Dostoevskii,

> You feel its terrible strength, which united here all these numberless people, who have come from all over the world, into one flock; you recognize its gigantic conception; you feel that here something has already been attained, that here there is triumph, exultation. It is as if you even begin to fear something. However independent you may be, for some reason you become terrified. Is this not, indeed, an attained ideal?, you think; is this not the end here? All of this is so solemn, victorious, and proud that you begin to crowd the soul. You look at these hundreds of thousands, at these millions of people who have submissively flowed here from all over the earth's surface, people who have come with a single thought, quietly, persistently, and silently thronging in this colossal palace, and you feel that here something has been accomplished once and for all, has been accomplished, and has come to an end. This is some kind of biblical tableau, something about Babylon, some sort of prophecy from Revelations that is being accomplished before your eyes. You feel that much everlasting spiritual repulse and negation is needed in order not to give in, not to submit to the impression, not to bow before the fact, and not to idolize Baal, that is not to accept what is for your ideal (Dostoevskii, 5: 69-70).

Dostoevskii's observations about Whitechapel resonate in Blok's Palace of Culture. Although the orators in *The Song of Fate* adopt a different tone, they treat the same themes. The newspaper boys trumpet the "triumph of human genius!" (4: 120) One of the orators, an Old Man, declares, "Today I pronounce for the sevety-seventh time a speech about the triumph of human progress. We scientists can boldly say that science is the sole path, on which humanity overcomes all the obstacles placed before it by nature." He goes on to say, "You see that knowledge has outstripped belief in the miraculous. There are no more miracles, kind sirs. There is nothing left for you to wish for after I acquaint you with the latest great discovery..." (4: 123-4). With nothing left to wish for, Blok's crowd is left in exactly the position described by Dostoevskii: they bow before what is.

[15] When critics discuss Dostoevskii's work in relation to *The Song of Fate*, they generally turn to *The Idiot* and find in Nastas'ia Filippovna a prototype for Faina. (See, for instance, Gromov 1961b, 503).

Dostoevskii, of course, had long before worked out the ideology of rebellion against scientific materialism and the crystal palace in *Notes from the Underground*. Certain of the Underground Man's remarks, in fact, seem *a priori* a direct response to the Old Man's contention that there is nothing left to wish for: "One's own unrestricted and free desire, one's own, even though the very wildest, caprice, one's own fantasy, irritated sometimes even to madness — all of this is that most left out, that most beneficial benefit, which does not fall under any classification and from which all systems and theories constantly fly all to hell. ... A person needs only *independent* desire, whatever this independence may cost and whatever it may lead to" (Dostoevskii, 5: 113). Like the Underground Man, Herman refuses to bow down:

> I can't and do not want to stand for this!
> So this is what the great banquet of Culture is!
> [...]
> So this is where the centuries
> Of lofty, lofty dreaming brought us
> (4: 129).

Despite his opposition to the ideology of progress, Herman does not advocate, or at least on the surface does not advocate the Underground Man's philosophy of the free personality. In fact, it is this schism between Herman's words and deeds that undermines the epic nature of his fate.

On the one hand, Herman espouses a rather different idea, namely duty. For example, after Faina has sung "The Song of Fate," Herman castigates the crowd for allowing her to smother "the strict voice of duty" (4: 129). Moreoever, this duty comes, as the allusion to Tolstoi suggests, from above. Herman confirms this in the fifth tableau when he tell his Friend, "At night I awaken suddenly, and someone's voice says to me: 'you are chosen, you are chosen'" (4: 146). He elaborates on this moments later: "I am not alone! I left not in my own name! The wind called me ..." (4: 148). All of this is consistent with the unitary nature of an epic hero, who acts not so much in accordance with his will, but with his fate, which is determined by some higher power. The philosophy of duty stands in stark contrast, however, to Herman's actions.

Herman acts in accordance with the Underground Man's precepts. For the Underground Man, suffering provides the key to human freedom. He argues, "In the crystal palace, it [suffering — TW] is inconceivable: suffering is doubt, is denial, and what is a crystal palace in which it is possible to feel doubt? And besides that, I am certain that man will never refuse true suffering, that is destruction and chaos" (Dostoevskii, 5: 119). Surprisingly, Herman is unable to turn away from suffering. Though Faina warns him to move away from the stage after his tirade about "The Song of Fate," Herman remains, clearly aware of the whip she holds in her hand. The gash across his cheek even becomes an emblem for him. As if the physical wound were not enough, he goes to Faina's dressing room to see her again. When she threatens to strike him again, Herman tells her to go ahead and hit him. Having destroyed his own happy home and having embarked on a sadomasochistic relationship with Faina, Herman could hardly be more in accord with the Underground Man's precepts.

It is true, however, that Herman tries to reconcile duty from above and freedom. Yet even here, Herman proves to be the Underground Man's devoted disciple. Genuine suffering, in this case, destruction lies at the heart of his striving: "Maybe one has to destroy all that is most tender, most cherished! After all spring too is destructive." Moreover, Herman's attempts to reconcile freedom and duty are characterized by striking, paradoxical language. "When the path is free," he tells his Friend, "one has to go inevitably" (4: 148). Likewise, the details of his freedom and his duty are given paradoxically. On one hand, he insists, "I am faithful! I am faithful! No one dares to mention betrayal" (4: 148). The fiery denial in this outburst seems an acknowledgment of his Friend's implied accusation that he has betrayed Elena who waits for him loyally. Even the epithet, "terrible happiness," which Herman describes his emotional state, partakes of paradox. The clear, unequivocal language of the epic hero escapes him.

To a lesser extent, doubles play a role in disrupting any monolithic, epic fabric. As Gromov argues in relation to the 1909 version, "Blok in the second variant of the play not only does not destroy the 'doubling' structure of the characters, but attempts to deepen and complicate it" (Gromov 1961b, 515). Gromov suggests that the Monk, Herman's Friend, and Faina's Companion, particularly in the first two versions of the play, serve as doubles (Gromov, 1961b, 515). Later critics, however, have generally not included Faina's Companion as a double. (See, for example, Kipnis, 88.) Critics have devoted less attention to the doubling in the female characters, but Elena is clearly counterposed to Faina.[16] Despite such extensive doubling, however, the images of the fool, clown, and rogue, by means of which the double undermines its referrent, are reduced to such an extent that these characters, as doubles, are hampered. For example, the Friend betrays some of the characteristics of a clown, but his mockery turns out to be merely cynical. Nonetheless, Herman, because he understands so little of the city he encounters, has some potential as a fool. This potential comes to nought, however, because he understands too well his Friend's cynicism and challenges it directly. Elena and Faina, on the other hand, seem well suited for one another as doubles. They represent radically opposed ideologies, and the potential for truly dialogic interaction seems great. Unfortunately, the two never meet, and the play's strongest dramatic potential is left untapped: Herman, at least in terms of ideology, presents no contrast to Faina.

If not in ideology, Herman, as hero, does contrast sharply with Faina. Though perhaps feebly, Herman follows the course of epic heroes. Faina, on the other hand, plays a rather different role, that of the carnival king. Indeed, Herman's epic quest falters the moment he encounters Faina, and for good reason. The single, unitary, and ultimately monologic ideology of the epic hero has nothing in common with the dialogizing influence of a carnival king. From her first appearance, Faina's role is clear. Her entrance into the Palace of Culture is a royal event. According to the stage directions, "Red footmen throw the gates of the Palace of Culture wide open. A huge black automobile decorated with roses

[16] Interesting in this regard is Prikhod'ko, who does not explicitly call Elena and Faina doubles, but nonetheless sees them as "the earthly and the heavenly incarnation of a single essence" (Prikhod'ko 1993, 45). Likewise, Wörn counterposes Faina as "Dionysian Eternal Feminine" to the "classical, Apollonian ideal of Elena" (Wörn, 517).

appears there. It slowly and noiselessly sails up to the stage. In the midst of the crowd's ceaseless roar within the walls and beyond the walls of the Palace, in the waves of the men's rapturous stares and the women's envious murmuring, Faina gets out of the automobile and quietly goes up to the stage." Although dressed in a simple black dress, she wears a mock crown: "In her hair shines a valuable gem." Nor does she lack a sceptre: "In her hand is a long whip" (4: 127). In the fourth tableau, a coterie of potential suitors waits to pay homage to their queen. Faina's actions likewise betoken a carnival king. Her address to the crowd turns out to be a mockery of romantic love and in couplets, no less:

> When I look into your eyes
> With a serpent's narrow eyes
> And lovingly, I press your hand,
> Hey, beware! I am all serpent!
> Look: for a moment, I was yours,
> And then I dumped you!
> To me, you are repellent! Go away!
> With another I will spend this night!
> Look for your wife!
>
> (4: 127).

From this standpoint, the lash she gives Herman across the cheek mocks the ceremonies of knighthood and initiates him into aristocracy, albeit a sadomasochistic one, of love.

Yet, just as elements of carnival interfere with Herman's epic intentions, the reverse is true as well. Because she remains the subject of Herman's serious and high-minded aspirations to duty, Faina is never subjected to a decrowning worthy of the name. The closest she gets to one is her misguided romance with Herman in the fifth and especially the seventh tableaux. In these scenes, Faina believes she has finally found the groom she waited for on the precipice while still in her native village, the one who will free her at last. However, even she seems aware that Herman is not that one, or if he is, that their time has not yet come. She tells him, "There, you are all that way... Exactly like mortals...." Later when Herman swears that he is ready to die for her, she upbraids him for the gap between his words and deeds: "Again words? You have lived too little to die! It is only in folktales they die!" (4: 161). In spite of her doubts, Faina remains with Herman until she hears a summons from beyond to leave. In the end, the match proves premature. Even so, Faina does not cease to be a carnival king. Her courtship bears within it elements of parody; but by itself, it cannot decrown her. As a result, the end of the play presents the spectator or reader with two unfulfilled rituals: Herman, as epic hero, fails to accomplish the valorous deeds that would secure him passage home and the play thematic focus, and Faina, as carnival king, retains her crown, leaving the play without the dialogizing upendings that might have enriched it.

In this sense, the title *The Song of Fate* aptly sums up the play's contradictions. On the one hand, fate in *The Song of Fate* is perhaps best understood in a serious and monologic epic sense, at least insofar as Herman is concerned. In Herman's mouth, no irony attaches itself to this idea. Where Faina is concerned, on the other hand, both the song and the fate it describes are intended ironically. Fate, in Faina's song, is reduced to biology: men are her playthings not because of some higher power, but because of their sexual desire. Had Herman put forth an ideology truly independent of Faina's, these contradictions might have been ambiguities; but as the play stands, he and Faina are too much in agreement for any dramatic conflict to exist.

More clearly than any other aspect of the play, this lack of drama in the relationships between Herman and Faina and Elena points not only to the play's weakness, but also to the differences between it and the trilogy of lyric dramas that preceded it. Here, one man and two women compose the underlying love triangle; whereas in the first three plays, it was always two men and one woman. The difference seems slight, but has far-reaching ramifications. If an implicit dramatic conflict between Elena and Faina arises, it never becomes manifest and never attains the tension, such as exists between Pierrot and Harlequin, the Poet and the Architect, or the Poet and the Astronomer. For whatever reason, Blok was unable to effectively oppose his lead female characters. It is a weakness he must have recognized intuitively: he returns to the old triangle of two men and a woman in *The Rose and the Cross.*

Still, the question of why Blok turned to the epic is an intriguing one, particularly in light of his growing preoccupation with the rift between the people and the intelligentsia. The fact that the Battle of Kulikovo occupies an important place in *The Song of Fate*, coupled with Blok's choice of an historical topic for *The Rose and the Cross,* points to a burgeoning interest in history. Perhaps it is in the epic's unrivalled capacity to express an historical era gone by that we will find the reasons for Blok's interest in the form. In Bowra's words, "We are forced to conclude that the full force of literary epic comes at the end of some great historical process and that the poet tries to sum up all that the process has meant" (Bowra, 28). If *The Song of Fate* is a farewell to the world of the hearth, it is also the first step toward the world that will replace it, the world of the Revolution and *The Twelve.*

CHAPTER SIX

FROM EPIC TO TRAGEDY: *THE ROSE AND THE CROSS*

I

The Origins of the Play

After the publication of *The Song of Fate*, nearly three years would elapse before Blok returned to drama. It is of no small significance that, as when he undertook to write *A Puppet Show*, a commission, not his own initiative, proved to be the catalyst. The commission was not, however, for the play that would eventually result, but for a ballet scenario. In March of 1912, with Aleksei Remizov acting as intermediary, Mikhail Tereshchenko, who had ties to the Director of the Imperial Theaters, broached the subject of a scenario with Blok. According to Blok's aunt, Mar'ia Beketova, Tereshchenko "hoped to stage in his own future theater some new, significant piece" (Beketova 1922, 173). Tereshchenko had already contacted the composer Aleksandr Glazunov who was to supply the music. The original proposal, however, was rather confused. Medieval Provence was suggested as a setting because Glazunov "loves the provençal troubadours of the XIV- XV centuries?!" (7: 136). As the punctuation of his diary entry indicates, Blok had spotted Tereshchenko and Glazunov's historical error and would eventually correct it by setting the action at the dawn of the thirteenth century.

The choice of a medieval theme was a fortuitous one. Blok had been fascinated by the Middle Ages from the time of his youth on. (See Blok's foreword to his mother's translation of Victor Hugo's *Legende du beau Pécopin et de la belle Bauldour* from *Le Rhin*, 6: 455.) The letters he wrote home while in Brittany in 1911 bear witness to an abiding interest in the Middle Ages, and experiences from the trip itself affect *The Rose and the Cross*. Medieval motifs frequently show up Blok's work, whether in such articles as "The Girl of the Rose Gate and the Ant Tsar" or in his lyric poetry. The influence of the Middle Ages, in fact, is perhaps strongest in the latter. The very attitude of the poet toward his beloved in Blok's first collection *Verses about the Beautiful Lady* reveals Dante's *Vita Nuova* to be a palpable influence. Blok was familiar with medieval literature not only from his philological studies at the university, but also from his work as a translator. Nikolai Evreinov's Theater of Antiquities, for instance, commissioned Blok to translate *Le Miracle de Théophile* by the trouvère poet Rutebeuf. The Old French trouvère tradition from which Rutebeuf issued and the Provençal troubadour tradition that helped shape it had a profound impact on Blok. His interest in the Middle Ages attracted Blok to artists whose work dealt with medieval themes and motifs. For example, Wagner, to whom critics have frequenly pointed in their discussions of *The Rose and the Cross* and to the strains of whose music Bertran's last soliloquy was set, was a favorite of Blok's.[1]

It comes as no great surprise, then, that Blok undertook the ballet commission with great enthusiasm. By March 27 he had already met with Tereshchenko personally. Within a week he was hard at work, and had the first version more or less mapped out by the end of April. This first outline falls into four parts (see 4: 455-6). In the first, which is set in winter, the mistress of a castle, entranced by the songs of a troubadour, secretly sends an emissary to find him. In the second, the emissary finds the troubadour, who turns out to be old and gray. He refuses the invitation proffered by the emissary. They quarrel. The troubadour agrees to go only if he can appear beneath the Châtelaine's window on a spring night so that she will not see him when he sings. The emissary returns with the troubadour's conditions, and the troubadour prepares for the road. In the third act, set on a spring night, the troubadour gallops up to the window of the Châtelaine with his face covered. He dismounts and sings. Overwrought with emotion, the troubadour uncovers his face, but the mistress thinks that it is the moon that has turned his hair silver. She throws down a rope ladder, but at this moment the emissary and several knights fall upon the troubadour, who is shackled. The mistress of the castle faints. The fourth act begins the next day as the lord of the castle orders that the troubadour be led in. In chains, he sings, but the Châtelaine does not recognize him. She says that she had a dream. The enraged lord kills the emissary. As the other knights approach the troubadour to throw him back in jail, he falls dead at the Châtelaine's feet. So ends the first version. Blok, however, appended a second plot on April 27. In this plot, a knight sets out to see his lady, but is killed along the way by a "crafty friend," who proves to be his double. On the issue of the double, however, Blok could not make up his mind. He also considered doing away with the double. Instead, the crafty friend would flatter the lady, but at the last moment the ghost of the murdered knight would arise before him. Blok quickly decided against this plot twist on the grounds that it could be either German or English, but not French. Apparently, this is the version that Blok related to Tereshchenko and Remizov on 3 May. (See 7: 142.)

The relation of this first "ballet" version to the final play has given rise to disagreement. According to Pavel Medvedev, "Even a cursory survey of these early initial plots convinces one of the following: first, both of them — and in particular the second — have nothing in common with the plot of *The Rose and the Cross*, and then both plots — and especially the first of them — are extraordinarily difficult for a ballet interpretation" (Medvedev, 99). Although Medvedev does not go into detail, the differences are numerous. The emphasis in this version falls on

[1] Names constitute a special problem in the study of *The Rose and the Cross*. Blok transliterated names into Russian from Provençal, Breton, and Old French sources. As a result, merely transliterating those names from Russian into English makes little sense, and I have instead gone back to Blok's sources. So, for example, Bertran, Alis and Archimbaut (or Archambaut) are given in their Provençal forms, while Aliscans, which derives from the chanson de geste *Aliscans*, is given in its Old French form.

the old troubadour, while in the play it falls on the emissary. Moreover, the figure of the emissary in his perfidy is utterly unlike the loyal Bertran of the play. Then too, the troubadour will become a trouvère in the play. Moreover, a host of minor characters are missing: Aliscans, the page who woos Izora, the mistress of the castle; Alis, Izora's lady-in-waiting; the Chaplain; and the Doctor. More importantly, the historical background of the Albigensian crusade is not yet apparent. Finally, the ending is different.

Despite all of these differences, one of the foremost authorities on Blok's dramaturgy, Pavel Gromov, maintains that Medvedev's position is a "profound error." According to Gromov,

> First and foremost Blok's manuscript speaks against this idea. In it the libretto is broken up into four acts with red pencil. Red pencil in the manuscripts of Blok's dramas always signifies the last authorial decision (at the very least for a given stage of work). Still more substantial is the circumstance that an objective analysis of the libretto itself testifies to the fact that this plan contains not only the actual kernel of the drama's conflict, but Blok's marking-out of it into acts corresponds (very schematically, of course) to the articulation of the conflict in the author's subsequent work right up to the final redaction (Gromov 1961a, 540).

In Gromov's view, the structure of the play remains stable, despite what he considers relatively superficial thematic alterations in the later drafts.

These two views go right to the heart not only of the drafts, but also of the play itself. On one side, some commentators have identified the play narrowly with the struggles of Bertran, the main protagonist. Without him, there is no play, or so the argument runs. On the other, some have pointed to the sophistication of the play as a play. Blok's contemporaries were especially sensitive to his growth as a playwright. Konstantin Vogak, for instance, wrote, "[T]he profound and wise content of the drama is poured into a finished and balanced scenic form" (Vogak, 56). Nearly all of the reviewers found *The Rose and the Cross* to be a "very stageworthy play" (B.G., 129). From this standpoint, a note that Blok included in the first sketch takes on great significance, even though it has been overlooked. Blok wrote at the end of his sketch, "One ought to consider it an *act*, where the *development* of the plot predominates. A *tableau*, where traits necessary for the characterization of the dramatis personae and their relations predominate" (4: 456). Structural considerations, then, appear to have been foremost in Blok's mind as he continued revising the play.

Those revisions were hard won. Tereshchenko's commission, though simple enough on the surface, proved difficult to fulfill. Glazunov turned out to be an unenthusiastic collaborator. Despite Blok's ardent desire to work with the composer, talks with Glazunov would come to nought, even though they dragged on through the middle of the summer of 1912. (See, in this regard, Blok and Remizov, 2: 103; and Blok 1927-32, 2: 214). Blok also encountered obstacles in the material itself. Already he had burst open the form of the scenario. To clarify his aims, in the middle of May he wrote up what he called "Considerations and Conjectures about the Play" (4: 456-59). Here Blok painted the psychological portraits of most of the major characters. This clarification, coupled with his work over the next several days, convinced Blok that he had an opera libretto on his hands. It was on May 17, in fact, that Blok first referred to the work as an opera (7: 144). This determination was hardly final, though. As late as May 30, Blok was still wondering whether it was opera or a ballet. In a list of things to be done, the first was: "Opera (Ballet?)" (7: 146).

At about the same time, Blok began to feel the need to delve more deeply into Provençal and Old French literature. To that end, he and Remizov met with the philologist Evgenii Anichkov, who had studied under the renowned Russian scholar Aleksandr Veselovskii and the famous French medievalist Gaston Paris. The meeting was a fruitful one, and as Blok put it, "Anichkov gave me many useful instructions and books" (7: 143).[2] One of the more important words of caution that Anichkov had for Blok was to rid the play of all pagan, especially Druid, themes.[3] Under the influence of the folklore of Brittany which he had visited several years earlier, Blok evidently planned to incorporate a Druid legend. This intention fell by the wayside in the course of his work, although vestiges of it are apparent still in the first full draft of the play, the opera libretto, especially in the speech of the second knight in the second act (4: 475-6). One measure of the seriousness with which Blok tackled the source material was that he held onto all eighteen books lent to him by Anichkov for two and a half months. At the beginning of August, he returned thirteen, but still retained five (Zhirmunskii, 31).

The draft that corresponds to the opera libretto came slowly. Blok wrote to Remizov on June 9, telling him that the first act was drafted (Blok and Remizov, 2: 106). Nearly two weeks had elapsed when Blok informed his mother, "Mama, my work nonetheless moves ahead, though slowly. Three acts have been written in rough draft. There remain the fourth act, the finishing touches, several small points, and several songs to be inserted" (Blok 1927-32, 2: 205). His work continued into July, but by the middle of the month the first draft of the opera was done. Blok read it to Tereshchenko on July 14, and he told his mother the next day that Tereshchenko had liked the play, making several observations, which Blok took into condsideration (letter dated 15 July, 1912 from Blok to his mother, Blok 1927-32, 2: 214). Blok gave much the same report to Remizov (Blok and Remizov, 2: 108). Tereshchenko wrote to Remizov to say that Blok "had gotten it right" (Blok and Remizov, 2: 108).

Blok apparently disagreed and would set off in a new direction about a month later. However, Tereshchenko was certainly correct in that, compared to the first plan for the ballet, the opera was fuller, more complex. Here his work on the source material stood him in good stead. Where the ballet had been vaguely medieval, the opera already took on the specific coloring of Provence during the time of the troubadours. The Albigensians and the crusade against them appear for the first time. Class tensions become clear as a result. The characters also assume

---

[2] Many of the books were specialized studies of the provençal troubadors. An incomplete list of those books was first published by Medvedev, 111-3. It was not until Viktor Zhirmunskii published his book on *The Rose and the Cross* that a complete list appeared (Zhirmunskii, 102-3). In general, Zhirmunskii's work is indispensable to the student of *The Rose and the Cross* and is far superior to the often unreliable Shelud'ko.

[3] See the excerpt, reprinted by Zhirmunskii, of Blok's notebook record of the conversation (Zhirmunskii, 102).

a greater depth. Bertran, the ridiculed knight, comes to the fore. The interaction of and interconnections between the characters become clearer as well. Izora and her page, for instance, develop a relationship, which was entirely missing from the first draft. The play's formal elements, though clearly connected to the first draft, evolve. For instance, Blok introduces the alternation of prose and verse in this draft for the first time. Nonetheless, in comparison with the finished play, this draft is rough. Although four acts remain intact from the ballet, they have not yet been broken up into scenes. The relationship between the two knights who will evolve into Bertran and Gaètan is still murky. Only further work would clarify these and a host of other problems.

As Blok embarked on the third stage of the writing of *The Rose and the Cross* and continued to rework the opera, he gradually realized that his opera had become a play. Already at the end of June, he had an inkling of the transformation that his work was undergoing. In a letter to his mother, Blok wrote, "[A]t one time it seemed to me that what was coming out was not an opera, but a drama: I was misled by one of the dramatis personae, who by character is rather more dramatic than musical; this is the failure, Bertran" (Blok 1927-32, 2: 207). Blok was convinced of this by his wife, who argued that the play was an opera, not a drama. Blok agreed that it was "too much a mosaic" to succeed as a drama. He had been misled, he thought, by his "unfortunate Bertran": "There is something in his character that outgrew opera" (7: 154). The problem of genre was persistent. As late as October, 1912, Blok himself still referred to the play as an opera. Describing his relations with Tereshchenko to Remizov, Blok wrote, "I do not know if I have the right feeling: I am ashamed that I am not finishing the opera; besides that, I think that this opera, which I am not finishing, was not ordered from me, strictly speaking; but a ballet after all was ordered!" (Blok and Remizov, 2: 112). It is perhaps typical of Blok that where his sense of duty was concerned, he always rose to the occasion. Tereshchenko gave Blok a deadline of three weeks on October 11 (7: 163). By the end of October, the opera was done. On October 31, Blok wrote in his diary noted that, except for a few songs, the opera was finished (7: 172).

One of the key moments in the transition from opera to play appears to have occurred toward the end of September. In a rather cryptic diary entry, Blok notes new ideas about finishing the play, but gives no details. He mentions only the "possibility" of a new act (7: 159). As the autumn of 1912 progressed, Blok penetrated more deeply into the core of the play. The relation of the Christian and Albigensian motifs seems to have been a particularly important problem for Blok since it shows up in unexpected places. For example, while outlining his disagreements with the modernists, he wrote, "I, for example, set forth in the opera everything that I am capable of in relation to one thing: *the fate of a failure*. At least in the Christian era to which we are contemporaries this is a constant. If I (or someone else) set forth all the diversity of my images in relation to Fate and the God of Greek tragedy, then I would be occupied with something unreal if I want to show this to others" (7: 164). Originally, the second knight, who would eventually become Gaètan, was to represent a "menacing Christianity"; however, in late October, Blok reconsidered (4: 458-9). This decision proved to be pivotal. The future Gaètan in the next redaction is already not so much a bearer of Christianity as a singer of a song. His role as singer becomes even more pronounced in the finished play, but it is already apparent at this stage.

Blok also devoted great attention to the penultimate act that he noted in his diary. However, he was mistaken about its position in the play. As he himself later noted, this revision would turn out to be the beginning of the fourth and last act (4: 459). Moreover, a comparison of his notes for the revision with the revised fourth act shows that Blok went far beyond his first intention. The fourth act, like the others in the draft finished on 31 October, shows greater articulation than its predecessors. Not only are the events broken into scenes, but several new scenes appear for the first time. Also significant is the way in which scenes involving one set of characters alternate with those involving another set. Blok's preoccupation with dramatic technique becomes especially evident in this new draft.

Despite these advances, Blok remained dissatisfied. A diary entry written several days after he had finished the second draft is symptomatic of his dissatisfaction. Describing a reading for Tereshchenko, Blok wrote, "He praised it, but I do not have a *sense of catharsis*. He says to write out the songs, dialogues, with which I am dissatisfied, to present it to Stanislavskii's 'Studio', and then to think about music for it" (7: 173). The absence of a feeling of catharsis disturbed Blok deeply, and he failed to take Tereshchenko's advice. Rather, he set to work on the third version of the play.

Soon Blok began to feel that one of the problems with the play centered around the figure of the Knight-Future, who would become Gaètan. Within a week of reading the play to Tereshchenko, Blok "understood decisively that the Knight-Future has to be redone" (7: 177). His diary over the next several days bears witness to the determination with which Blok approached the problem. He noted in his diary the next day that he discussed the knight with his mother (7: 177). The following day he wrote that he had reconsidered the function of the Knight (7: 180).

However, the more he thought about the Knight, the more he began to feel dissatisfied with the whole play. He soon decided "to redo the *whole* play, break up the unity of place, from which the act will become more tense and more natural — separate scenes. I began a plan. I am smiling, but there is a lot of work. It still will be necessary to put off the deadline — again" (7: 180). The new plan was hardly complete, though. The next day he was forced to concede, "I continue not to know the *end* of Bertran's fate."

At least in part, it was the traditional meaning of such symbols as the rose and the cross that interfered with a clear conception of Bertran's fate. Nowhere is this clearer than in his reaction to a suggestion his wife made about the ending: "This morning Liuba gave me an idea: Bertran dies building the chapel of the Holy Rose. Having agonizingly thought this situation over, I came to the conclusion that I do not have the right to speak of the mystic Rose. What makes that perfectly clear is the simple fact that I do not have sufficient spiritual strength to examine the confused symbols of the Rose and the Cross only 'for beauty', only artistically" (7: 181).[4] By early December, Blok was even more resolute in turning away from the allegorical, traditional meaning of these symbols toward the human condition of his protagonist: "No, in my present state (cruelty, awkwardness, adulthood, illness), I do not know how to and I do not have the right to speak more than about the

[4] Despite Blok's explicit renunciation of the rose and the cross as symbols, some scholars persist in searching for their mystical meaning. For a particularly earnest and thoroughgoing attempt, see Prikhod'ko 1994, esp. 47-50.

human. My theme is not at all 'the Cross and the Rose' — I have not mastered that. Let it be — the human fate of a failure, and if I succeed in 'diminishing myself' before art, then — something bigger — can flash through my theme to someone. That is: my strictness to myself and 'humility' with all my strength can help the play to become a work of art, but a work of art is a being that moves, and not a corpse in repose" (7: 186). With such thoughts in mind, Blok set to work again.

Within a week, he had written a new plan for *The Cross and the Rose*, as he then called it (7: 191). The day after finishing the plan, he began a third redaction (7: 191). In another two weeks, he "had written a new ending" (7: 196). Two days later he added two new scenes (7: 197), and by 4 January, he had returned to the fourth act (7: 204). Now work on the play was winding down. Two days later he "set to verse some new scenes" (7: 205). The following day he noted, "Everything is written — only a few more 'brush strokes' and Izora's monologue with the apparition. At night I am reading it to Liuba. She likes it, as do I" (7: 205). On January 9, he wrote, "This morning I wrote the last scene — Izora, her monologue. Only the finishing touches remain. I sent a telegram to M.I. Tereshchenko" (7: 205). The finishing touches were to continue on for another ten days. On 16 January Blok wrote, "To the melodies of Wagner I set the last scene in verse" (7: 208). Finally, the play was finished on 19 January (7: 209). He gave readings on January 30 and February 3 to enthusiastic friends and acquaintances, Meyerhold among them. Blok was now finally content with the play. However, when Blok returned to the play in June to prepare it for publication, he suggested that, had he the strength, he would revise the play to give the Second Knight, with whom Bertran battles, a substantial role. This revision never came into being, and he sent it off be copied on June 7, 1913 (4: 463). The play appeared in the first almanac of the Sirin publishing house in August of that same year.

II

The Plot and its Sources

The play that resulted contains nineteen scenes, divided into four acts.[5] As is typical of Blok's dramas, the principle of symmetry is everywhere apparent in formal matters. The first and last acts, for example, consist of five scenes each. The second and third, though they are not symmetrical in the strict sense, display great order in their disproportion: the third contains exactly twice as many scenes as the second. The play also reveals a carefully articulated stratification of prose and verse among the characters. The speech of those characters whom Blok dubbed "quadratic" — that is, characters who are consumed by commonplaces of everyday

[5] *The Rose and the Cross* has twice been translated into English. See Greene 1986b and Vogel 1983.

life and who are stunted spiritually — tends to be in iambic pentameter or in prose. The main characters who are alive spiritually tend to use unrhymed accentual meters in soliloquies and when they speak to each other. When characters from the two different groups meet, their speech tends toward iambic pentameter (Rudnev, 294-334 passim, but especially 306-7). This highly nuanced graduation proves to be not only a technical tour de force, but also an effective theatrical device. Those moments during which the main protagonists slip into prose are also moments of spiritual fall and acquiescence to convention.

The play opens in the courtyard of a castle in Languedoc at twilight. Here Bertran delivers a soliloquy, in which all of the major motifs are sounded for the first time. The opening lines are actually a quotation from a song which had entranced the lady of the castle, Izora, when it was sung by a jongleur the previous summer. Bertran, like the other inhabitants of the castle, can only partially remember the song that continues to torment Izora. In no small measure, what we learn about the main characters depends on what they remember from the song and how they interpret what they remember. A strange admixture of woe and duty remains in Bertran's case: "Everywhere misfortune and losses, / What awaits you ahead?" (4: 169). Bertran comments on the song and focuses on the image of the cross, which will be associated with duty for him: "A strange song about the sea / And about a cross burning above the snowstorm" (4: 169). The association of the cross with the snowstorm hearkens back to Blok's lyric cycle *The Snow Mask*, where snow is linked to baptism in the poem "The Second Christening". That same imagery is intoned, as we have seen, by Herman in *The Song of Fate*. Indeed, Bertran and Herman share the same concern — how to reconcile duty with desire. This theme is sometimes obscured and complicated by Herman's guilt about his privileged position in society. Bertran, who comes from the lower rungs of the social ladder, suffers no such guilt, and a much clearer exposition of this theme results in *The Rose and the Cross.*

Bertran goes on to compare his fate to that of an old apple tree in the courtyard. Not unlike Tolstoi's Andrei Bolkonsky on his first visit to the old oak tree, Bertran contrasts the greenery and the blossoming all around to a weather-beaten and aged tree. In that tree he sees his own fate reflected. To explain the source of his own fate, he returns to the song: "What does the strange song prophesy? / 'There is one indisputable law for the heart — / Joy is only suffering!'" (4: 171). The first scene comes to an end when Alis, Izora's lady-in-waiting, interrupts Bertran's ruminations and asks him to get away from the window because his singing unsettles Izora. Bertran acquiesces and moves away.

The second scene, which is entirely in prose, shifts attention from the main characters to the secondary. In a passageway Alis is frightened by the unexpected appearance of the Chaplain. Alis asks the Chaplain's reasons for lurking in the dark passageway only to find that he has designs on her. Only the fortuitous appearance of the page Aliscans saves her. The Chaplain, afraid of scandal, runs off. Aliscans, however, proves to be almost as lacking in chivalric virtue as the Chaplain. Alis asks the page for help because she feels faint. Aliscans refuses, perhaps sensing that Alis's own motives are not pure. He tells her to lead him to Izora: "She thirsts for the sounds of my lute" (4: 173).

The third scene opens in Izora's quarters, where the lady of the castle, like Bertran in the first scene, is preoccupied with the jongleur's song, of which she remembers only snippets: "The snow swirls ... / A momentary age rushes by ... /

A blissful shore appears in a dream ..." (4: 173). Frustrated, Izora cannot remember the song beyond these few snatches. The Doctor diagnoses Izora's ailment as melancholy.[6] She tells him to leave her alone and returns to the song: "'An indisputable law for the heart ... ' is to love and wait. 'Joy is suffering...' yes, and suffering is joy with your sweetheart! ... Isn't that so, Alis?" (4: 174). Izora and Alis begin a game of chess, and Izora asks Aliscans for a song, telling him to sing whatever he wants. In the early drafts, Blok puts into Aliscans's mouth a variation on the Old French song "Bele Aaliz main leva", a prose translation of which he found in Evgenii Anichkov's book on spring ritual poetry (Anichkov, 151-2). The song evolved, and as Viktor Zhirmunskii has pointed out, "In the final redaction of the drama, Blok created Aliscans's song completely independently, having elevated and improved it in the spirit of a somewhat stylized troubadour romanticism not bound to medieval tradition, having preserved only the poetic name Aèlis 'for its consonance with the name Alis' in Anichkov's 'transcription', as is stated in the notes" (Zhirmunskii, 48).[7] Aliscans's song fails to brighten Izora's low spirits, the source of which remains mysterious. Alis and Aliscans's best efforts to cheer their mistress fall short, and Izora leaves, despondent. Alis assures the page that no one, not even Izora, will intrude at such a late hour, and they embrace.

The fourth scene takes place in the Count's quarters, and it is here that Blok expounds the historical context of the play for the first time. He was deliberate in his choice of the Albigensian Crusade as a backdrop for *The Rose and the Cross.* The setting in the first draft is not so much medieval, as stylized in a medieval manner. However, with each successive draft, Blok worked into the play greater and greater historical detail. For instance, in the course of the fourth scene, the Chaplain refers to the Albigensians as the "devil's weavers" (4: 180). As Blok points out in his notes, a large portion of the Albigensian congregation, especially in Toulouse, consisted of weavers, and the term was popularly used to designate any Albigensian believer.

The Albigensian faith itself and its place in the play is a thorny problem.[8] At this juncture in the first full draft, Aliscans delivered the soliloquy which in the final version begins the fourth act. In the first version of the soliloquy, the Albigensian belief system is treated explicitly. Aliscans, a child of privilege, mocks the notion that "our beautiful world was created by the devil!" (4: 485). For the final version,

---

[6] As Blok points out in his notes to the play (4: 511), the diagnosis is authentic for the time. The term itself was taken from a medieval manuscript on medicine. See Salmon.

[7] For Blok's own note, see 4: 512. I have transliterated the name "Aèlis" from the Russian so as to give a sense of the sound qualities Blok found in Anichkov's transcription of the name.

[8] The question of Albigenianism as an ideology has received only scant attention in the scholarship on the play. (However, see Lewitter, especially 436.) Blok himself expressed a lively interest in various gnostic sects. To give but one example, he accompanied his half-sister Angelina to a talk on the dualistic underpinnings of the Orthodoxy. A certain Professor Nikol'skii argued, in Blok's paraphrase, "The gloomy essence of the Orthodoxy [...] arose from the dualism of the Bogomils with their teaching about Satanail, about how the world was either created or penetrated by an evil fundament (hence their asceticism)" (7: 182).

Blok cut this remark and honed the speech to focus on Aliscans's vanity. Nonetheless, in structural terms, scene four of Act One remains that juncture at which Blok treats the Albigensian Crusade. The changes Blok introduced deal not just with which characters participate in the scene, but also with the manner of presentation. In the first draft, Aliscans presents the topic in a monologue, and there is no response to what he says. The final version, however, is structured dialogically so that the issue of the Albigensian belief is presented as a conflict. The Count fumes over the advances of forces he and his Chaplain consider heretical. The Chaplain eggs him on, saying, "Send a new detachment of knights, and the unruly villains will be annihilated" (4: 178). It is also the Chaplain who first intones the name of Simon de Montfort, the de facto leader of the crusade. (Arnald-Amaury, abbot of Cîteaux and eventually archbishop of Narbonne, was named the nominal leader of the crusade, but Simon de Monfort soon came to the fore amongst the military leaders.) In so doing, the Chaplain very clearly sets forth the religious and socio-economic allegiances shared by those under the Count's dominion. In religious terms, they are Catholic, and as such are vehemently opposed to the dualism of the Albigensians. In socio-economic terms, they belong to the aristocracy and look down on a movement that is decidedly popular. Although largely popular, the Albigensian movement was not exclusively so. Bertran will shortly announce that one of the Archimbaut's neighbors has gone over to the Albigensian cause, a circumstance that is based in historical fact. Particularly in Languedoc the local aristocracy converted to the "heretical" faith in significant numbers.

A dialogically opposed view comes out the moment that the Count calls for Bertran. Perhaps the most striking formal change is that the scene suddenly moves from prose to verse as soon as Bertran sets foot on stage. An ideological shift accompanies this formal shift. Unlike his lord and master, Bertran is from the lower rungs of the social ladder. As he tells Gaètan in scene two of act two, he is the "son of a simple weaver from Toulouse" (4: 199).[9] Although he has become a knight, Bertran remains sympathetic to his own. He is painfully aware of the scorn visited upon the Albigensians by the nobility. He, for instance, takes note of the "neighboring peasants, who are here contemptuously called 'weavers'" with a certain sympathy (4: 521).

In this regard, it seems more than mere coincidence that the first news of Simon de Montfort's opponent, Raimond VI [Ramon VI], issues from Bertran's lips. Raimond VI himself, who was vilified by his Catholic accusers as a blasphemer and heretic and who was accused of such outrageous acts as allowing his jester to preach in a church, receives a more sympathetic treatment here. According to Blok's note, "Raimond VI 'the elder', count of Toulouse, was born in 1156, had stormy disagreements with the holy throne in regard to Albigensianism, which he secretly sympathized with" (4: 512). Although Blok does note Raimond's two excommunications and the murder of Pierre de Castelnau which was ascribed to him and which served as the pretext for the Albigensian Crusade, the treatment Raimond receives in Blok's note is quite free of the sensationalism that sometimes accompanies his biography. The sensational does make an appearance, but Blok places it in the mouth of a character who is ideologically opposed to Raimond. It is

[9] Blok reiterates this point in "Bertran's Notes Written by him Several Hours Before his Death", in which Blok sought to check the realism of Bertran's motivation (4: 521).

the Chaplain who reviles the count of Toulouse: "Five wives — and not a single legitimate son ..." (4: 178).

Blok's intent seems to have been to portray both ideologies as autonomous. Had he chosen any other period in the Albigensian wars, such autonomy would have been difficult to portray clearly. The Crusade's early successes, which were affirmed by the Council of Lateran in 1215, effectively put Provence under foreign hegemony. Although Simon de Montfort's army consisted of Catholics of many nationalities, the people of Provence saw the occupying army as French. Foreign occupation, therefore, aroused not only a nationalistic fervor, but also a hatred of France. Consequently, whereas the ideological struggle at the beginning of the Albigensian Crusade can be elucidated along religious lines, it had changed so radically by the Council of Lateran that the battle between Catholicism and Albigensianism no longer sufficed to explain it. Provençal nationalism ran so deep, in fact, that with the death of Simon de Montfort during the battle for Toulouse in 1218, Raimond VI was able to reverse his fortunes and restore sovereignty to his land. This shift in the nature of the ideological conflict becomes nowhere clearer than in attitude of the French monarchy to the Albigensian Crusade. From the beginning Philip Augustus abstained from any involvement. Not even the entreaties of Pope Innocent III could sway him. With the ascension to the throne of Louis VIII, however, the posture of the French monarchy toward Languedoc changed. Dissatisfied with the efforts of Amaury de Montfort, who had succeeded his father as the leader of the crusaders, Louis VIII set out to subdue the south in 1226. The king himself was to die in the process, and it was left to his widow and son, Louis IX, to complete his mission. This they did, and the subjugation of south to north was formalized by treaty in 1229. In terms of ideology, especially that portrayed in *The Rose and the Cross*, it is true that the Albigensian Crusade accomplished what Innocent III set out to do — eradicate the so-called Albigensian heresy. However, the consequences of the crusade were so extensive that the ostensible ideology out which it grew fails to explain the beliefs of those who subjugated Languedoc. To judge by their actions, the French were after nothing less than the eradication of provençal culture. The French language, government and administrative system were all imposed on Provence. Provençal was suppressed, and the great heritage of troubadour poetry was lost along with it. It seems the northern French sought to make Frenchmen of their southern neighbors.

That Blok chose the very beginning of the Albigensian wars as a setting suggests that he wished to keep the ideologies of nationalism at bay. Without a doubt, nationalism and nationalist tensions make themselves felt in *The Rose and the Cross*. The key point here, however, is that they never become the focus of ideological conflict in the play. The importance of the tension between the Catholic and Albigensian belief systems becomes especially clear in a rather interesting mistake Blok makes in dating the action of the play. According to Blok's note on Simon de Montfort, "This campaign began in 1208, to which one must set the time of the action of *The Rose and the Cross*" (4: 512). Blok explains that this is the year when Simon de Montfort's forces gathered in Lyon, an occurrence which Bertran brings to the attention of the Count (4: 179). However, as a matter of historical accuracy, the chronicle and most historians set the date of the rendezvous about a year later, in July, 1209. What did happen in 1208, though, was the murder of Pierre de Castelnau and the first excommunication of Raimond VI. Blok appears then to have attached relatively more significance to the religious than to the military aspects of the Albigensian wars.

Despite their importance, the Albigensian and Catholic positions by no means exhaust the spectrum of ideological struggle in the play. Another ideological stance makes itself in an apparently simple remark Bertran makes soon after informing Archimbaut that Simon de Montfort and his forces have gathered in Lyon. He tells the Count, "You know I am always ready to serve / Both my lady and you ..." (4: 179). Here the ideology and historical development of chivalry prove to be fundamental to Bertran's perception of the world. Bertran, in fact, would be the incarnation of an ideal knight, had he not been unseated at his first tournament. His failures notwithstanding, he remains a standard-bearer for the ideology of ideal chivalry and the cult of the lady. In the scene five, Izora will be surprised by Bertran's courtly love when he says, "I would swear by the rose, / You are more beautiful than all roses" (4: 188). In the course of the scene, he will swear his faithfulness to Izora and undertake a quest for her sake. By the end of the play, he will have sacrificed his love for Izora's happiness and his life in the defense of the castle and his lady. Blok was nothing short of scrupulous in his research on chivalry and knighthood. Zhirmunskii points out, for instance, that paid close attention to the characterization the knight Guillems [Vilelme] de Nivers (William de Nevers) in *Flamenca* (Zhirmunskii, 42). Paradoxically, however, it is the consonance between Betrand's beliefs and his actions that leads to ideological conflict.

The problem that Bertran encounters is the waning of chivalry as an ideology. The condescension the other characters display toward the unfortunate knight stems not only from his lowly origins, but also from a radically different attitude toward chivalry. What Bertran takes seriously they view with irony. (Aliscans's cynical treatment of Alis in scenes two and three may serve as a typical example.) Bertran, in their eyes, stands out as a somewhat comical figure, who is out of step with his time. In this, he shares a certain kinship with Don Quixote inasmuch as time had changed a belief system both attempt to preserve. This change is apparent in the sources Blok used, especially in the provençal novel *Flamenca*. Composed soon after the period in which the action of *The Rose and the Cross* takes place,[10] *Flamenca* reflects a somewhat ironical attitude toward chivalry. In this regard, Viktor Zhirmunskii has drawn attention to Paul Meyer's opinion that "for Guillaume de Nevers his love adventure is not so much high passion as a worldly amusement obligatory for a young knight in his position (although he manifests his feeling in the usual forms of courtly-love service to a lady); for Flamenca her love romance is before all else a means to revenge herself upon a coarse, uncourtly husband for his jealous suspicions, unworthy of a worldly,

---

[10] Disagreement exists about the date of composition. Paul Meyer, who edited and translated the version of *Flamenca* that Blok used, argues that it was written between 1220 and 1250 (Meyer 1865). Merton Jerome Hubert and Marion E. Porter, on the other hand, put the date slightly later, "toward the third quarter of the thirteenth century" (Hubert and Porter, 5). Perhaps the salient point here is that Blok in all probability accepted Meyer's opinion as authoritative and took *Flamenca* as a portrayal of courtly manners more or less contemporary to the action of *The Rose and the Cross*. In this, I follow the implicit assumption of Viktor Zhirmunskii. See Zhirmunskii, 36-7.

cultured person" (Zhirmunskii, 37 and Meyer, X ff.). Such attitudes are far from Bertan's, but close to those of Aliscans and Alis. In fact, one of the principal ideological conflicts between the main characters and the characters Blok calls "quadratic" (Archimbaut, Aliscans, Alis, the Chaplain all belong to this group) arises in their differing attitudes towards courtly love. *Flamenca*, incidentally, became required reading for the cast of the Moscow Art Theater when they began work on a production of *The Rose and the Cross* (Dinesman, 72).

In this ideological struggle, Izora is decidedly in Bertran's camp. Indeed, the remainder of scene four of act one pivots on Izora's attitude toward courtly love. After Bertran's departure, the Chaplain informs the Count that Izora has been reading the romance *Floire et Blanchefleur* instead of her prayerbook. He attributes this influence to Alis. When Alis enters soon after this revelation to tell Archimbaut about his wife's melancholy, the Count and the Chaplain try to act as if they do not know about the romance. The new information about his wife, however, has fueled the fire of Archimbaut's jealousy. In Alis's account of Izora's malady, he pays scant attention to Izora's suffering, but latches onto the fact that she repeats a name over and over. "Whose name?," demands the Count. Alis replies that it is the Wanderer who composed the song that Izora can only partially remember (4: 182).

A discussion of the song ensues. Archimbaut asks about the song's content, but before Alis can answer, the Chaplain suggests that the content of the song is known beforehand. It is, according to him, "about the nightingale and the rose" (4: 183). As Zhirmunskii has pointed out, however, this comment represents one of the very few anachronisms in the play. The nightingale as the lover of the rose is characteristic of Persian, not troubadour poetry (Zhirmunskii, 53-4). Blok apparently introduced the anachronism consciously since Charles Joret makes this point explicitly in an article that Blok consulted during his work on *The Rose and the Cross* (Joret, 294 and Zhirmunskii, 54). The image of the nightingale is an important one in Blok's own work and in that of poets in the Russian Romantic tradition, such as Fet and Tiutchev, whose poetry wielded enormous influence over Blok in his formative years. The image reaches its zenith in Blok's work several years after the composition of *The Rose and the Cross* in his long poem *The Nightingale Garden* [*Solov'inyi sad*]. Blok's purpose here then appears to be the reinforcing of the romantic motifs associated with the image of the rose. (Much the same purpose explains, incidentally, the liberties Blok took with the chronology of events. Simon de Montfort's army did not gather until July, but Blok clearly sets the action of the play in early spring. Spring proved too important thematically for Blok to sacrifice it to historical exactitude.)

Alis points out that the Chaplain is mistaken in another regard too: "No, about the rose and about the nightingale there is not a word there" (4: 183). She goes on to emphasize the song's incomprehensibility. Although the song will turn out to be enigmatic, the Count immediately interprets the apparent meaninglessness of the song and Izora's endless repeating of it as signs of her psychic instability. The Doctor reaffirms that the root of the problem is melancholy and that the only cure is patience. The fourth scene ends as Archimbaut turns to the Chaplain for advice.

The fifth and final scene of act one is set again in Izora's quarters. There she recounts for Alis a dream she has had about the Wanderer. In the dream she sees him, but is unable to touch him. Nor does he answer her entreaty to tell her his name. Alis suddenly realizes that someone is eavesdropping, and at that moment the Chaplain bursts into the room, threatening Izora with imprisonment in a tower. Izora and Alis panic over what steps to take. Alis again hears someone, this time by the window. It turns out to be Bertran, whom Izora invites in. After questioning his faithfulness, she entreats him to find the composer of the song that torments her and to bring him to her. Bertran agrees to find the Wanderer or to die in the attempt. Izora then asks him to take an oath. In the process, she compels the unfortunate knight to acknowledge that she is his lady. In a sense, they are ideological allies, at least insofar as they maintain an unironic attitude toward courtly love.

Their ideological alliance is further underscored by a formal device. The scene opens in verse as Izora recounts her dream. The moment the Chaplain enters, though, everyone's speech turns to prose. When Bertran enters, the characters return to verse. They revert to prose once more when the Count enters after Bertran has sworn his oath. Archimbaut demands to know why Bertran is there and assumes that the knight has designs on Alis. The Count sends his wife to the Tower of the Inconsolable Widow and orders Alis to share Izora's fate for abetting her. All exit, but Bertran, who reiterates his intention to carry out his quest or die. Bertran leaves, and the curtain falls on Act One.

The setting of Act Two is far different. Where the other acts are set in the south with its fair climate and bountiful countryside, Act Two is set in the north on a forbidding coast in Brittany. A late spring storm envelops Bertran, who urges on his weary horse. Bertran remarks on the snow that blinds him and the wind that whistles in his ears. The same motif recurs in the song, whose singer Bertran seeks. In a note to the song, Blok writes that he drew on a retelling of the Breton story "Noël des Chouans" by Anatole le Braz for this image (4: 520).[11] Blok may have overstated his debt, since the images of snow and wind arise in his own work from the beginning of his so-called second period to the very end. Be that as it may, these images set the tone for Blok's portrayal of Brittany as a harsh, forbidding land.

Bertran moves on, disappearing behind a rock. Closer to the shore appears Gaètan, whose first entrance is as enigmatic as his final exit. He sings a song, which begins, "Don't believe the madness of love! / Behind joy is suffering! / Behind joy is suffering!" (4: 192). A nearby fisherman recognizes the song and sings the next verse. The song concerns the legend of Ker-Is, which was flooded when Dahu, the daughter of King Grallon, stole from her father the key to a secret door in the well that protected the city from floods in order to let her lover in. Water inundated the city, and only Grallon's horse escaped. In his notes, Blok writes that he relied on Villemarqué's collection of Breton folklore as the source for his version of the legend. A prose translation based on Villemarqué's text certainly supports this. However, Blok does not use the forms of the names that Villemarqué uses. Blok, for instance, gives the king's name as Grallon and his daughter's as Dahu, whereas Villemarqué offers Gradlon and Dahut (4: 514 and Barzaz-Breiz, 39-49). However, the forms Blok uses do coincide with those of

---

[11] Blok mistakenly renders the title as "Nôel des Chouans." See also Zhirmunskii's treatment of the motif (Zhirmunskii, 84-5).

Paul-Yves Sébillot, whose work was also available to the Russian poet (Sébillot, 202-3). A third source arises in the work of Anatole le Braz noted above.[12]

The exposition of the Ker-Is plot takes place gradually through the second act and not always in the form of Gaètan's song. For instance, when they stop singing, Gaètan asks the Fisherman if he knows where Ker-Is was. The Fisherman points to a mound of rocks as he begins to explain how to get to Ker-Is. Gaètan responds, "I see it. In front there is a lion and then a steed...." The Fisherman cannot hide his surprise: "There is no steed there, but simply rocks" (4: 194). The steed that Gaètan sees in the ocean mist is, of course, that of King Grallon. Gaètan lives, as it were, his song. Throughout the play, he will make puzzling comments that only make sense when interpreted in terms of his song. (See, for instance, Bertran's comic attempt to understand Gaètan in Act Three, scene four.) Because he lives in the world of his song, Gaètan is viewed as an eccentric. The Fisherman, for instance, describes for Gaètan the eccentric seigneur of Troménec only to discover that the seigneur stands before him. The Fisherman escapes any untoward consequences for his words when Bertran wanders back onto the scene. He and Gaètan, to the horror of the Fisherman, begin fighting, and Bertran forces the older knight to submit. Despite their fight, they become friends, and Gaètan invites Bertran back to Troménec, which serves as the setting for the second scene.

A courteous host, Gaètan entertains his guest with his song about Ker-Is. They talk and become friends, each relating his story to the other. Bertran relates the story of his life first. As noted earlier, he tells Gaètan that he is the son of a Toulouse weaver, who had to go into service at an early age. His tale is one of misfortune as he relates how, at his first tournament, he was unseated by "a lumbering giant with a dolphin in his coat of arms" (4: 200). Though he asked that his heart be pierced, his life was spared when his lady waved her kerchief. Bertran goes on, "No one since that time has made way for me, / Everyone laughs in my face" (4: 200). Gaètan laments his friend's suffering.

Bertran then turns to the immediate reason for his trip to the north, the whereabouts of Simon de Montfort's forces. Gaètan remarks that he would not serve if called upon. This elicits from Bertran a statement that perhaps captures the contradictions of his ideological makeup at their most acute: "Brother, that means you believe / That in our veins / There is one holy French blood?... / Cruel Montfort with that very sword / Which felled the unfaithful / Spills fraternal blood" (4: 201). In point of historical fact, Bertran's belief in "one holy French blood" is an anachronism. Even Catholics in Provence had misgivings about a crusade led by a Frenchman. However, this belief is characteristic of Bertran inasmuch as it reveals to what an extent he is an outsider in his own land. Bertran is at one and the same time a knight who has renounced his Albigensian origins and the son of an Albigensian weaver who is not accepted in the Count's court. On the one hand, he tells Gaètan that he never personally participated when poor peasants, who were Albigensians in all likelihood, were hunted down for sport. He rails against Montfort: "I, like you, do not believe in the new campaign. / Montfort's sword is not in God's hand" (4: 201). On the other hand, he will not renounce his duty to the Count, no matter how cruel Archimbaut is. Gaètan remarks, "Heavy they must

[12] Blok's use of these sources as he reworked the drafts is intricate. Zhirmunskii's work remains the most reliable guide. See Zhirmunskii, 76-83.

be, / These earthly bonds" (4: 201). The irony in these words would not have been lost on Bertran, who was reared on the teachings of Albigensianism.

Bertran refuses to explain why he left the via Tolosana once he had discovered Montfort's whereabouts.[13] Gaètan lets the matter drop and begins his own story. Unlike Bertran's story, which is replete with rich detail of life in medieval Languedoc, Gaeatan's has little to do with the realia of medieval Brittany. For Gaètan's biography, Blok relied heavily on the Lancelot legend (Blok's notes to the play, 4: 517). Like the hero in the Arthurian legends, Gaètan was raised by a fairy, who was loath to let him return to this world. Lancelot was taught to be a knight before he appeared in King Arthur's court. Gaètan, on the other hand, learns a song. As he relates the song to his guest, Bertran suddenly realizes that his quest is at an end, that Gaètan is the Wanderer whom he sought. The second scene ends with Bertran's tears, which express both the joy of finding Gaètan and relief that the seigneur of Troménec is an old man. The third and last scene of Act Two finds Gaètan and Bertran once more on the coast, this time mounted on their steeds. Gaètan continues to hear and see things Bertran does not. Bertran urges his friend on.

In Act Three the action and Bertran return to Languedoc. The first scene opens in the Count's quarters, where Archimbaut is receiving Bertran, who has seen Montfort's standard and army himself. Bertran announces that Simon de Montfort is already in Béziers. Despite Archimbaut's happiness concerning Bertran's report, an ideological tension makes itself felt in the differing reactions the two men have to the events Bertran relates. A certain horror is perceptible when Bertran says, "They are now in Beziers. / They burn, beat the residents mercilessly: 'Slaughter them all!" — / Said the legate: — The Lord will know His own'" (4: 207). His sympathy for the innocent is implicit. Archimbaut, on the other hand, rails against the residents of Beziers: "That's what they deserve!" (4: 208). Bertran, by the way, echoes the Russian historian Osokin, to whose work Blok referred during the composition of *The Rose and the Cross*. Osokin likens the barbarity of Montfort's forces to that of the Golden Horde (Osokin, 143).

Because Bertran does not argue, the ideological conflict over Albigensianism remains beneath the surface and gives way to a similar divergence of opinion about chivalry. The immediate cause arises when the Count pardons Bertran and tells him to name his reward. Bertran reminds Archimbaut that the following day is the first of May and informs him that he has returned with a jongleur. Bertran then asks for his reward. To the Count's dismay, it is not for himself that Bertran makes his request. Rather, as a good knight should, Bertran implores the Count to release Izora from the tower. Archimbaut is dumbfounded: "From where did you get it into your head / To ask about this?" (4: 209). His cynical view of courtly love makes such a sacrifice incomprehensible.

The setting shifts to the kitchen of the castle for scene two. Here, as in many of the scenes that include the "quadratic" characters, the tone is decidedly lower than in the scenes that deal with Bertran, Izora, or Gaètan. For example, according to the stage directions, "The cooks behave disgracefully" (4: 209). Their conduct seems appopriate to the tone of the conversation between the Doctor and

[13] Blok surmised that Montfort, and hence Bertran, moved along the via Tolosana (4: 517). Historians suggest otherwise. For more on this question, see Zhirmunskii, 55-6.

the Cook, who are discussing the Count. Much of the Count's behavior is reminiscent of that of his namesake in *Flamenca*[14] The Cook observes that Archimbaut sleeps with keys to the tower. The Doctor replies, "And have you seen what is on his head? — Like a devil in a picture. He hasn't cut his hair for two months. When he smiles, he bares his teeth like a dog. He doesn't believe anyone besides his Reverence" (4: 209). The same low tone is maintained throughout the rest of the scene. The cooks, under the direction of the Doctor, are busily preparing for Izora a pastry stuffed with, among other ingredients, a purgative. The Chaplain walks in unexpectedly and demands to know for whom the dish is being prepared. When he finds out that it is for Izora, the Chaplain asks to taste it. Before the Cook hands the dish over to the Chaplain, however, Aliscans enters on the pretext of checking with the Chaplain on the arrangements for his initiation into knighthood. His real purpose, however, is to surreptitiously pass on a pastry stuffed with a note to the Cook. As the scene ends, the Chaplain leaves with the dish the Doctor had intended for Izora, and the Cook is left with Aliscans's creation.

The third scene is set in the Tower of the Inconsolable Widow, where Izora still suffers from melancholy. Alis suggests a game of chess or checkers to divert her mistress, but Izora refuses. Instead, she takes off on a flight of fantasy, much to Alis's surprise. Izora imagines herself in a church, where a scoundrel follows her and a cleric with prayer book in hand approaches her. "Give the book to her!," she demands. Alis compliantly hands over the romance *Floire et Blanchefleur*, which the Chaplain had railed against in scene four of Act One. With Izora in the role of Flamenca and Alis as Guillems, the two women proceed to act out a scene from *Flamenca*.

This provençal romance proves to be pivotal, in fact, not just for this scene, but for the entire plot of *The Rose and the Cross*. Since Viktor Zhirmunskii has analyzed in great detail the similarites between the Provençal romance and Blok's play, I will summarize only the most important features. (For Zhirmunskii's discussion of the two works, see Zhirmunskii, 35-43.) Izora and Flamenca are both locked in a tower by a jealous husband. In both instances, the husband's name is Archimbaut. Both husbands, as noted above, sleep with the keys to the tower and become gradually more and more unkempt with time. The towers in which the two heroines are incarcerated both have secret passageways. The earlier drafts of *The Rose and the Cross* also share with *Flamenca* a triangle that includes a neglected wife, her jealous husband, and the knight who wishes to free her. In the final version of the play this similarity is somewhat obscured because the role of the knight bifurcates in two, into that of Gaètan and that of Aliscans. Blok also drew on *Flamenca* for imagery, such as the nightingale and the rose, and for the spring fesitivities that open Act Four.

Yet, perhaps the most obvious borrowing arises in the playacting of scene three. Izora quite consciously models this play within a play on *Flamenca*. In the romance, Archimbaut allows Flamenca out of the tower only long enough to attend mass. Guillems hits upon a subterfuge by means of which to communicate with Flamenca. He disguises himself as a cleric and approaches Flamenca. Each time they meet, they utter a single exchange out of caution. Their conversation, as a result, goes on for months. Izora foreshortens the time span, turning the episode

[14] Zhirmunskii was the first to observe this connection. See his exhaustive treatment of the parallels (Zhirmunskii, 38-40).

into a more ordinary conversation. The borrowing becomes particularly emphatic when Alis presents Izora not with a prayerbook, but with a copy of *Floire et Blanchefleur*, which Flamenca also kept by her bedside.

The playacting is cut short by a knock at the door. Afraid that they have been overheard, Izora runs out. Archimbaut and the Chaplain enter. The Count asks to taste the pastry dish only to discover that the Chaplain has beaten him to it. His Reverence explains that he ate not out of hunger but to make sure that the food was not poisoned and that it contained no secret notes. The Count forgives the Chaplain and inquires about Izora's whereabouts. Alis replies that she saying her evening prayers. She also remarks on how much Archimbaut has changed in two months. The Count insists that he knows what he is about. He then turns to the question of his wife's health. Alis describes Izora's sleeplessness and loss of appetite. To the Count's questions about Izora's dreams, Alis says that her mistress still dreams of a knight, but that the night before the knight's features recalled the Count's own. She goes on to make a request on Izora's behalf, namely that she be allowed to pray in church. The Count is pleased, but when Izora returns, he notices her beautiful hair and, like his namesake in *Flamenca*, threatens to cut it off. He brings the conversation back to Alis's request that Izora be allowed to go to church. Izora quickly catches on to Alis's subterfuge and goes along with it. The Count then cruelly dangles the prospect of freedom before his wife, only to abruptly exit, leaving Izora to her supper. Alis cuts open the pastry and discovers a note. Alis insists that it is not meant for Izora, who believes Bertran has finally returned. With this dilemma unresolved, scene three comes to a close.

Scene four is set outside in the rosebushes, where Bertran tells Gaètan to bed down for the night. A rather intricate counterpoint develops as their conversation proceeds. At every step along the way, Gaètan poses a question related to the myth of Ker-Is, and Bertran attempts to answer in terms of the everyday world about them. Thus, when Gaètan asks if he will sing for the king, Bertran answers that he will sing for the Count. When Gaètan asks if the woman in question is the daughter of old Grallon, Bertran informs him that she is the daughter of a simple seamstress. The conversation continues in this manner until it breaks down in a complete lack of understanding. As Bertran remarks, "After all it is all the same to you who you will / Free with your song" (4: 219). Bertran asks again if it was a fairy who taught Gaètan his song. Gaètan replies in the affirmative. Bertran then asks Gaètan to interpret the song for him. "How can suffering become joy?," he asks. Gaètan replies simply, "You know the song. What more is there for me to say?" (4: 220). Bertran laments the fact that he cannot penetrate the song's meaning. He leaves to take up the guard duty assigned to him, and the scene ends.

The fifth scene returns us to the Tower of the Inconsolable Widow at midnight. Izora despairs because no one has come. Alis reminds her mistress that the note was not intended for her. Izora then tries to conjure the knight. She hears rustling in the rosebushes and has a vision of the Wanderer. She speaks to the vision but receives no reply. She lets drop a rose and then faints. Alis and the Count enter to find her unconscious. Archimbaut suddenly repents and frees his wife: "She is free, — tell her! Tomorrow is May! Bertran has brought back a jongleur! We will cheer her up! Just bring her around!" (4: 222). So ends the fifth scene.

Bertran's brief soliloquy in scene six brings the third act to a close. He again addresses the apple tree: "And are you, old comrade, happy for spring?" (4: 222). He then prays for Izora's well-being: "O, Lord, send her peaceful dreams... / Free young Izora's ardent breast / From obscure images..." (4: 222). With Bertran's prayer, the curtain falls on Act Three.

The beginning of Act Four finds Aliscans in a meadow at dawn. He laments the hard night he has spent on guard. His soliloquy, which begins in verse, now switches over to prose as he berates the lady who, he believes, received his note, but gave no sign. He returns to verse as soon as his tirade ends: "O, how sweetly the nightingales sing!... / The fragrance of the roses, like Izora's breathing..." (4: 224). Spurred on perhaps by his impending initiation, Aliscans begins to contemplate his lot in life. As his soliloquy develops, the complete and utter breakdown of the ideology of knighthood becomes apparent. Aliscans wonders, "Is it for these beautiful fingers to clench / The rough shaft of a lance? / No, not for this was I born!" (4: 224). Aliscans separates the roles of lover and warrior, the combination of which was fundamental to the knighthood at its zenith. He imagines the court of Arras as an ideal. No one there, according to Aliscans, would stoop to jealousy and "disturb the merry-making of those at court" (4: 225). As the soliloquy continues, Aliscans notices his reflection in a pond. Not unlike Narcissus, he admires his own reflection and imagines spending his nights with Izora.

If in scene one Blok portrays the breakdown of the ideology of knighthood, he juxtaposes scene two to it as counterpoint. Bertran continues on the quest set for him by Izora. As the scene opens, he returns to the thicket of rosebushes where he left Gaètan the previous evening. The older knight is still fast asleep. Bertran notices that a black rose has fallen onto Gaètan's chest as he slept. Even in his sleep, Gaètan mutters about the legend of Ker-Is, which remains a reality for him whether he is awake or asleep. Bertran rouses Gaètan and reminds him of his request, which the Breton knight promises to fulfill. Bertran asks one more small favor, that Gaètan give him the black rose that had fallen on his chest. Gaètan gladly complies. Bertran hands him a jongleur's outfit, and scene two ends.

In the third scene the action returns to the meadow, where girls sing May Day songs. In the drafts Blok titled this section "May Calends." Although eliminated from the final version, this subtitle once more points to the influence of *Flamenca*. The author of the Provençal romance uses the term "kalenda maia," which literally means the first day of May, to designate songs sung in celebration of May Day.[15] Blok's use of the plural suggests that he too refers to the songs and not only the day. The song the girls sing, however, was based on a translation of a "trimouzette," or spring greeting song, by Anichkov. Blok himself makes this clear in a note (4: 519; see also Zhirmunskii, 44). The singers, among them young men and women and more rarely children, would go from house to house. Their song typically consisted of a stylized refrain of praise for the first day of May, good wishes for the host and hostess, a request for some reward, and prayers to Christ for a bountiful harvest. Blok's version differs from the traditional trimouzette in two respects. First, it is sung exclusively by girls. Secondly, perhaps because it is

[15] For more on this matter, see Zhirmunskii, on whom I rely here. Zhirmunskii also points to *Guillaume de Dole* and Anichkov as sources for these scenes (Zhirmunskii, 42-3).

sung to a large group generally and to no one in particular, it omits the wishes for the health and prosperity of the host and hostess.

As the song is being sung, the participants in the festival gather after mass. The Count with various members of his court, his vassals, guests, and knights and Izora with her ladies arrive in the meadow to the sound of trumpets. Archimbaut greets his guests in a rather strange manner. Not bounded by mere praise for spring, the Count's words take on an ideologically strident tone: "May brings us happy news! / Montfort, the hero of Palestine, / [...] / Burns and routs the treacherous weavers / And will soon be here!" (4: 228). As he has whenever the discussion turns to the Albigensian Crusade, Bertran enters into a disagreement with the Count. He points out that "Albi, Carcassonne, and Val d'Aran are enveloped by the uprising" and that Montfort is still not far along the via Tolosana (4: 228). The Count dismisses Bertran's concerns out of hand and goes on to initiate Aliscans into knighthood. When Aliscans asks Izora if she will allow him to serve her, she acquiesces, and he sits down at her feet.

A minstrel comes forward to sing. As Blok himself notes, he based the song on the first, second, and fourth stanzas of a sirventes by the renowned troubadour Bertran de Born (4: 519). Blok's adaptation is a technical tour de force, which preserves the complex rhyme scheme of the original. Of all the troubadour poetry from which Blok could have chosen, this sirventes turned out to be a felicitous choice. Although the May Day festivities seem innocent enough, Bertran is quite correct to voice concern about the possibility of an attack from the forces of Raimond VI. A sense of foreboding pervades. In its military spirit the sirventes Blok chose enhances this sense of foreboding.[16] The Minstrel's song begins with a seemingly innocuous description of what he loves about spring. His tone changes almost immediately, however, when to the delights of nature he adds preparations for war. In the second stanza the minstrel describes the destruction he enjoys.[17] In the final stanza stanza, he praises the military spirit of the hero and his courage.

The Count, unaware of what is fomenting around him, is taken aback by the minstrel's military spirit and calls forth the Second Minstrel. As Zhirmunskii has shown, for this song Blok again relied upon Anichkov, whose translation of a pastoral by the trouvère Willaume le Viniers [Guillaume le Vinier] (Zhirmunskii, 46-7). Conventional in both form and content, the pastoral suffers when compared to Bertran de Born's sirventes. The singer tells of meeting two beautiful women while out riding. The rest of the poem is devoted to their singing and dancing. Like the vast majority of trouvère poetry, this poem simplifies the complex attitudes toward courtly love expressed in the best troubadour poetry. It also simplifies the

---

[16] In his military spirit, Bertran de Born's work shatters the traditional image of troubadour poetry. On this aspect of his work, see Goldin, 224-7 and Klein.

[17] As Zhirmunskii points out, an interesting misinterpretation led Blok to a striking image. Although he had access to Bertran de Born's work in the original and to Anichkov's reliable Russian translation in prose, Blok also consulted a German translation by Friedrich Diez. In the last lines of the second stanza in the original, Bertran de Born expresses delight at the thought of the enemy being surrounded by ditches at the water's edge. Diez rendered the phrase "by ditches" accurately as "von Gräben," but Blok interpreted the German as "von Gräbern," or "by graves." This suggested to Blok his rather free adaptation, "a pensive row of lonely graves" (4: 230). See Zhirmunskii, 46.

dialogic structure of the troubadour poem. The troubadour addresses his poem not to a single, unified audience, but to single, unified groups within his audience in successive stanzas. The trouvère poem, such as the pastoral Blok chose, is addressed to a single, unified audience (Goldin, 108-25 passim). This song pleases Aliscans as surely as it unsettles Bertran. In essence, Blok's choice of source material again bears ideological content. Perhaps the clearest evidence of this assertion lies in the reaction of the Count, who rewards the singer with his best shirt for such a "sweet song" (4: 231). Archimbaut goes so far as to invite the Second Minstrel to remain at court for the entire summer.

Izora, however, has no patience for the first two singers. She eagerly awaits the new arrival. Her anticipation ebbs, though, when Alis points out that Gaètan's hair is gray. Izora indifferently listens as Gaètan begins his song. As Blok himself notes, Gaètan's song is his own creation, although he borrows several motifs Breton folklore. In particular, Blok points to a didactic dialogue between a Druid and a child (Barzaz-Breiz, 2 ff. and Zhirmunskii, 70-1). In that dialogue, the Druid tells the child, "There is only one Necessity, Death, the father of Sorrow; nothing before, nothing after." The Druid's remarks are reflected quite clearly in the early drafts. However, Blok talked the matter over with Anichkov, who strongly advised him to drop the passage. According to Blok's notes on the conversation, Anichkov said, "Not in any case can any pagan (druid) traditions remain" (Zhirmunskii, 102). What remained was the part of the song Bertran remembers at the beginning of the play: "There is one indisputable law for the heart — / Joy is only suffering!" (4: 171, 233). Other motifs in the poem were suggested by Blok's trip to Brittany. Blok's sense of the ocean as an elemental force, in fact, sets the tone of the whole song: "The hurricane roars, / The ocean sings, / Snow whirls ..." (4: 232). Alis, Aliscans, and the Count all denounce the song because it is strikingly out of place. Taken as a whole, Gaètan marks out an ideological territory that threatens his audience. The very collocation of joy and suffering undermines the frivolous romantic games that Alis and Aliscans indulge in. Although Archimbaut believes the danger of an uprising is past, he vaguely perceives the implications of this collocation when it is applied to a peasantry that believes in a dualistic religion. The entire company, of course, is acutely aware of the dissonance between the images of snow in Gaètan's song and the spring holiday they are celebrating. It is as if Gaètan were bringing into question their assumptions about spring as a time of renewal.

Gaètan's song affects Izora strongly, and she faints. She awakens, mumbling the words of the song. Aliscans remarks that Gaètan has disappeared, and the Count calls for jongleurs to amuse his wife. As they try to distract Izora, Aliscans is busy wooing her: "Like Narcissus in love, / I am reflected in your eyes ...." One of the jongleurs catches on to the irony Aliscans misses: "And that is how Narcissus looked into the water and drowned ..." (4: 235). Izora, suddenly freed of her melancholy by Gaètan's song, becomes more and more receptive to the knight's advances. Aliscans, in fact, is on the verge of success when a knight sounds an alarum. Raimond's forces attack, and Bertran rushes into battle with the cry, "Sancta Rosa!" (4: 236).

The fourth scene takes place in a passageway after the battle is over. From the returning knights the audience learns that Bertran unseated a giant with a dolphin on his shield — perhaps the very one who unseated him at his first tournament. As soon as Bertran forced the giant to capitulate, Raimond's forces scattered, according to the knights. One of them observes, however, that Bertran was wounded. Aliscans, they note, never took the field. The Count then enters and rejoices over their victory. When one knight gives credit to Bertran, Archimbaut is dismissive, saying that their opponents were bandits, an opponent unworthy of a knight. He also makes light of Bertran's wounds. They disperse, and Alis and the Chaplain enter. They arrange a rendezvous and exit. Then Bertran enters. A knight praises his bravery and offers to relieve him from guard duty. Bertran gently refuses both his praise and his offer. The knight leaves, and Izora enters. Bertran, despite his wounds, expresses concern over Izora's peace of mind because she is not asleep. He clutches to his breast the rose he took from Gaètan. Izora asks what it is, and Bertran tells her that it is the "rose of my faithfulness" (4: 239). She points out that all were saved by his faithfulness. Bertran replies that it was only duty. Izora responds, "The Lord will reward you for this... / You, Bertran, He created faithful, / And me — treacherous ..." (4: 239-40). Bertran assures her that she is not to blame. Izora then asks her faithful knight to stand guard while she and Aliscans meet. The sound of a sword falling to the ground is to be the sign, should anyone approach.

The final scene opens in the castle courtyard, where Bertran stands guard. He helps Aliscans climb up the trunk of the apple tree to Izora's window. Left alone, Bertran begins a soliloquy that will be interrupted periodically. Several times Izora appears at her window overwhelmed by the passion that now pulses through her veins. The Chaplain and Alis enter, and his Reverence offers the lady-in-waiting a present. They depart when they finally notice Bertran. Throughout all of these interruptions, Bertran weaves motifs from Gaètan's song together with those of Izora and the rose. As he is about to die, he comes to understand the mysterious song that had so long eluded him. At the moment of his death, Bertran lets his sword drop and in this way alerts Izora and Aliscans of approaching danger. Aliscans escapes just as the Chaplain arrives with the Count in tow. Suspecting that something is amiss, the Chaplain had awakened the Count in order to see what Izora was up to. The mistress of the castle pretends to have been asleep. They discover Bertran's corpse, and Izora begins to weep. Archimbaut asks why she is crying. "I am sorry for him. He was after all a faithful servant" (4: 246). With Izora's pronouncement, the curtain falls.

III

Ideology and Elements of the Carnival-Grotesque

Like its predecessors, *The Rose and the Cross* belongs to the realm of the serio-comic (Bakhtin 1984b, 108-9). The three major characteristics noted by Bakhtin are all apparent here. First, the play has an immediate relation to the present that is not at first apparent. As Blok explained to the actors of the Moscow Art Theater, "The first thing that I want to emphasize is that *The Rose and the Cross* is not a historical drama. When I wrote the drama, it was not the epoch, or the events of French life of the beginning of the thirteenth century, or the style that concerned me first and foremost. ... Thus, the gist of the matter is not that the action takes place in 1208 in southern and northern France, but that the life of the feudal lords of the west, peculiar in its mores, coloring, and details did not in its rhythm differ at all from the life of landowners of any country and any century" (4: 530-1). As he wrote in his notebook, "One has to stick to history knowing, however, all the time that the characters are 'contemporary' people. Their tragedy is our tragedy" (Blok 1965, 285). He explained that he did take a contemporary subject "because contemporary life appears many-colored in my eyes and its sounds run together in my ears" (Blok 1965, 288). Though he chose a different century and culture, Blok was still writing about his own time and country.

In this sense, the cynical exposé of thirteenth-century beliefs in *The Rose and the Cross* is posited on Blok's own time; yet, it would not be convincing were it not grounded in historically accurate detail. Blok made this point emphatically. The artist Mikhail Dobuzhinskii, who created the stage design for the production of *The Rose and the Cross* at the Moscow Art Theater, recalled how Blok "insisted on the reality of the staging" (Dobuzhinskii, 256, 280). The exposé of thirteenth-century beliefs is thoroughgoing as we have already seen: Bertran, in his conversation with Gaètan at Troménec, remarks on the savagery of a crusade that purports to be Christian. Aliscans makes a mockery of the ideals of knighthood, reducing the role of the knight to that of a lover. His failure to even enter the battle in Act Four shows the shallowness of an initiation that is barely over. Amongst other examples, the Chaplain's appetites, especially his sexual appetite for Alis, undermine any moral authority his position might afford.

Blok's lampooning of these characters and their beliefs finds a formal echo in his rejection stylistic unity, the third characteristic of serio-comic literature. *The Rose and the Cross* is a potent mixture of prose and verse. Generally, Blok reserves prose for the "quadratic" characters, such as Archimbaut and the Chaplain. Verse serves two rather different functions. Ternary meters are reserved in most instances for the three characters who strive spiritually, Bertran, Izora, and Gaètan. Binary meters, and especially iambic pentameter, serve for functional scenes and become a sort of common ground between quadratic and spiritual characters.

This admixture has enormous ramifications in terms of style and points in the direction of the grotesque. Meyerhold and those sympathetic to him quickly picked up on the play's grotesque elements. Konstantin Vogak, for example, wrote, "In general, the banal atmosphere surrounding Izora is depicted vividly, and at times this depiction even bears traits of the grotesque" (Vogak, 57). Scenes in prose tend to be low in style and treat the banal, the mundane, or the crudely comic. Archimbaut's ravings illustrate this point well. His tirades about the Albigensians and his wife are in prose for the most part. The romantic encounters in which the chief interest of the participants is sexual also tend to be treated in prose. The meetings between the Chaplain and Alis and between Aliscans and Alis all illustrate this point. Finally, the cruder comedy also appears in prose. The scene in which the Doctor supervises the preparation of a purgative in the kitchen is entirely in prose.

On the other hand, high style usually goes hand in hand with ternary meters in *The Rose and the Cross*. It arises in relation to such themes as love, chivalry, religious belief, and the mystic. For example, Izora's exclamations during her tryst with Aliscans in the last act are in verse. The same applies to the scene in which Izora recounts her dream of the Wanderer in Act One. Chivalric acts also receive treatment in verse. The various conversations between Izora and Bertran, for instance, are carried on in an elevated tone and in verse. Finally, Gaètan's songs, all divorced from the concerns of this world, carry a rarefied air.

This motley approach to style suits the variety of ideologies portrayed in the play. Every character in the play interprets the ideologies of Albigensianism, Catholicism, chivalry, feudalism, populism in their own manner. Their varying interpretations lead sometimes to conflict, sometimes to mere disagreement or incomprehension. Yet, Blok does not array the ideological forces haphazardly. *The Rose and the Cross*, in fact, marks a return to the structures of his trilogy of lyrical dramas. There, as here, doubles served to bring ideology into question.

The most important set of metaphoric doubles, without a doubt, is that of Bertran and Gaètan. The friendly relations they enjoy in the final version mask their subtle failure to understand one another. As one critic has pointed out, "The poet in the drama turns out to be a distinctive double of the hero, Bertran: both close to him and in some ways alien, even hostile" (Ogneva, 142; see also Thomson, 298 and Prikhod'ko 1994, 38). Their relationship as doubles is much clearer in the drafts. In his first plan, Blok conceived of the two more simply as antagonists. The emissary in that version is described as a "clever devil," who issues his lady's invitation with "devilish laughter" (4: 455). When the singer, a troubadour in the first version, appears under the lady's window, the "devilish emissary" sets upon the unsuspecting poet with the help of other knights. When the lady fails to recognize the troubadour the next day, the Count kills the emissary, and the poet, with no explanation falls dead at the lady's feet. A sketch for a second plot appended to the first makes the knights' adversarial relationship even more vivid. In it, a knight sets off to see his lady but is killed along the way by his "perfidious friend." The friend, using their mutual resemblance to his advantage, takes the knight's place, "like his double" (4: 455). The later drafts portray a similar relationship between the two. After the first plan, Blok in his "Considerations and Guesses about the Play" described the future Gaètan as the "bearer of a menacing Christianity" (4: 455). Bertran, the son of Albigensians, is by upbringing opposed to him. This conflict is reflected in the first full draft, when Bertran says to the knight, "Your are a devil in a knight's mask" (4: 488).

A comparison of the relationship between Bertran and Gaètan with that of the metaphoric doubles in the trilogy adds heft to this argument. In each of those plays, a triangle emerges between the two doubles and a woman. The doubles, in one sense or another, compete for her. The metaphoric double in each of those plays holds sway over the woman, but his power is as inexplicable as it is undeniable. Gaètan, through his song, has a power over Izora that is similar to the power that allows Harlequin to whisk Columbine away even after she has sworn her faithfulness to Pierrot. Perhaps the closest parallel, however, is that between the Astronomer in *The Stranger* and Gaètan. His knowledge of the stars gives him much the same power over Mariia that Gaètan has over Izora. The drafts reveal other similarities. In the second full draft, the future Gaètan takes off his cloak and beret: He is wearing "blue clothes, strewn with stars" (4: 498). This motif hearkens back to the Astronomer's clothing. Then too, Gaètan upsets the atmosphere of the May Day celebration in much the same way that the Astronomer's arrival marks the demise of the soirée in *The Stranger*. Finally, both disappear mysteriously, leaving the other characters to wonder what happened to them.

As in the relationship between the Poet and the Astronomer, the relationship between Bertran and Gaètan is not simple. There, as here, metonymic doubles complicate the relationship between the metaphoric doubles. The most important of Gaètan's metonymic doubles is Aliscans. In the drafts, Bertran and the future Gaètan are both romantically interested in Izora. By the final draft, Gaètan's interest has been ceded to Aliscans. A number of details bind the two together. First, Aliscans's success is predicated on Gaètan's performance. Their relation is metonymic in temporal terms: As soon as Gaètan finishes and disappears, Izora begins to respond to Aliscans's advances. Blok himself underscores their relation: "If Gaètan is not a person, but a spectre and, as it were, a *pure call*, a singer who himself does not know what he sings about, then Aliscans is also not a person, but a beautiful animal, which knows too well where it is calling" (4: 529). Likewise, in the drafts, the future Gaètan's "menacing Christianity" echoes Aliscans's negative attitude toward Albigensiansim. Finally, Izora underscores their kinship in an offhand comment. To one of Aliscans's compliments, she responds, "It is true, a fairy taught you / To make declarations of love" (4: 175). Gaètan, of course, tells Bertran that he was literally taught by a fairy. Gaètan and Aliscans then are related as metonymic doubles in much the same way that the Astronomer and the Gentleman are in *The Stranger*.

Gaètan has a second metonymic double, who never actually appears on stage, the giant who unseated Bertran. His image is invoked in two contexts: Bertran's first tournament is one, and the other is the battle that erupts at the end of the third scene in Act Four. Although no direct link between the giant and Gaètan appears in the final version of the play, the drafts clearly indicate their relation in structural terms. In the first drafts where Bertran and the future Gaètan are conceived of as simple adversaries, the two meet in physical combat. In the first plan, the "devilish emissary" jumps the troubadour. In the plot appended to that plan, the double kills his friend. In the second full draft of the play, Bertran cries out at the end that he has been slain by his nemesis. And, of course, it is the giant who inflicts the fatal wound in the final version. The original image of the second knight in this manner splintered, and the giant maintained the role of physical opponent. The giant does preserve some traits of the knight in the drafts. For instance, Bertran in the notes written before his death says that the giant unseated him with a "foul blow" (4: 521). While he is perhaps not the devil the knight of the drafts is, the giant is nonetheless not pure. Blok himself underscores the giant's evil side. Soon after finishing the play, Blok considered possible changes to the play and wrote, "The Second Knight might repent that he laughed at Bertran" (4: 463). Gaètan and the giant thus share a common heritage.

As in the plays of the trilogy, the doubles don the masks of fool, rogue, and clown and in so doing bring the ideology of their referrent into dialogic juxtaposition with their own (Bakhtin 1981a, 400-10 passim). Aliscans and the Chaplain, as clowns, undermine chivalry and the Catholic faith respectively. They do so by polemically not understanding the ideologies they attack and then by bending them to their own purposes. Thus, Aliscans is initiated into knighthood but cannot comprehend why he should take up arms a few moments later. Knighthood becomes a mere pretext for his amorous designs. Likewise, the Chaplain does not see any conflict between his abuses of power and the spiritual office he invested with. To his mind, what is good for the Chaplain is good for his office.

Strong as these images are, the most common mask in *The Rose and the Cross* is that of the fool who misunderstands or simply does not understand. For instance, to the consternation of his audience, Gaètan fails to ascertain that his song is not appropriate to the celebration of spring. His failure calls into question the festivities themselves. The ideological function of Izora's melancholy follows a similar pattern. Her malady is, in a sense, a polemical failure to acknowledge her husband's jealousy as legitimate. By not acknowledging its legitimacy, she shows his position to be outlandish. Similarly, Bertran's orthodox belief in the knighthood calls into question all those who, like Aliscans, have betrayed it. In no small measure, it is Bertran's failure to recognize how the world has changed that leads to this polemical standoff.

Because he is a fool, Bertran is difficult to define. As is the case for the main characters in *A Puppet Show*, it is easier to say what he is not than what he is. This negative description gives rise to the principle of non-coincidence, which provides the only adequate means to characterize Bertran's position in the play. For instance, at one and the same time, he both is and is not a knight. Although he went through the initiation rites, no one treats him like a knight. He remains an outsider at court. Again, he both is and is not an Albigensian. On the one hand, as the son of a weaver from Toulouse, he was born an Albigensian. In the second full version of the play, Bertran fights against the crusaders and is referred to as a "heretic" (4: 510). As Blok himself noted, Bertran is the "son of a Toulouse weaver, and in his veins flows the blood of the people, the blood of a heretic, [an Aligensian], a Cathar" (4: 534; brackets as in original). Yet, on the other hand, Bertran believes in one France and considers it his sworn duty to to fight his own in order to protect the Count and his family. He remains non-coincident with himself because none of these positions exhausts his character. In fact, the pathos of Bertran's life stems from the coherence he gives to these contradictions.

Non-coincidence renders Bertran's character ambiguous. At once he is tragic and pathetic. In this and other ways, Bertran is not unlike Don Quixote. Both fall in love with Spanish women from the lower strata of their society who literally or figuratively rise to the status of ladies. As Bertran tells Gaètan, Izora is the "daughter of a simple seamstress" (4: 219).[18] Both, donning the masks of fools, believe in the ideology of knighthood, though the world has long since changed. Both are honest as only a fool can be. As Blok put it, Bertran "is inexorably honest, difficultly honest, and with such honesty it is almost impossible to live in this world; and everyone around you, using this honesty to all ends, mocks at it and considers it idiotic" (4: 534).

If there is a difference between Bertran and Quixote, it is one of awareness. Bertran recognizes the painful foolishness of his position to a greater extent than Quixote. Bertran describes himself as a "freak derided by all" (4: 171). Abuse is heaped upon his head as it is upon Quixote's. Both reveal the world in its reverse aspect. In his physical appearance, Bertran is a parody of a knight. He is aging as his gray hair shows only too well. Moreover, he is not of noble birth. In fact,

---

[18] This transformation is underscored in the fourth scene of Act Three when Gaètan, in his imagination, transforms Izora into Dahu, the daughter of King Grallon (4: 219). The transformation of Aldonza into Dulcinea was a recurrent motif in the work of Fedor Sologub, whose play *The Triumph of Death* [*Pobeda smerti*] may have influenced Blok here.

Bertran is a mock epic hero, whose every triumph reveals defeat. He fulfills Izora's seemingly hopeless quest. Yet, his triumph turns to nought when Aliscans wins Izora's affections because of Gaètan's performance, and his lofty dreams of his lady are frustrated. Even his ultimate victory over the giant turns ironically to defeat when he is mortally wounded. We recognize in Bertran a carnival king in the abuse he receives, in his status as a mock epic hero, in the carnivalistic upendings of his every act.

Blok was well aware of Bertran's special status. In one description of *The Rose and the Cross*, Blok wrote, "It is, in the first place, the drama of the *person* Bertran; he is not a hero, but the reason and heart of the drama" (4: 529). In his role as carnival king, Bertran brings together the ideological strands that bind the play. His death, like his life, is ambiguous. On the one hand, he sacrifices himself unselfishly for Izora. As Blok would have it, Bertran "died for her like a *Christian*" (4: 530; italics in the original). On the other hand, death releases Bertran from the evil he has suffered his entire life. As Blok told an interviewer, "Bertran's consolation is found only in Death" (4: 530). This latter statement is consistent with the beliefs of the Albigensians. In the end, perhaps Bertran's great triumph is that his character is not exhausted by these ideologies. Where the quadratic characters accept the confines of their narrow ideologies, Bertran must acknowledge opposed belief systems in their dialogic opposition. The rose and the cross, as emblems of Provençal and French culture, mark the historical crossroads, at which Bertran stands.[19]

IV

From Puppet Shows to the NaturalisticTheater

The failure of *The Song of Fate*, particularly in Stanislavskii's eyes, affected Blok strongly. Rejection by the Moscow Art Theater deepened his misgivings about his own dramaturgy, a circumstance that, at least in part, led him to abandon drama for nearly four years. Yet, the abandonment of drama did not mean the abandonment of theater altogether. Rather, the four years that lay between *The Song of Fate* and *The Rose and the Cross* constitute a period not of rejection of the theater, but of continuing, if not growing familiarity with the theater. It could

[19] Western readings of the play have often been reductionist in this regard. Commentators have tended to diminish the role of Albigensianism and to interpret the ending exclusively in Christian terms. (See Thompson, 345-50 passim; and Thomson, especially 305.)

hardly have been otherwise, since it was at this time that his wife resolved to become an actress.

The relation between Mendeleeva-Blok the actress and Blok the playwright has been oddly slighted by critics, even those who have noted the influence of other actresses, such as Natal'ia Volokhova, with whom Blok was romantically involved. The omission is especially striking, given that from the very beginning their relationship centered around the stage. Theater took on a vital meaning for both, but especially for the young Mendeleeva. She studied acting assiduously in Petersburg. By the time she and Blok were engaged, she had already formed very definite ideas about acting and the theater, ideas that already showed a decided disinclination toward realism. Recounting a successful performance in Gogol's *The Marriage* in her memoirs, she goes so far as to rue this disinclination as an impediment to her career:

> Even afterwards I continued to perform very successfully in *The Marriage*, but here, probably, is one of my basic mistakes in life: playing realistic roles did not satisfy me. True, I enjoyed putting into them my ability to make fun of things, my powers of observation, and my love for the colorful details of life, but this was not my full range. More important than this and what I needed personally was the grand gesture, the ornamental and picturesque pose, the effect of costumes and impressive declamation — in other words, the heroic plane (Mendeleeva-Blok 1982b, 34).

Whatever its effect on her career, Mendeleeva-Blok's aversion to realism took shape early. In part, she was influenced by ideas that were prevalent at the time, especially in the circle that she and Blok frequented. Her empathy for Meyerhold was perhaps to be expected as a corollary of both personal acquaintance and ideas held in common. Mendeleeva-Blok's determination to become an actress was not iron-willed, but it was abiding. So it was in February, 1908, while Blok was in the last stage of his work on the first redaction of*The Song of Fate*, that Mendeleeva-Blok set out on a tour of the provinces with a troup led by Meyerhold, whom Komissarzhevskaia not long before had dismissed as director of her theater.

Although Mendeleeva-Blok's experience in the theater left little trace on *The Song of Fate*, its negative impression has important ramifications for *The Rose and the Cross*, considered by some the most stageworthy of all of Blok's plays. At a time when his wife, under Meyerhold's sway, grew increasingly enamoured of the non-realist theater, Blok himself, having grown estranged from Meyerhold, puppets, and the theater of the grotesque in the narrow sense, became more and more concerned with psychology and realistic motivation. As he later noted of *The Rose and the Cross*, "One of my main 'inspirations' was *honesty*, i.e. the desire to not dissemble 'mystically.' So that it would be possible to explain everything psychologically, 'simply'" (Blok 1965, 285).

Such a rift was bound to have consequences, both personal and creative. In regard to the former, it exacerbated the tensions in an already troubled marriage. Infidelities on both sides threatened the marriage at times. It is perhaps worth noting that one of the most volatile periods for poet and actress came at the time *The Rose and the Cross* was being written. Blok grew increasingly distressed over Mendeleeva-Blok's involvement with the actor Konstantin Tverskoi, who appeared under the stage name Kuzmin-Karavaev. While the disagreements between husband and wife about theater did not cause such infidelities any more than the infidelities caused such disagreements, nonetheless the personal became inextricably bound up in the professional.

From the very beginning, Blok did little to support his wife as an actress, and she, out of pride, refused to ask for his help. Surveying her career as a whole, Mendeleeva-Blok wrote,

> Now it seeems idiotic to me that I did not take advantage of Blok's position to attain my goals, and it was all because of that same fastidiousness. But it is also true that Blok, as though deliberately, did not do anything to help me along in my career, and, consequently, he even hurt me, because his non-involvement appeared to be a conscious dismissal of my talents stemming from a lack of confidence in me. This could have aroused strong scepticism about me, but if I had only asked him, if I had only explained my feelings to him — certainly he would have helped, that I know. Yet his attitude stirred my pride even more and I tried to make it on my own. Everything that I achieved in the theater I achieved not only on my own, without any outside help, but also in spite of the great handicap of two overwhelming names: those of my father and my husband (Mendeleeva-Blok 1982b, 58).[20]

Blok could even turn spiteful at times. For instance, about a month after completing *The Rose and the Cross*, Blok wrote to his wife who was in Zhitomir with Kuzmin-Karavaev. After a devastating critique of Meyerhold's version of *Elektra* at the Mariinskii Theater, the criticism took on a personal coloring, and he continued, "I do not like actors, dear. It is constantly painful for me that you want to perform. There is something *shameful* here. *Only genius* saves it; without genius, it is shameful, boring, unnecessary. Theater of genius is art; theater without it is thankless craft" (8: 410-1). Blok's attitude toward his wife as an actress would change. In time, he would applaud her appearance in popular theater as a “good and important pursuit" (Blok 1927-32, 2: 271). By 1918, he would even venture a cautious recommendation of his wife to Iurii Iur'ev for the role of Lady Macbeth (Blok 1964, 528). However, so long as she was under Meyerhold's spell, Blok's assessment of his wife's abilities remained vitriolic.

Similarly harsh judgments were meted out to Meyerhold. Strange as it may sound, Meyerhold, without the least romantic intention, became a bone of contention in their marriage. Moreover, with time Blok's attitude toward Meyerhold worsened in a seemingly inexplicable manner, given Meyerhold's enthusiastic admiration for Blok and the number of times Meyerhold came to Blok's aid, particularly in regard to *The Rose and the Cross.* Without a doubt, Blok and Meyerhold were growing apart artistically, but the tenor of Blok's criticism of Meyerhold was uncharacteristically strident and would remain so until Meyerhold's 1914 production of *A Puppet Show* and *The Stranger.* The source of his stridency was at least partly personal. As Avril Pyman writes,

[20] Mendeleeva-Blok's father was, of course, none other than Dmitrii Mendeleev, who created the periodic table.

> It seems more than probable that Blok's stubborn inability to 'see' Meyerhold as an artist was bound up with his resentment of the great director's influence on his wife. The men who had loved her — with the exception of Andrey Bely ('whom I most probably hate') — he did not recognize as rivals. But Meyerhold — without intending to, without effort — was taking Lyuba away from Blok far more effectively than any Kuzmin-Karavayev, drawing her into a world of sparkling make-believe and calculated effect that really was deeply alien to her husband, whose whole being was now concentrated on 'restoring integrity to Russian life', on the problem of how to restate simple ethical truths in a way so new, so exquisite, and so indirect that people would feel they had rediscovered them for themselves (Pyman 1980, 2: 191).

The question of why Mendeleeva-Blok's lovers caused Blok relatively less distress than Belyi and Meyerhold is perplexing, but surely hinges on artistic authority. The others were merely lovers, while Belyi and Meyerhold were masters, Blok's equals in art. Modernist theater, in the guise of Meyerhold, took on a personal meaning for Blok. As he himself noted, the modernists more and more separated wife from husband (7: 163). Perhaps it was because Blok's self-image rested so centrally on Blok the poet that he reacted negatively to the challenge Meyerhold represented.

In the final analysis, Blok's reaction against Meyerhold's ideas became inextricably bound up in the disruption of his personal life. Blok began to criticize nearly everything that involved Meyerhold, from his productions to his studios. For instance, in 1911 he told the poet and art critic Konstantin Siunnerberg that he had "disliked terribly" Meyerhold's *Don Juan* (8: 381). In describing the première of Meyerhold's *Elektra* to his wife, Blok wrote, "falsehood as we expected" (8: 410). The tone of his diary entry on *Elektra* is even more dismissive: "For me it was if there were nothing" (7: 222). The production proved even worse in retrospect. A month later when he wrote about the play in his diary, Blok referred to *Elektra* as *"VAPID RUMORMONGERING"* (7: 239; capitals and italics in original). In his tirade about Meyerhold's *Elektra*, he recalled other disappointments, such as "the Meyerholdian spoiling of Sophocles and Lermontov" (8: 410). Even the productions he did not see were not immune to indictment. He roundly criticized, for example, Meyerhold's production of D'Annunzio's *La Pisanelle* in Paris on the grounds that Meyerhold knew no French. Apathy was again evoked by a visit to Meyerhold's for a theatrical evening: "*Love for the Three Oranges* compiled by Meyerhold, Solov'ev, and Vogak according to Gozzi's scenario produced no impression whatsoever: dry and motley" (Blok 1978, 299).[21]

Nor did Mendeleeva-Blok's participation in Meyerhold's productions ameliorate Blok's judgments. In the summer of 1912, she acted in Meyerhold's production of a short play by Cervantes. As Blok wrote to his mother, "Besides that, there were two pantomimes, of which she took part in one — she danced; the

---

[21] Vladimir Nikolaevich Solov'ev was a director and ally of Meyerhold's, and Konstantin Vogak taught in Meyerhold's studio. Vogak's name is spelled incorrectly in the letter as printed in the Collected Works (8: 413). It appears correctly in Blok 1978, 299.

pantomime, in my opinion, was foolish and was thought up and put on by Meyerhold in an uncommonly banal manner" (8: 392). But his most vicious attacks on Meyerhold were reserved for his wife as when he wrote to her, "It is better we do not speak about Meyerhold. ... I do not need born plagiarists with their soul's *wretched contents* and their sensitivity that creates the impression of talent" (8: 419). Much the same tone predominates when Blok contrasts the Moscow Art Theater studio with Meyerhold's: "In any case the spirit of *work* (solely instructive) exists only there, and all the rest (and Meyerhold especially) is just ignorance inside" (8: 420). Meyerhold's requests to stage *The Rose and the Cross*, even with Mendeleeva-Blok's intercession, elicited only reluctance from Blok. As Blok wrote to his wife point-blank, "Inwardly I do not at all feel his being as an artist, and I am very afraid of him outwardly, since I know that at the Aleksandrinka there is such a 'director'" (8: 427).

In all of these remarks, separating the personal from the artistic proves difficult. What becomes clear, however, is that Blok was not objective. Blok the critic was characterized by sharp vision and acute insight. A single volume would suffice for him to catch the scent of a major poet, such as an Akhmatova or a Khlebnikov.[22] Yet, after a relatively brief period of understanding during their collaboration at the Komissarzhevskaia Theater, Blok consistently, almost willfully misconstrued Meyerhold and his theater. Moreover, the Meyerhold whom Blok attacked was changing. Meyerhold, after all, was nothing if not protean. But Blok missed the director's evolution. Herein rests the core of the saddest chapter on *The Rose and the Cross.* Partly for personal reasons, Blok turned away from Meyerhold toward Stanislavskii.

To understand just how badly Blok misjudged the two we need only contrast their theaters. The Moscow Art Theater, after its celebrated productions of Chekhov in the early years of the century when it could lay claim to the title of the country's foremost theater, was on the wane, having turned increasingly to the classics, producing fewer and fewer original works. One historian of theater has estimated that in the first seven years of its existence (1898-1905), the Moscow Art Theater put on three new plays for every old one. In the second period of seven years (1906-1913), the number of new and old plays was nearly equal. In the third, the numbers for the first period were nearly reversed, as old plays outnumbered the new by a margin of more than two to one (Èfros, 304-5). The theater was experiencing a crisis brought on by the challenge of such directors as Meyerhold, Evreinov, and Tairov. In time, the challenge would be met, but the process of sorting out artistic aims took years. Along the way, a number of experiments were undertaken. Nemirovich-Danchenko turned to musical drama, a move that helped to keep the theater afloat through the difficult years immediately after the revolution. Evgenii Vakhtangov was installed in the studio theater, and he would eventually clarify the Moscow Art Theater's relation to non-realist theater. Vakhtangov's innovations would be consolidated after his death when the First Studio was reorganized as the Second Moscow Art Theater. Vakhtangov's clarification, in its turn, would allow the main theater to return to its naturalist core;

---

[22] To the former, he inscribed one of his books of poems with a madrigal and the other collections he gave her simply, "To Akhmatova from Blok," a subtle compliment first noted by Pyman 1980, 2: 193. Of the latter, Blok noted in his diary, "I suspect that Khlebnikov is significant" (7: 232).

and in the mid-twenties with the lungs of playwrights like Bulgakov, Vsevolod Ivanov, Valentin Kataev, and Leonid Leonov, it would gather its second wind. Yet at the time Blok was wooing the Moscow Art Theater, all of these changes were in the future. The theater that Blok approached was in the throes of a major crisis.

On the other hand, Meyerhold was just hitting stride. His productions at the Aleksandrinskii, especially *Don Juan* and *Masquerade*, were among the most important between the two revolutions. His innovative approach turned a moribund imperial theater into one of the leading theaters in the country. At the same time his experimental studio productions and classes were breaking important theoretical ground. Meyerhold's continuing interest in the *commedia dell'arte* bore fruit not only in his production of *A Puppet Show* and *The Stranger*, but also in a series of harlequinades and pantomimes, as well as in specialized studio classes on the *commedia dell'arte*. In these productions and in his classes, Meyerhold worked out the basic tenets of techniques he would deploy in the future. The seeds of constructivism germinated in his work on *The Stranger*. Ideas developed in classes on movement would later crystallize into biomechanics. In short, Meyerhold seemed indefatigable through these years. Given his accomplishments, his mastery of non-realist theater, his empathy for Blok and his work, Meyerhold would seem to have been the natural choice for *The Rose and the Cross*.

However, when Blok finally relented and acquiesced to Meyerhold's desire to stage the play, outside forces intervened, and *The Rose and the Cross* never made it to the stage of the Aleksandrinskii. Preparations included submission of the play to the censor, who proved to be "pigheaded concerning *The Rose and the Cross*" (Blok 1965, 227, 233). The censors were particularly troubled by the title of the play (Pyman 1980, 2: 323) and by several passages in which the image of the cross is invoked (Meierkhol'd 1976, 164-5). Fortunately, Blok had already worked with one of the censors, Baron Nikolai Osten-Drizen, with whom the poet remained on cordial terms. Osten-Drizen, together with Nikolai Evreinov and Aleksandr Sanin [Shenberg], had made possible the production of Rutebeuf's *Le Miracle de Théophile* in Blok's translation at the Starinnyi. Now, largely through Osten-Drizen's intercession, *The Rose and the Cross* passed the censor (see Zaborova, 41-2). One more obstacle stood in the path of the production, and it proved insurmountable: The director of the imperial theaters, Vladimir Teliakovskii, refused to sanction a production of the play at the Aleksandrinskii (Dolinskii 1985, 185). Teliakovskii's intransigence appears to reflect his own, somewhat arbitrary, personal opinion. A little more than a year later, in November, 1915, the Theatrical-Literary Committee of the Imperial Theaters would find the play "suitable for production on imperial stages" (Konechnyi, 5: 86).

The failure of Meyerhold's production to materialize was not, for Blok, a personal catastrophe. In fact, it may well have come as a relief, given the tensions between him and Meyerhold. One critic goes so far as to suggest that in general Meyerhold's "cold, aesthetic pathos was foreign and even objectionable to Blok" (Alpers, 159). Certainly by this time, Blok's doubts about modernist theater had solidified. If he now found truth in theater, it was Stanislavskii's truth. Although relations between poet and director were sometimes troubled, Blok's desire to work with Stanislavskii never flagged. With an almost quixotic fervor, Blok withstood even Stanislavskii's most damning critiques. Turned down once with *The Song of Fate*, he tried again with *The Rose and the Cross*. Turned down again, one last opportunity presented itself, and Blok jumped at it. There was in Blok's attitude toward Stanislavskii something compulsive. Perhaps, the turn away from Meyerhold necessitated a corresponding turn toward the director of the Moscow Art Theater: To work with anyone else would have been a step down.

This is not to suggest, however, that Blok's desire to work with Stanislavskii was calculated. In fact, it was sincere and emanated from a deep respect for the director's work. His reactions to Stanislavskii's productions very often had been ecstatic. In the spring of 1909, for instance, Blok saw four plays that the Moscow Art Theater put on while on tour in Petersburg. Of the four, he reacted to Chekhov's *Three Sisters* most strongly: "And in the evening I returned utterly shaken from *Three Sisters*" (8: 280). Yet his reaction to Stanislavskii grew out of personal, as well as professional, respect. One sign of this respect appeared in 1911, when Blok, usually reserved and restrained emotionally, asked one of Stanislavskii's friends to tell the latter that he "thought about him with tenderness and gratitude" (8: 377). In Stanislavskii, Blok valued very greatly the bond between man and artist. Writing about a performance of Tolstoy's *Living Corpse*, Blok noted in his diary, "All of them are actors, singular and excellent, but actors. Stanislavskii alone, again both as an actor and as a person, is a miraculous combination of life and art" (7: 138). It is perhaps symptomatic that as Blok formulated his rejection of Meyerhold and his predilection for ethical art as he broadly construed it, Stanislavskii plays a pivotal role: "Again everything that concerns *Meyerholdism* is painful to me. I irrepressibly like 'healthy realism,' Stanislavskii, and Musical drama" (Blok 1965, 209).

Blok first turned to Stanislavskii with the play in the spring of 1913, when the Moscow Art Theater was on tour in Petersburg. In the middle of April, Blok wrote to Stanislavskii, "I have a play, *The Rose and the Cross*. If you were to agree to listen to it, you would afford me the greatest joy" (8: 415). Blok went on to tell Stanislavskii that he wished to read the play to him alone, with only Aleksei Remizov in the room. As always in his dealings with Stanislavskii, Blok was exquisitely polite, offering to go to the director if that were more convenient. Stanislavskii quickly agreed to meet with Blok and Remizov (Stanislavskii, 7: 569).

The reading, however, was nothing short of disastrous. Blok described some of the difficulties in a diary entry: "It was especially difficult for me to read, and I read poorly, feeling that Konstantin Sergeevich was listening intensely, but was not grasping it. From our conversations it turned out that this was actually so" (7: 240-1). Stanislavskii reacted only slightly better to *The Rose and the Cross* than he had to *The Song of Fate*. "You — Stanislavskii said to me — hide, conceal from the spectator (and from the actor) the most effective places, there where it is possible to show Bertran's figure at its full height, where Bertran becomes a *role* and even an *independent* one — a Hamlet or a Don Quixote (?)" (7: 243). Blok took Stanislavskii's critique to heart. Particularly Stanislavskii's doubts about Bertran's motivation worried Blok, and they led him to write the knight's autobiography in order to test the accuracy of his portrait. (For more on this matter, see 8: 457.) Stanislavskii appears to have regretted his own reaction. As Blok noted, "The evening ended with Stanislavskii excusing himself. He was afraid that he had injured me. He took back his own words. He said that he had not stepped back from my scheme — 'we (directors) need to learn to speak with authors' — that he had not said anything to me, that he had not caught on to even a quarter of the play, that it is necessary to consider that he had heard from me only the scheme of a future play" (7: 244). Despite the compliments Stanislavskii tacked on for

Blok's sake on his way out, the upshot of the reading was painfully obvious: "Apparently, nothing will happen with the Art Theater, and it will be necessary to print *The Rose and the Cross.* But the time to mount it on stage has not come" (7: 245). A conversation he had several days later with Nemirovich-Danchenko seemed to hammer the last nail in the coffin. In regard to it, Blok wrote to his wife, "I met with Vl. Nemirovich-Danchenko in the studio, and in highly polite form gave him to understand everything that I think about him (the conversation was about *The Rose and the Cross* which he wanted to know). I think that the path to the Art Theater is closed to me definitively, and now I am very miserable from a lot of things and from this too" (8: 420).

For several years after its publication, *The Rose and the Cross* lay dormant. Offers to stage it continued to come in, one of the more significant from the Svobodnyi, or Free Theater of Konstantin Mardzhanov [Mardzhanishvili]. The intention of the Svobodnyi to stage *The Rose and the Cross* was apparently one of long standing. Blok first heard about the theater's interest in his play in May, 1913 (7: 248). A year later he heard about it again from a different source (Blok 1965, 227). Another year would pass before rumors of the Svobodnyi's plans to stage *The Rose and the Cross* in the 1915-16 season reached Blok's ears (Dinesman, 5: 76). The rumors proved false, and the production was never realized. The failure of the play at the Svobodnyi owes at least in part to opposition from several of its most important members. The actress Mariia Andreeva, for instance, railed against *The Rose and the Cross*, vehemently arguing, "This is simply a bad play, artificial and false, written in poor verse and poor language" (Andreeva, 553). However, the play also found staunch supporters at the Svobodnyi. Among them were Mardzhanov himself, Aleksandr Tairov and Stanislavskii's favorite pupil, Alis Koonen. Their interest in the play would have important ramifications. Mardzhanov seems to have mounted a production of *The Rose and the Cross* at the Dramatic Theater in Kiev in 1919 with the help of Pavel Il'in (Sholomova, 5: 49). Little is known about the production, and it has received only the most cursory attention. The interest in the play expressed by Tairov and Koonen, on the other hand, constitutes one of the most interesting, if unfortunate chapters in the legacy of *The Rose and the Cross* as a piece for theater.

Tairov and Koonen left the Svobodnyi to create the Kamernyi or Chamber Theater in Moscow. Some two years after Stanislavskii's rejection of *The Rose and the Cross* Tairov broached the subject of staging the play at the Kamernyi with Blok. Tairov's interest in Blok's work was enduring, and in fact, the poet and director had known each other personally for some time. They first met when Tairov was beginning his acting career at Komissarzhevskaia's theater. Tairov, although he did not originate the role, played the man in the first pair of lovers in Meyerhold's production of *A Puppet Show* (Tairov, 68). At the time, Blok presented a copy of his *Verses about the Beautiful Lady* to "the blue mask of *A Puppet Show* to whom I am warmly disposed" (Morderer and Parnis, 3: 131). While never close, Blok and Tairov remained on friendly terms. Those relations were clouded, however, by the shadow of Meyerhold. It was certainly not coincidence, but a deeply felt spiritual kinship that led Tairov to Komissarzhevskaia's theater when he arrived in Petersburg from Kiev. Despite their sometimes rancorous and contentious disagreements, Tairov throughout his career followed a modernist path first blazed by Meyerhold.

Thus, when Tairov met with Blok on 23 April, 1915, very distinct differences, if not oppositions, made themselves felt. The enthusiasm Tairov brought to bear on *The Rose and the Cross* was not reciprocated. That is not to say, however, that Blok was hostile, but rather that he remained unconvinced by modernist theater. The sheer difference in how Blok and Tairov reacted to their meeting is striking. Blok noted the meeting in his notebook without comment and treated it as he would any other piece of ongoing business (Blok 1965, 261). The notebook entry indicates neither that an agreement had been reached, nor that Blok had refused Tairov. Blok apparently anticipated further negotiations.

Tairov left with an altogether different understanding. With great enthusiasm he immediately announced plans to stage the play. Blok reacted to the announcement with consternation. In his notebook, he wrote, "In *The Russian Word* it has been made public that *The Rose and the Cross* will be performed at the Kamernyi Theater — ?!" (Blok 1965, 262; punctuation as in the original). Such mutual incomprehension characterized the history of *The Rose and the Cross* at the Kamernyi. Unaware of the misunderstanding that loomed over the production, Tairov was already hard at work. Roles were assigned, and actors began to learn their lines. Alis Koonen, whose sparkling performance in Tairov's production of Kalidasa's *Sakuntala* was the talk of Moscow, undertook the role of Izora. Music was sought, preliminary sketches of costumes were made, and Aleksandra Èkster began work on stage designs (Dolinskii 1985, 186). Tairov and company were well along in their preparations when they found out that Blok had given the play to another theater.

This second theater could have been none other than the Moscow Art Theater. In large measure, the invitation from the Art Theater owed to the advocacy of Leonid Andreev: "It was he who pointed out to the Art Theater Blok's *The Rose and the Cross* as repertory material valuable to it" (Èfros, 300). In November, 1915, Andreev's advice came to fruition, and Nemirovich-Danchenko wrote to inform Blok of the decision. When Tairov heard about the Art Theater's production, he and members of his cast sent Blok a flurry of letters. In February, 1916, Tairov wrote to Blok, "I was confident after our conversation last summer that the play had been given to us. I have worked with it, gotten used to it, and I didn't stage it this season only because I have fallen very much in love with it, and I was afraid to present it in an unworthy guise. ... We dreamed of opening next season with the play.... That we were readying the play has been in all of the newspapers. It has been discussed in conversations about the theater, in which Bal'mont, Briusov, Sologub, Berdiaev, Viacheslav Ivanov have participated. ... Is it really necessary that all this be destroyed?" Alisa Koonen sent Blok a telegram and implored him, "Arrange it somehow so the play will be ours. We are in horrible despair." Tairov followed up with a telegram of his own: "You cannot imagine our distress and sorrow. We hope you will confirm the play for the Kamernyi" (cited by Bongard-Levin, 74; compare to Dolgopolov, 4: 588).

Blok, however, disregarded Tairov's entreaties. His refusal turned out to be a poor decision. In part, Blok underestimated Tairov and the Kamernyi, who were just finishing their inaugural season when negotiations for *The Rose and the Cross* began. Although the productions of that first season had begun to set the Kamernyi apart from a host of other, fledgling theaters, Blok may well have opted for the Moscow Art Theater because of its prestige. Though understandable, Blok's attitude towards the Kamernyi was short-sighted because Tairov had already made and would continue to make theatrical history. His production of Kalidasa's *Sakuntala* was the theatrical event of the 1914-15 season in Moscow. The following season, Tairov's staging of Innokentii Annenskii's *Thamyris Kitharodos* caused a sensation, and not only because of the diaphanous costumes that graced the actors. Considerations such as these have suggested to at least one critic the great potential lost in Tairov's unrealized production of Blok's play: "It is possible that both for Blok and for Tairov such a meeting would have proven a fortunate one" (Rudnitskii 1990, 234). Tairov, whose attention to concrete detail and "classical clarity" has led to comparisons between him and the acmeists, was sympathetic to Blok's impatience with Symbolist theater (Rudnitskii 1987, 187).

Blok, however, cared little about the Kamernyi once the Art Theater had made an offer; or perhaps it would be more accurate to say, once Stanislavskii's theater had made an offer. The Moscow Art Theater was not, for Blok, an institution. It was the singular creation and achievement of one man. Stanislavskii's participation was crucial for Blok, even though it was quite limited in the beginning. Nonetheless, Blok would not have been as eager to participate himself, were Stanislavskii not involved. Nowhere is this clearer than in Blok's reaction to an offer from the Third Studio of the Moscow Art Theater to stage *The Rose and the Cross*. Evgenii Vakhtangov, the director of the Third Studio, approached Blok through an intermediary. Annoyed that the offer had come secondhand, Blok rejected it outright. In his diary, he even made a disparaging comment about Vakhtangov's rather unusual last name (7: 239). Blok's reaction was utterly different when the offer came from the Art Theater itself: He threw himself into preparations for rehearsals. He left Petersburg for Moscow, arriving on 29 March 1916, and set right to work. Not only did he read the play for the directors and the cast and discuss it with them no fewer than eight times (Èfros, 144), he also compiled a special "Explanatory Note for the Art Theater" (8: 530-8). Blok gave unstintingly of himself while in Moscow. The impression he made was lasting, and his stay became something of an event.

The question of Stanislavskii's attitude toward the play is a difficult one. It may very well have been that he never overcame the doubts he expressed to Blok in 1913. According to Ol'ga Gzovskaia, who was to play Izora, Nemirovich-Danchenko recounted a "great struggle" that erupted between Stanislavskii and himself over Blok and *The Rose and the Cross* (Gzovskaia, 247). Certainly Stanislavskii's distance from the production in its early stages supports such a contention. Although he was present when Blok read the play to the actors, Stanislavskii turned the play over to Nemirovich-Danchenko, who worked in close association with Vasilii Luzhskii [Kaluzhskii] on the play (Èfros, 302). Luzhskii, in fact, was at times the *de facto* director. (For more Luzhskii's role, see Dinesman, 5: 69-75 passim).

The question of exactly who would direct the play complicated the entire history of *The Rose and the Cross* at the Art Theater. When Blok was first informed of the Art Theater production, Stanislavskii was consumed with work on a stage adaptation of Dostoevsky's *The Village of Stepanchikovo*, and Nemirovich-Danchenko apparently became director in order to free Stanislavskii for that production (Stroeva 1973, 334). However, Stanislavskii would eventually relieve Nemirovich-Danchenko of his directorial duties, but not before "a large part of the play was rehearsed and worked out" (Èfros, 302).

Stanislavskii's decision to take over was unfortunate for a number of reasons. First, the years associated with his work on *The Rose and the Cross* mark a period of alienation from the Art Theater: Whereas Stanislavskii insisted on experimentation and studio productions as the necessary means to renew the Art Theater, the older members of the troupe, the so-called "shareholders," were unwilling to take risks (Stroeva 1973, 334). Just as important are the personal crises Stanislavskii underwent during this period. A number of failed productions, but especially the poorly received staging of several of Pushkin's *Little Tragedies*, convinced Stanislavskii of the need for a new direction. Most important of all, however, was the death of his associate and close friend, Leopol'd Sulerzhitskii. An early enthusiast and staunch supporter of Stanislavskii's directorial innovations, Sulerzhitskii provided support for Stanislavskii at every step along the way. His death came as a severe blow (Stroeva 1973, 336-7). All of these factors complicated Stanislavskii's work on Blok's play. Even Blok was compelled to recognize that Stanislavskii and *The Rose and the Cross* were poorly suited to one another. Blok never doubted the director's genius, but as he wrote to his mother before Stanislavskii assumed the helm, "*The Rose and the Cross* is utterly incomprehensible and unnecessary to him; while praising the play, he dissembles (he is being cunning with himself). He would only torture himself over it" (8: 485). Indeed, when Stanislavskii began work on the play, he found Nemirovich-Danchenko's production unsatisfactory and started over again from scratch. In consequence, the cast's morale fell (Èfros, 302), and many of the roles were reassigned.

Problems of casting, in fact, had plagued the production from the very beginning. The cast originally ran as follows: Aleksandr Vishnevskii as Archimbaut, Ol'ga Gzovskaia as Izora, Mariia Lilina and Ol'ga Pyzhova as Alis, Luzhskii himself as the Chaplain, Aleksandr Shakhalov as Gaètan, Vasilii Kachalov as Bertran, and Ivan Bersenev as Aliscans.[23] Almost immediately complications arose. Shakhalov could not manage the difficult role of Gaètan, and Nemirovich-Danchenko asked Kachalov to take his place. Kachalov, whose Bertran was already well formulated (Gzovskaia, 206), was loath to give up the role, but did so anyway for the sake of the production. Nikolai Massalitinov then assumed the role of Bertran. Another difficulty arose because, as one commentator put it, "Blok remained dissatisfied with Gzovskaia's work" (Dinesman, 5: 83), seeing in her performance only a "pale picture" (8: 483). Nonetheless, Gzovskaia's eventual departure from the Art Theater contributed to the demise of the production. Perhaps the most difficult role to fill, however, was that of Aliscans. The first to undertake the role was Ivan Bersenev [Pavlishchev], whose portrayal of Aliscans pleased Blok but not Nemirovich-Danchenko. The director then gave the role to Nikolai Tseretelli, who abruptly departed for the Kamernyi Theater. The role passed to Nikolai Chuzhoi [Èfros], who would become in time the first historian of the Art Theater. However, he too failed to create a persuasive Aliscans. Stanislavskii next offered the role to Vladimir Gaidarov. After Gaidarov, Evgenii Kaluzhskii, the son of Vasilii Luzhskii, rehearsed the role. Perhaps Gzovskaia summed up this

[23] Dolgopolov (4: 589) and Vilenkin (2: 593) mistakenly identify Vasilii Kachalov as the first Gaètan and Vladimir Gaidarov as the first Aliscans. Aleksandr Shakhalov and Ivan Bersenev respectively were the first to attempt the roles. See Gaidarov, 72-3 and Gzovskaia, 247.

revolving door of casting best when she quipped to Stanislavskii that in such revolutionary times, she would not take responsibility for the corps of pages that had formed around Izora (Gaidarov, 72-3).

Like other elements of the production, set design proved problematic, and work on it was protracted. In the early stages, the sculptor Nikolai Andreev worked with Luzhskii on the architectural construction of the sets. Although "witty," the construction turned out to be too complicated and bulky to realize on stage (Dobuzhinskii, 256). Nemirovich-Danchenko then asked the renowned artist Mstislav Dobuzhinskii to design the sets and costumes. By this point, the artist had established a reputation for himself independently of the World of Art group, with which he had been associated earlier in his career. Although in posterity he would perhaps be remembered best as a member of the World of Art group or as Vladimir Nabokov's drawing teacher, his portraits and his stage design for other Art Theater productions had won him high praise from his contemporaries. Such high expectations transformed the first dress rehearsal into a calamity. The sheer bulk of the sets themselves and the large number of set changes necessitated an equally large number of intermissions, which destroyed the unity of the production (Bertenson, 250). Stanislavskii absolutely refused to employ the sets.

The crux of the problem, however, centered as much on Stanislavskii's reconsideration of the function of sets and set design as it did on the number and bulk of Dobuzhinskii's sets. As one commentator has pointed out, Stanislavskii sought and experimented with new principles of stage design throughout the years 1916-1920 (Vinogradskaia, 215). His dissatisfaction with Dobuzhinskii's sets may have stemmed from such theoretical considerations. Others praised Dobuzhinskii's work. Sergei Bertenson, who assisted Stanislavskii at the time and who had spent much of his career in the Imperial Theaters in Petersburg, remarked on the "high quality of the production" (Bertenson, 250). Still others praised the designs, but harbored reservations. Blok would later find that "some are very good. All are a little wooden" (7: 420).[24] In his memoirs, Dobuzhinskii assented to Blok's opinion, acknowledging that the difficulty of the set design owed to the large number of rapid set changes (Dobuzhinskii, 256).

Rumors of Stanislavskii's dissatisfaction with Dobuzhinskii's sets and costumes circulated even before the dress rehearsal, and Dobuzhinskii grew so disheartened that he abandoned Moscow for Petersburg, where he learned of the demise of not only his work, but Nemirovich-Danchenko's as well (Dobuzhinskii, 256-7). Stanislavskii took Dobuzhinskii's departure as a sign that the artist would be unwilling to redo the sets. For a short time Stanislavskii considered Anatolii Arapov (Zolotnitskii, 102), but in the end resolved to work with an artist whose first allegiance was to the theater. No one fit that description better than Dobuzhinskii's assistant, Ivan Gremislavskii, whose first allegiance was not just to any theater, but to the Art Theater itself. The son of the Art Theater's own makeup artists, Gremislavskii had grown up in the Art Theater. *The Rose and the Cross* was, in a sense, his big break. However, because Gremislavskii had never been responsible for an entire production before, Stanislavskii asked Bertenson to

---

[24] Nonetheless, Blok supported Dobuzhinskii. Not only did he recommend Dobuzhinskii in the first place, but he also encouraged the former Nezlobin Theater to use the artist's designs in a later production. For more on the Nezlobin production, see below.

supervise the young set designer's progress. Stanislavskii insisted on the supervision because he was introducing a new principle of set design: Instead of a traditional set, a series of drapes would be used in order to facilitate set changes. In this way, sets could be changed, Stanislavskii thought, "just as quickly as the pages of a book are turned" (Bertenson, 250-1). In practice, Stanislavskii's principle proved difficult to execute, and Gremislavskii's work drew a mixed reaction. The execution of the work also proved difficult because of a dearth of available materials in the postrevolutionary period (Zolotnitskii, 102).

Complications also arose in regard to music for *The Rose and the Cross.* At first, following the path of least resistance, the Art Theater considered the opera *The Rose and the Cross* by the young and unknown Iurii Bazilevskii. In early February, 1914, Bazilevskii had written to Blok about his intention to create an opera out of *The Rose and the Cross* (Dinesman, 5: 75). Within several days, the two met (Blok 1965, 209). Bazilevskii's work apparently moved along well because Blok recommended it for a proposed staging of *The Rose and the Cross* in Kharkov in November of the same year (Sholomova, 5: 46).[25] Although Bazilevskii is largely forgotten now, at the time he was establishing a solid reputation as a composer. The renowned conductor Sergei Koussevitzky included several of Bazilevskii's works in his concerts and proposed to perform the young composer's operatic rendering of Blok's play. Although the plan never came to fruition, it did have at least one important consequence. Bazilevskii asked Blok to write a short note about the play for Koussevitzky's program. Blok's note, of course, never appeared in any of Koussevitzky's programs; however, it formed the basis of an explanatory note that appeared in the press at the time of the Moscow Art Theater's production of *The Rose and the Cross* (4: 527-30). Bazilevskii's music was eventually performed for the Art Theater (Dinesman, 72), but it was rejected as too operatic and too modernist (Dinesman, 81).

At about the same time, the Art Theater was considering other composers for *The Rose and the Cross.* Luzhskii, in a letter to Blok, mentioned two in particular, Sergei Vasilenko and Boris Ianovskii (Dinesman, 72-3). Blok responded, "Everything that you write about Dobuzhinskii and Vasilenko makes me happy" (8: 460). A collaboration with Vasilenko, a professor at the Moscow Conservatory, pleased Blok because the composer was deeply interested in medieval music and poetry. The subject matter of Blok's play and Vasilenko's cycle "The Songs of the Troubadours of XII-XIV centuries" pointed to a commonality of purpose. Despite these convergences, Vasilenko turned down the Art Theater's offer for reasons that remain unclear. Ianovskii, by contrast, proved an avid collaborator, composing music for most the play, in fact. The quality of the compositions, however, appears to have come into question, and Luzhskii and Nemirovich-Danchenko did not avail themselves of Ianovskii's work.

From the beginning, Nemirovich-Danchenko attributed great importance to the music, and he now set his sights higher: He invited Sergei Rachmaninov to compose the music (Freidkina, 319). Rachmaninov in the end refused, but Nemirovich-Danchenko was still trying to persuade him four months later. His persistence suggests the high value the theater put not only on the music, but on Blok's play itself. Despite his refusal, Rachmaninov, by all accounts, was quite interested in *The Rose and the Cross*, and the contention that Rachmaninov

---

[25] For more on the Kharkov staging, see below.

dismissed Blok's work because of its Symbolist tendencies appears misguided (see Khoprova, 61). In fact, the composer made some interesting observations. Nemirovich-Danchenko and Rachmaninov decided that "music in the ordinary sense, as this is always done, is not needed here at all." In its stead, the director and composer proposed "a splendid romance of genius (of a Scriabinesque tone) for Gaètan," and instead of an orchestra, "a combination of some three, four, five instruments (violin, cello, piano) in the hands of *splendid* musicians." Rachmaninov also recommended to Nemirovich-Danchenko another composer, Nikolai Metner (Nemirovich-Danchenko, 2: 190-1). Metner, however, also turned down Nemirovich-Danchenko's offer.

Next, the services of the composer Mikhail Gnesin were enlisted. Blok, however, reacted negatively to his compositions, especially his theme for Gaètan. In his notebook, Blok is emphatic: "*Not* Gnesin (or at least not his Gaètan)" (Blok 1965, 287). Eventually, the Art Theater turned to Sergei Pototskii, who later became the head of the music section for the Second theater. The score suggests that in all likelihood, Pototskii built on Gnesin's work (Polkanova, 5: 68). When finished, Pototskii's music garnered a generally favorable reaction (Polkanova, 5: 63).[26]

As if problems within the theater were not enough, the production was plagued from start to finish by problems from without. Complications arose in regard to Blok's participation. Work was slowed in the early stages when both Blok and Dobuzhinskii were drafted. At a later stage, Blok was so overwhelmed by bureaucratic responsibilities assigned to him by the new government after the revolution that he had to refuse an invitation from Stanislavskii in the fall of 1918. As a result, interest in *The Rose and the Cross* dissipated somewhat (Bertenson, 256). Then too, pressure from the censors did not end with the revolution. Whereas prerevolutionary censors objected to the possibly blasphemous connotations of the cross imagery, postrevolutionary censors worried that the quashing of a popular rebellion would send the wrong message to a revolutionary society (Stroeva 1977, 19). In the end, the greatest complication was precipitated by the civil war. A small group from the Art Theater, led by Kachalov and Bertenson, went on tour in the south of Russia. They soon found themselves caught behind White Army lines. Unable to return to Moscow, they spent the next several years on tour in Europe. Although Stanislavskii had stopped rehearsing *The Rose and the Cross* on 13 December, 1918, months before the departure of Kachalov and company, hope remained that the play would be mounted the following season (Freidkina, 340). Without Kachalov, those hopes were dashed.

These problems, taken together, proved insurmountable. All told, the Moscow Art Theater held over two hundred rehearsals of *The Rose and the Cross*; yet, the key to a successful production was never found. As one critic has noted, *The Rose and the Cross* was one of more than ten plays for which the Art Theater failed to find "the means of artistic expression" (Markov, 142). The overly long intermissions of Nemirovich-Danchenko's production and the inability of the Art Theater to effect Stanislavskii's stylization doomed the play. Despite this failure,

---

[26] Undoubtedly, the most important composer to actually undertake a score for *The Rose and the Cross* is Al'fred Schnittke, who composed the music for a projected television production of the play in either 1962 (Ivashkin, 297) or 1969 (Èlik, 261).

Nemirovich-Danchenko apparently never completely gave up on the play. At several different times in later years, productions of *The Rose and the Cross* were discussed. For instance, in 1923, Nemirovich-Danchenko promised to help the Second studio with a production that was never realized (Freidkina, 372). Nemirovich-Danchenko was not content, however, to leave the play to the studio theater. Writing in 1924, the first chronicler of the Art Theater asserted, "I know that Nemirovich-Danchenko is again dreaming about *The Rose and the Cross*" (Èfros, 304). Nemirovich-Danchenko pursued this dream for some time. Over a year later the repertory-artistic board of the Art Theater selected *The Rose and the Cross* for "preliminary discussion" (Markov, 526). Discussions, however, never got past the preliminary stage.

Blok always pinned his hopes for *The Rose and the Cross* on the Moscow Art Theater. However, the spring before Blok's death brought with it an intensification of the illness that would eventually kill him. In dire financial straits, he cast about for money and permission to go abroad in order to recuperate. Primarily out of financial need, Blok asked for an advance on the still unrealized production from the Moscow Theater while he was in Moscow on a reading tour. The three hundred thousand rubles the theater offered did little to alleviate Blok's financial woes. With part of the troupe abroad and separated from the main troupe by the civil war, Stanislavskii and Nemirovich-Danchenko conceded that *The Rose and the Cross* could not be taken up again until the entire troupe was back and together in Moscow.

Out of concern for Blok's condition, they helped Blok sell the play to the former Nezlobin Theater, officially the second theater of the Moscow Union of Popular Education [MONO]. The negotiations proved to be involved, but they proceeded quickly. Semen Brailovskii, who negotiated on behalf of the Nezlobin theater, at first offered a sum of no more than one-and-a-half million rubles. Stanislavskii felt that this offer was too low and turned to the Korsh Theater. On behalf of the latter, Morits Shlugleit offered half a million up front if Blok agreed to break off negotiations with the Nezlobin. When Brailovskii heard about the Korsh offer, he immediately set out to find Blok, who was still in Moscow for a reading. The next morning Brailovskii showed up at Blok's door with an agreement and a million rubles. (See 7: 418-9).

Of the nine conditions set forth in the contract, eight favor Blok and only one the Nezlobin Theater. Being unfamiliar with both the theater and its management, Blok was careful to safeguard both his artistic and financial interests. In regard to the latter, he secured the sum of two million rubles, half of which was to be paid as an advance. In regard to the former, he reserved final judgment on every aspect of the production, from casting to the director. He went so far as to stipulate that the stage design and costumes were to be prepared from the sketches Dobuzhinskii had made for the Moscow Art Theater. In return, Blok agreed to prohibit the production of the play by any other Moscow theater for a period of two years. (For the text of the 10 May, 1921 agreement, see Superfin and Timenchik, 411. See also 8: 539.) As was the case at the Moscow Art Theater, complications arose, and the production at the Nezlobin was not realized. By the end of the following season, the Nezlobin Theater was a thing of the past, and Nezlobin himself had left for Riga (Zolotnitskii, 103).

However, *The Rose and the Cross* did make it to the stage during Blok's lifetime, and therein lies a certain irony: Although Blok carefully distanced himself from the leading experimental directors, including Vakhtangov, Tairov, and Meyerhold, the first productions were staged by their lesser followers in the provinces. For example, the first two productions of *The Rose and the Cross* took place in a Kharkov studio theater. Pavel Il'in, the director of the studio, sought to keep up with the latest developments in theater and was considered "a progressive-minded person for his time" by his most illustrious pupil (Iutkevich, 520). As one scholar has noted in regard to the studio theater production of a play by Jacinto Benavente y Martinez, Il'in worked "under the obvious influence of the directorial devices of Meyerhold, whose theoretical works he followed attentively" (Dolinskii 1976, 43). Il'in apparently approached *The Rose and the Cross* differently, although he still put a premium on the modernity of the staging: "The play was staged sparingly in the style of Gordon Craig's Shakespearean productions" (Dolinskii 1976, 44). Il'in's studio attracted the best actors in Kharkov, some of whom went on to achieve national recognition. Foremost among them was Dmitrii Orlov, who started as Aliscans and eventually worked his way up to the role of Bertran (Orlov, 55). Behind the scenes, a teenager named Sergei Iutkevich honed the skills that would one day bring him renown as a film director (Dolinskii 1976, 43-5). Blok knew about the Kharkov production (Blok 1965, 247) and replied to the studio theater's request to stage *The Rose and the Cross*: "I have nothing against a production of it in an intimate theater," but cautioned against the play's difficulty (Sholomova, 5: 46). The Kharkov production of *The Rose and the Cross* was successful, entering into the studio's repertory (Sholomova, 5: 47).

Il'in's production, for all its success, was still an amateur staging. The first production of *The Rose and the Cross* by a professional troupe took place just months before Blok's death. Iurii Bondi, Meyerhold's co-director on the 1914 production of *A Puppet Show* and *The Stranger*, staged *The Rose and the Cross* in Kostroma at the municipal theater during the 1920-21 season. This was not the first time Bondi had attempted to put on Blok's play. While working at the Malyi Dramatic Theater in 1919, he approached Blok in regard to *The Rose and the Cross* (Blok 1965, 472). Blok refused Bondi (Blok 1965, 473), but the director persevered. After the revolution, the Malyi went on tour and eventually made their way to Kostroma. Some members of the troupe, including Bondi, decided to remain in Kostroma, and it was in this way that the opportunity to stage *The Rose and the Cross* finally materialized. The production enjoyed a small measure of success, running for a total of fifteen performances. As was the case for productions of Blok's other plays, audience reaction was mixed, although memoirists suggest that many spectators returned to see the play more than once. They also suggest that Blok knew of the production, but the poet left behind no indication of his attitude toward Bondi's production (Dolinskii 1985, 189; see also Dolgopolov, 4: 593).

Even without documentary evidence, Blok's attitude is hardly mysterious. Although Blok was well disposed toward Bondi personally, he rejected the director's modernism. His refusal of the offer from the Malyi stemmed from questions of repertoire and approach. Bondi remained a proponent of modernist theater and Meyerholdian theater in particular, despite problems in his personal relationship with Meyerhold. The Kostroma production could hardly have satisfied Blok because Bondi employed many of the techniques he had learned while working with Meyerhold. In fact, accounts of Bondi's staging sound as if they could have been lifted out of descriptions of a Meyerhold production. For example, one spectator wrote, "Everything here was unexpected and new: the proscenium, the entrance of the actors through the curtain, the special towers by the sides of the portals, the violet-rose-green color, the fantasy decoration, and, the most important thing, the theatrical servants" (cited by Rubtsov, 115). This impression is bolstered by program notes written by Iurii Bondi's brother, Sergei, who insisted, "This production of *The Rose and the Cross* is built on the principle of renouncing 'realism' and the imitation of real life" (cited by Dolgopolov, 4: 593). Bondi and company were clearly abreast of the latest developments in theater; however, their production in isolated Kostroma produced no resonance in the theatrical centers, and its influence was negligible.

Even the relatively successful productions of *The Rose and the Cross* by Il'in and Bondi fail to overshadow the failed productions attempted by Stanislavskii, Meyerhold, and Tairov. Blok's antipathy toward modernist theater explains why Meyerhold and Tairov were unable to bring productions to fruition. It does not, however, explain the protracted collapse of the play at the Moscow Art Theater. There, the reasons stemmed largely from difficulties inherent in the play itself. Practitioners of the theater who have studied *The Rose and the Cross* generally agree about the nature of those difficulties. For example, the artist Dobuzhinskii attributed complications in the play's production to its numerous settings and concomitant scene changes (Dobuzhinskii, 256). The director Nikolai Evreinov echoed Dobuzhinskii when he wrote, "... Works that are too spectacular are not to the playwright's advantage. For example, Blok's *The Rose and the Cross* is not playing anywhere because of this" (cited by Timenchik, 5: 30).

Yet, what constricts in one medium may yield in another. The cumbersome set designs and scene changes that burdened the theater might provide fertile soil for the cinema, for example. Perhaps out of considerations such as these, Meyerhold returned to *The Rose and the Cross* and was the first to discern in Blok's play a film (Fevral'skii, 56). Blok, an avid moviegoer, was intrigued by the idea (8: 482.) Meyerhold arranged a meeting with Paul Thiemann, who had founded a movie company together with Max Reinhardt. Blok and Thiemann, after some haggling, came to an agreement (Blok 1965, 320). Despite their agreement, the film was never made. However, a director from Thiemann's company, Nikolai Volkov, did not give up (Dolinskii 1985, 307). After leaving Thiemann's employ and not long after Blok's death, Volkov approached Mstislav Dobuzhinskii in regard to the art direction of a proposed film version of *The Rose and the Cross*. Volkov's movie, like Meyerhold's, remained unfilmed. Nonetheless, his tenacity points to an untapped potential in the play.

The period immediately after Blok's death proved barren ground for *The Rose and the Cross*. Perhaps because it deals with a period of cultural crisis, the play was not taken up by any of the major theaters in the twenties. The literature of the new society looked to the new man and had no time for Bertran's Hamlet-like self-lacerations. Theater, like the society it issued from, became revolutionary. Matinées were replaced by mass demonstrations. In this regard, it is difficult to suppress the impression that a certain consonance exists between the creator and his creation. Blok too stood at a crossroads, that of the naturalistic and the modernist theaters. At different times, he was sympathetic to both, but belonged to neither. What Meyerhold or Vakhtangov or Tairov could have done with *The Rose and the Cross* is, in a certain sense, a moot point. Blok's decision not to work with them, however, is not. In the end it was precisely Blok's refusals that may have done the most harm to his reputation as a playwright.

CONCLUSION:
BLOK AS DRAMATIST

I

After The Rose and the Cross

The Rose and the Cross marks a milestone in Blok's career: With his fifth play, Blok's dramatic output diminished to a trickle and nearly ceased altogether. His life in drama and theater did not end; however, it underwent an important shift, a shift away from creative work. In other areas of theatrical life, Blok's involvement continued unchanged or even increased. For example, his very personal interest in actresses did not abate and found an outlet in an affair with the opera singer Liubov' Andreeva-Del'mas. His professional interest in theater also found outlets. As his involvement in the proposed Moscow Art Theater production of *The Rose and the Cross* attests, Blok remained profoundly interested in the workings of theater itself.

After the revolution, this interest was channelled into administrative work. Blok served on the Theatrical-Literary Commission, the Theatrical Division of the People's Commissariat for Education [Narkompros], the board of directors for the Bol'shoi Dramatic Theater in Petrograd, and the short-lived Theatrical Soviet (Ivanova, 5: 134-222 passim, and Gerasimov, 321-43 passim). He eventually became chair of both the Repetory Section for the Theatrical Division and of the board of directors for the Bolshoi Dramatic Theater. Blok worked tirelessly, attending meetings, drafting protocols, giving speeches to actors about dramatic tradition from Shakespeare to Mæterlinck and reviewing plays by everyone from Kuzmin to Meyerhold. His diaries and notebooks in the years after the revolution are eloquent testimony to a superhuman capacity for committee work. The enormous amount of time and energy consumed by such administrative work is astounding. One scholar suggests that Blok's work in the Theatrical Division alone took away "almost a year of his creative life" (Ivanova, 5: 134). A simple lack of time partly explains the precipitous decline Blok's creative output after the revolution.

That decline was not an absolute cessation, however, in terms of either poetry or drama. Blok turned to drama for the last time at the behest of the "Commission on the Compilation of Historical Tableaux." Under the aegis of Gorkii's publishing house World Literature, the commission sought to illustrate world history through a series of historical dramas and appealed to some of the foremost writers of the day. Little came of the venture, and Zamiatin's *Attila* is probably the only work of literary merit to issue from it. However, as one critic has pointed out, the size and ambition of the project are typical of the period just after the revolution (Volkov 1926, 137). The range of subjects, for example, just in what Blok undertook is formidable. He sketched out drafts and plans for periods as far flung as ancient Egypt, medieval Provence, Rimini during the Renaissance, and Russia both at the battle of Kulikovo and during Ivan Kalita's reign. Blok clearly sought to build on the history he knew intimately, and almost all of these drafts have some relation to earlier work. In the Provence play, Blok sought to explore the same territory he had mapped out in *The Rose and the Cross*. The Kulikovo play marks a clear return to the themes of his cycle *On the Field of Kulikovo*. Given the importance of that cycle to *The Song of Fate*, the Kulikovo play might have had an intrinsic relation to Blok's fourth play. The other drafts are tied to Blok's work more tenuously. The image of Ivan Kalita, for example, appears in only one poem (3: 131-2). Likewise, the ties of the play set in Rimini to Blok's earlier work are loose. However, one commentator suggests that the theme of this play has nonetheless "a remote and very indistinct correspondence in the theme of Italy, which finds expression in lyric poetry in *The Italian Verses* and in prose in *Lightningbolts of Art*" (Fedorov 1980, 167). Other plans point to favorite themes. The fragment based on the legend of Tristan and Isolde, for example, reflects Blok's longstanding interest not only in medieval legend, but in Wagner as well.

Surprisingly, none of the projects with an organic basis in Blok's work came to fruition. Blok, despite his many attempts, completed only one play. Seemingly distant from all of his previous work and adjudged "unreadable" even by those sympathetic to the poet (Pyman 1980, 2: 338), *Ramses* reveals nothing so much as Blok's utter incapacity for didactic forms. And yet, he saw didacticism, broadly construed, as the goal not just of *Ramses*, but of all the historical tableaux in the World Literature series. The impasse between educated and uneducated, Blok argued, could only be surmounted through enlightenment. For this, "... newer and newer means are being sought to enlighten life, to put it in order, to solder life and education into one. Pedagogy proposes new means of teaching, in the form, for example, of the theatricalization of it. Theater has been recognized as a powerful means of enlightenment (in Russia, in essence, for the first time)..." (6: 422). Blok tempers these remarks, suggesting that theater cannot be purely the instrument of enlightenment. Above all, Blok hoped to inculcate in the audience a sense of history as something personal. He refers with approbation, for instance, to Carlyle's ideas on the importance of individuality in history. Blok's approach to history must surely have raised eyebrows and ruffled feathers amongst Marxist purists, but his exposition is unequivocal.

Oddly, Blok followed his own dicta only haltingly in *Ramses*. Set in Thebes in the reign of Ramses II, the play offers nothing that would allow this history to become something personal to the audience. None of the dramatis personae, for example, develop beyond the limits of character type. If Carlyle's ideas about the individual in history make any impression here at all, it is a purely negative one. Composed in prose, the play is prosaic in conception and lacks precisely what Blok said the historical tableaux must have, namely "that poetic feeling, which makes the whole world intimate and familiar and, by means of that, more mysterious and fascinating" (6: 424). Formal problems plague the play as well. The seamless integration of sources that characterizes *The Rose and the*

Cross is alien to *Ramses*, and the impression that it is a lightly dramatized version of the scholarly books Blok used in his research becomes overwhelming as the play progresses.[1] As Volkov observes sharply, *Ramses* "is not in its essence the work of a playwright since no dramatic principle sets its flow in motion" (Volkov 1926, 140). A brief synopsis will clarify Volkov's point:

The curtain opens on the market square with the house of the town governor, Psaru. As the play begins, Psaru complains that his stomach hurts, that his head burns, and that he has a bitter taste in his mouth. He upbraids his steward Khamoizit. While Psaru was away on the Pharaoh's business, Khamoizit, it seems, was carousing and not tending to his duties. In the course of the ensuing incriminations and self-justifications, the two characters inform the audience about the political unrest in Thebes. Khamoizit, for example, reminds Psaru, "You know, master, that the workers on the new construction projects are constantly in revolt" (4: 250). With the exposition of the political situation completed, Psaru's house guest makes an entrance. Psaru explains that he cannot show his guest around the city due to ill health. He entrusts his guest to Khamoizit and retires to his house.

The next scene, which is not separate from the scene that precedes it or the ones that follow, depicts their tour of the market square. It is in this scene that Volkov's criticism becomes particularly pertinent. Khamoizit and the guest do not say a word to each other as they make their way around the square. The multitudinous and variegated square offers ample opportunity for the depiction of a sociological cross section of ancient Egyptian society. Lacking dialogue, however, the scene is better suited to screen than stage: It takes place in its entirety in Blok's stage directions. The scene comes to an end with Khamoizit, laden with the guest's purchases, ushering his charge into Psaru's house as eager merchants swoop down and circle this wealthy prey.

After Khamoizit and the guest retire, the square is filled with people strolling by. From amongst the crowd, a Clerk emerges and walks up to an Officer, whom he engages in conversation. Each of them bemoans his lot in life and rails against the injustice of the Pharaoh's state. They are followed by a Prophet who tells of the woe awaiting Egypt and its people. Psaru makes the mistake of looking out of his window at the wrong moment and gets the evil eye from the doom-saying Prophet. Psaru ducks back in, but too late. He is soon confronted by a crowd of masons who complain of hunger and ask for his help. At first, he puts them off; however, when he learns that the Pharaoh is coming, Psaru compels Khamoizit to open his own grain stores to the masons.

Ramses then makes his entrance, and Psaru prostrates himself before the Pharaoh until the latter allows him to arise. Ramses, his wife, and daughter hang heavy necklaces around Psaru's neck in recognition of his good services. Psaru, who can hardly stand up under the weight of the valuables, sings in praise of the Pharaoh. Upon learning of a disturbance in another part of his kingdom, Ramses leaves. In his wake, Psaru collapses and is carried away from the square. News of his quick death reaches the square in short order. The crowd then turns on the

[1] The first draft, in fact, is littered with references to Boris Turaev's work on ancient Egypt. It is perhaps telling that Blok begins his notes to the published version of the play with the admission that the "scenes" were compiled from the work of Gaston Masperot and Turaev.

Prophet who gave Psaru the evil eye. It remains to Khamoizit to arrange for the embalming of Psaru's body. In the last scene, he haggles with embalmers, and news of the Prophet's death comes. A voice in the crowd cries out, "For a dog, a dog's death!" As evening approaches, the play ends, and Sirius, the Dog Star, looms on the horizon.

Ramses departs so radically from Blok's other plays that it seems barely credible that it could have issued from the same pen. And yet, it did, of course. Closer examination, in fact, points to certain parallels between *Ramses* and the earlier plays, especially*The King on the Square*, the only other play in which Blok addresses the problem of political power directly. It is no coincidence that Meyerhold planned at one point to stage *Ramses* and *The King on the Square* together as part of an evening of Blok's work. Meyerhold's plan went unrealized, but he astutely assessed the kinship between the two plays (Dolgopolov, 4: 574, 594). In both a few have concentrated power into their own hands, and the many do their bidding. Those few rule in the name of a greater power, before which the many bow. That power manifests itself ritually, whether in the form of idolatry of the living or the inanimate.

Such thematic, and relatively superficial similarities, give way to reveal deeper, generic affinities. Volkov points out, for example, that the grotesque plays a pivotal role in *Ramses.* Blok prepares for the grotesque in his characterizations. For instance, Psaru, who is small and stout, finds his comic opposite in Khamoizit, who is long and gaunt.[2] The grotesque makes itself elsewhere too. Volkov argues that the scene, in which the Prophet first proclaims the doom of Egypt and then gives Psaru the evil eye, is informed by what he calls the "device of the *sublime et grotesque.*" In yet another instance, Volkov sees the grotesque in the scene in which Ramses ladens Psaru with valuables. Although Volkov does not argue the point explicitly, he also notes the contrast between Psaru's comic death and the tragic murder of the Prophet (Volkov 1926, 141-44). By their gradual accumulation, these grotesque elements hearken back to the earlier plays, even if they never come to inform *Ramses* as grotesque elements informed Blok's best plays. As different from Blok's other plays as it may seem at first blush, though, *Ramses* clearly flows from the same spring.

Nonetheless, *Ramses* follows another channel and departs radically from the earlier plays. Whereas all of the major plays, except *The Song of Fate*, center around a triangle of two men and a woman, *Ramses* does not. Its focus on the socio-political is narrow, and the absence of any sense of personal life renders it one-dimensional. It also lacks the ideological complexity of the other plays. The Prophet may herald the demise of Egypt, but he in no way questions its underlying belief system. Even the Clerk and the Officer, for all their complaining, blame fate, not Egypt. None of these characters assume the masks of the fool, the rogue, or the clown, which all figure prominently in the other plays. There is only the ideology of the state. This generally reductive tendency separates *Ramses* from Blok's other plays, and nowhere is this so clear as in the ending. The symbol of the Dog Star, which foretells the fall of Egyptian civilization, deteriorates into allegory. Rigid, heavy-handed, this use of Sirius betrays a clumsiness uncharacteristic of Blok. Such infelicities, so rarely met elsewhere in his work, are

---

[2] It is on the basis of such traits as this that leads Volkov to define the play as a comedy. (Volkov 1926, 141).

accompanied by the absence of Blok's characteristic strengths. Seen from this vantage point, the play suffers from the surprising absence of female characters. After the revolution, Blok's enervation as a creative artist never asserted itself so strongly as it does here. That the poet of the Beautiful Lady and the Stranger could renounce the feminine presence in his work altogether signals a decline. It is as though Blok's art died alongside Katya in *The Twelve*.

The drafts for other plays that Blok left behind are similarly disengaged. In the drafts for the other historical tableaux, Blok seems to go over ground he has already covered. Aside from the historical tableaux, there is also extant a draft for a play Blok thought to call *The Boat*. It is something of a curiosity because in it, Blok eschews what had been his increasing predilection for realism and reverts to a manner that at one and same time is reminiscent of early Symbolism and looks ahead to futuristic works like Zamiatin's *We*. Blok conceived of the play as a battle between culture and the elements, a conflict that informs much of his work both before and after the revolution. A family finds itself on the banks of a river in a barren land. Across the river, which they hope to cross, lies a "blue country". From their side of the river, the family can make out a land filled with fruit and peaceable animals. Their repeated attempts to ford the river end in failure and the drowning of one of them. Subject to attacks by wild beasts, the family eventually takes to the trees. The fragment that Blok left behind ends with the images of the children perishing when attacked by a wild beast, of a serpent, and of hunger. The difference between the mythical setting of this fragment and and the impulse toward historical accuracy in the historical tableaux is profound. *The Boat* brings to mind the plays of Leonid Andreev, not the realism of Maksim Gor'kii. Perhaps more than anything else Blok wrote in his last years, *The Boat* bears witness to a Symbolism that Blok could never completely renounce.

Yet for all his activity on behalf of the theater and all of the unfinished drafts he left behind, Blok's career as a dramatist had come to end with *Ramses*. The year 1918 saw a new edition of Blok's *Theater*, which brought together the trilogy of lyrical dramas and *The Rose and the Cross*, and with 1919 came the publication of the revised *Song of Fate*. *Ramses* finally came out in 1921. Editorial and administrative work replaced creative work. All that remained to Blok after the revolution, it appears, was tidying up.

II

Blok's Place in Russian Drama

Blok's preeminence as a poet brooks no opposition. His place, his reputation, his legacy as a playwright, on the other hand, yield to question after question. If discussion is limited to just his own plays, then three of them — *A Puppet Show*, *The Stranger*, and *The Rose and the Cross* — safeguard for Blok a major place in the history of Russian drama.[3] *The Rose and the Cross*, in fact, is

[3] Blok's place in the history of Russian theater, on the other hand, is more modest, largely because of his decision not to work with modernist directors on *The Song of*

arguably the finest play of the period. Economical, if not Shakespearean, in structure, infused with the essence of Blok's lyricism, *The Rose and the Cross* attains an immediacy, in spite of its medieval setting, that the esoteric revivals of Greek drama and theater by Ivanov and Annenskii lack; its attention to detail, both historical and psychological, rescue it from the abstraction that mars many of the best plays by Sologub and Andreev; its moral and psychological incisiveness lend it a depth that is missing from Kuzmin's enchanting, but coquettish, dramas; its tragedy transcends moralism and could not be more antithetical to Gor'kii's work.

Viewed in relation to the theater of his day, Blok occupies a unique position. Nearly every director of note expressed interest in staging one or more of Blok's plays. Figures as disparate as Meyerhold, Stanislavskii, Nemirovich-Danchenko, Tairov, Vakhtangov, Evreinov, Mardzhanov, and Komissarzhevskii recognized Blok's importance for the stage. Then too, Blok, sometimes successfully, sometimes not, dealt with the leading theaters of his day: the Moscow Art Theater, the Komissarzhevskaia Theater, the Starinnyi, the Kamernyi, and even the Aleksandrinskii. For his contemporaries, if not for posterity, Blok was a commanding theatrical presence. Even Stanislavskii, whose doubts about Blok's plays were manifest, gave Nemirovich-Danchenko to understand that Blok and Andreev were the foremost Russian playwrights of their day (Nemirovich-Danchenko, 2: 186). Nemirovich-Danchenko went further and implicitly put Blok on the same footing as Chekhov. For the twentieth anniversary of the Moscow Art Theater, he even proposed that the rose and the cross be adopted as emblems of the theater. On one side of the stage, a curtain with the Chekhov seagull would mark the first twenty years of the Art Theater, and on the other side Blok's rose and cross would point to its future (Freidkina, 332; Polkanova, 5: 64). With the failure of the Art Theater's production of *The Rose and the Cross*, such a proposal became untenable. The very fact of the proposal itself, however, should give us pause.

To some extent, Nemirovich-Danchenko may have been paying tribute to a great poet, and not a dramatist. Blok's drama suffers, if compared to Chekhov's. In part, this judgment issues from the consistency of Chekhov's achievement: Once Chekhov hit stride, he never faltered. From *The Seagull* to *The Cherry Orchard*, Chekhov delivered— and delivered as have only a very few. Blok's dramas, by comparison, chart a course through peaks and valleys. *The King on the Square* and *The Song of Fate*, though fascinating in their failure, disclose an unresolved poetic, one still in the making. Even the consummation of that poetic in *The Rose and the Cross* is undermined by *Ramses*, which vouchsafes its dissolution.

To no small degree, the persuasiveness of Chekhov's poetic derives to some extent from actual productions, from his interaction with a real theater. To disengage Chekhov from the Moscow Art Theater is to dabble in abstraction. Undoubtedly Chekhov's plays would have commanded a reading audience had they not been performed, but it was through the conduit of the Moscow Art Theater that

---

Fate and *The Rose and the Cross*. However, the Fomenko Studio's 1994 production of *A Puppet Show* and *The Stranger* attested to the relevance of Blok's work to contemporary theater. The production, which ran under the common title *A Puppet Show* and which was directed by Ivan Popovski, fit into a cultural trend: the assimilation of the culture of the Silver Age. In this respect, Blok's dramas may have a significant role to play in the development of post-Soviet, Russian theater.

they reached a worldwide audience. Chekhov, after all, was a staple not only at home for Stanislavskii and Nemirovich-Danchenko's troupe, but also abroad. On both European and American tours, Chekhov's plays became a focal point for the Moscow Art Theater. The troupe's work on the Chekhov plays also became a proving ground for Stanislavskii's much vaunted system. For better or worse, the constellation of Chekhov's plays, the Moscow Art Theater, and the Stanislavskii system attained a luminosity that made their conjunction seem inevitable. By means of these associations, Chekhov's plays reached and influenced audiences they would otherwise have missed. Chekhov's reputation, especially his international reputation, grew because the Moscow Art Theater in a sense proselytized in the name of the Chekhovian gospel.

Blok's reputation is likewise tied to the theaters that staged and tried to stage his work, and no matter how much Blok railed against Meyerhold and his ideas in later years, he owes no small part of his reputation as a dramatist to the founder of biomechanics. Meyerhold's production of *A Puppet Show* at the Komissarzhevskaia Theater marks a pivotal moment in the history of Russian modernism. *A Puppet Show* upended more than just the immediate targets of its parody: an entire system of imperial theaters toppled down with the scenery around Pierrot. The constraints and limitations of the imperial theaters, their histrionic actors and their officially approved plays, were knocked down by Meyerhold with the battering ram of Blok's little play. After *A Puppet Show*, only the militantly obtuse could return to the theater and fail see its artifice anew. In an important sense, *A Puppet Show* at the Komissarzhevskaia Theater is the first step on a road that would lead to Meyerhold's appointment as a director in the imperial theaters several years later.

Meyerhold's later production of *A Puppet Show* and *The Stranger* at the Tenishev school auditorium in 1914 also advanced Blok's reputation, but for somewhat different reasons. Limited as it was to a restricted cross section of the theater-going public, the production did not make Blok the playwright a household name. Rather, the production grew in importance in posterity, when Meyerhold pointed to it as the first bloom of constructivist theater. From the construction of the bridge in the second vision to the servants of the proscenium whose kneeling figures and raised candles formed human footlights to the acrobatics and the juggled oranges of the intermission, Meyerhold's endless capacity for invention added polish to the plays' inherent luster. As Meyerhold's reputation grew, so did that of the plays by dint of association.

Meyerhold, in fact, proved a more strident advocate for Blok than Stanislavskii for Chekhov. Blok figures prominently in Meyerhold's writings before the revolution. The very similarity between the titles of Meyerhold's seminal article, "A Puppet Show" or "Balagan", and Blok's play, *A Puppet Show* or *Balaganchik*, speaks volumes. True, as would any major artist, Meyerhold recast Blok in his own image, but Blok's own qualities are still apparent. Meyerhold's Blok is an iconoclast, who returns to the traditions of the *commedia dell'arte* and the romantic theater in order resuscitate theater as theater. As late as 1930, Meyerhold would insist, "Blok interested me because his plays all were built on theatrical devices..." (Meierkhol'd 1968b, 231). Meyerhold's vision of Blok proved so persuasive that Blok the playwright is usually thought of as the author of *A Puppet Show*. Certainly for their contemporaries, Blok and Meyerhold were inextricably bound to one another. When Evgenii Vakhtangov, who has been characterized as "a poet of theater, a Blok of the stage" (Smirnov-Nesvitskii, 550), expressed his admiration for Meyerhold, he singled out his productions of Blok's plays (Vakhtangov, 326).

Counterbalance to Meyerhold's Blok should have come in the form of the Moscow Art Theater production of *The Rose and the Cross*, but did not, of course. The failure of the production turned out to be disastrous not only for Stanislavskii, Nemirovich-Danchenko, and their struggling troupe, but also for Blok's subsequent reputation as a playwright. If Stanislavskii could not stage *The Rose and the Cross* — or so the argument would seem to run — then who could? The failure of *The Rose and the Cross* in Stanislavskii's hands played in to old biases. It lent credence to the idea that Symbolist plays were meant to be read, not acted.

Without doubt, *The Rose and the Cross* presents the theater a challenge, but to pronounce it unstageable is to ignore how unsuited Stanislavskii and Nemirovich-Danchenko were to the play. Stanislavskii, of course, recognized this when he refused to stage the play when Blok first presented it to him. Well aware of his own predilection for Chekhovian mood and psychology, he seemed to understand that, although psychologically consistent, *The Rose and the Cross* was not impressionist or psychological drama. His assessment of the play and of his ability to stage it showed an uncanny astuteness. When Blok left behind the hearth of nineteenth-century Russian literature, he attended less and less to individual psychology and more and more to social upheaval. Even *The Song of Fate* follows not so much the fate of one man as that of an epoch. Similarly, Bertran interests Blok not because of his complex psychology, but because his life is emblematic of his time, an epoch at a crossroads, caught between opposing historical forces, the emblems of which are the rose and the cross. In this context, Stanislavskii's desire to elicit each character's past as a guide to motivation could not have been more misplaced.

Blok, in the final analysis, must bear considerable responsibility for the ebbing of his reputation as a dramatist. In a fundamental way, he misjudged his own art. He mistook a burgeoning interest in the social reality outside of him for realism in his own work. As a result, he set his sights on the most realistic director and theater available. Blok's insistence on realism bordered on the quixotic. Even the most cursory examination of his plays reveals how little they rely on realism: Bertran, as war approaches, sets off from southerly Provence in search of the singer of a song in northerly Brittany. Herman, happy and contented with Elena, abandons her just as soon as a monk has told him about Faina, a woman he has never met or talked to and will have to search for. The very artifice of these plots begs for the artifice of theater, not the illusion of reality.

Meyerhold implored Blok for a chance to stage *The Rose and the Cross*, and Vakhtangov and Tairov expressed ardent interest, but Blok gave them scant encouragement. Whether their productions would have altered the history of theater and the course of Blok's reputation is a magnificent, but sterile question. That Blok would have been better served by any of these directors than by Stanislavskii seems beyond debate. Perhaps it is fitting in the end that Blok's last plays, whose heroes seek but never find the fulfillment of their dreams, still await their ideal productions.

WORKS CITED

Aleksandr Blok. Novye materialy i issledovaniia. Literaturnoe nasledstvo, vol. 92, 5 books (Moskva: Nauka, 1980-93).

Alpers, Boris. "Teatr sotsial'noi maski." In his *Teatral'nye ocherki v dvukh tomakh. Tom pervyi. Teatral'nye monografii* (Moskva: Iskusstvo, 1977), 27-162.

Andreev, Leonid. Letter to Blok, 2 March, 1909. In Daniil Andreev and Vera Beklemisheva (eds.). *Rekviem. Sbornik pamiati Leonida Andreeva* (Moskva: Federatsiia, 1930), 86.

Andreeva, Mariia [Mariia Iurkovskaia-Zheliabuzhskaia]. Letter to Ivan Ladyzhnikov, Moscow, 4 December, 1913. In Konstantin Mardzhanov [Kotè Mardzhanishvili]. *Tvorcheskoe nasledie, pis'ma, vospominaniia, i stat'i o K.A. Mardzhanishvili* (Tbilisi: Literatura da khelovneba, 1966), 553.

Anichkov, Evgenii. *Vesenniaia obriadovaia poè ziia na Zapade i u slavian*, chast' I (Sankt-Peterburg, 1903).

Avel' [Lev Vasilevskii]. "Teatr Komissarzhevskoi." *Molodaia zhizn'*, no. 5, 2 January, 1907, 4.

Azov, Vladimir. [Vladimir Ashkinazi]. "Teatr Komissarzhevskoi. ('Balaganchik.' 'Chudo strannika Antoniia.')." *Rech'*, no. 1, January 1, 1907, 5.

B.G. [Boris Griftsov]. "'Roza i krest.'" *Sofiia* 1(1914): 128-30.

Bakhtin, Mikhail. [1965] 1986. *Tvorchestvo Fransua Rable i narodnaia kul'tura srednevekov'ia i renessansa* (Moskva: Khudozhestvennaia literatura, 1965; reprint, Orange, CT, Dusseldorf: Antikvariat, 1986).

Bakhtin, Mikhail. [1968] 1984a. *Rabelais and his World*, translated by Hélène Iswolsky (Cambridge, MA: MIT Press, 1968; reprint, Bloomington, IN: Indiana University Press, 1984).

Bakhtin, Mikhail. 1981a. "Discourse in the Novel." In his *The Dialogic Imagination*, translated by Michael Holquist and Caryl Emerson (Austin, TX: University of Texas Press, 1981), 259-422.

Bakhtin, Mikhail. 1981b. "Epic and Novel." In his *The Dialogic Imagination*, translated by Michael Holquist and Caryl Emerson (Austin, TX: University of Texas Press, 1981), 3-40.

Bakhtin, Mikhail. 1984b. *Problems of Dostoevsky's Poetics*, trans. and ed. Caryl Emerson, Theory and History of Literature, vol. 8 (Minneapolis, MN: Univ. of Minnesota Press, 1984).

Balakian, Anna. *The Symbolist Movement* (New York: New York University Press, 1977).

Barzaz-Breiz. *Chants populaires de la Bretagne*, 10th ed., compiled, translated, annotated by the Vicomte Hersart de la Villemarqué, (Paris: Perrin, 1903).

Bazarov, Vladimir. "Misteriia ili byt?" In *Krizis teatra* (Moskva: Problemy iskusstva, 1908), 54-81.

Beketova, Mariia. 1922. *Aleksandr Blok. Biograficheskii ocherk* (Peterburg: Alkonost, 1922).

Beketova, Mariia. 1982. "Iz 'dnevnika' M.A. Beketovoi." *Aleksandr Blok. Novye materialy i issledovaniia*, 3: 598-634.

Beliaev, Iurii. "Teatr Komissarzhevskoi. ('Balaganchik' A. Bloka. 'Chudo strannika Antoniia' M. Meterlinka)". *Novoe vremia*, no. 11067 (3 January, 1907): 13.

Belyi, Andrei [Boris Bugaev]. "Oblomki mirov. Liricheskie dramy Bloka," *Vesy* 5 (1908): 65-8.

Bennett, Virginia H. 1982a. "Russian *pagliacci*: Symbols of Profaned Love in *The Puppet Show*." *Drama and Symbolism*, Themes in Drama, vol. 4 (Cambridge: Cambridge University Press, 1982), 141-71.

Bennett, Virginia H., trans. 1982b. *The Puppet Show*, by Aleksandr Blok. *Drama and Symbolism*, Themes in Drama, vol. 4 (Cambridge: Cambridge University Press, 1982), 172-8.

Bertenson, Sergei [Bertensson]. *Vokrug iskusstva* (Hollywood: n.p., 1957).

Bezrodnyi, M. V. 1987. "Poètika èpigrafa (iz kommentariia k drame Bloka 'Neznakomka'". *Uchenye Zapiski Tartuskogo Universiteta* 748 (1987): 143-9.

Bezrodnyi, M. V. 1991. "O proekte postanovki 'Neznakomki' v Parizhe." In Iurii Gerasimov, N.Iu. Griakalova, and Aleksandr Lavrov (eds.). *Aleksandr Blok. Issledovaniia i materialy*. (Leningrad: "Nauka," 1991), 228-31.

Blok, Aleksandr. 1909. *Pesnia sud'by*. *Shipovnik* IX (1909): 193-252.

Blok, Aleksandr. 1925. *Pis'ma Aleksandra Bloka* (Leningrad: Kolos, 1925).

Blok, Aleksandr. 1927-32. *Pis'ma Bloka k rodnym*, 2 volumes. (Leningrad: Academia, 1927-32).

Blok, Aleksandr. 1960-3. *Sobranie sochinenii v vos'mi tomakh*. (Moskva-Leningrad: Gosudarstvennoe izdatel'stvo khudozhestvennoi literatury, 1960-63).

Blok, Aleksandr. 1964. "Neizvestnye pis'ma Bloka," edited by Iurii Gerasimov. In Iurii Lotman (ed.). *Blokovskii sbornik: Trudy konferentsii, posviashchennoi izucheniiu zhizni i tvorchestva A.A. Bloka, mai 1962 goda*, [vol. 1], (Tartu: Tartuskii gosudarstvennyi universitet, 1964), 522-9.

Blok, Aleksandr. 1965. *Zapisnye knizhki* (Moskva-Leningrad: Gosudarstvennoe Izdatel'stvo khudozhestvennoi literatury, 1965).

Blok, Aleksandr. 1978. *Pis'ma k zhene*. *Literaturnoe nasledstvo*. vol. 89, (Moskva: Nauka, 1978).

Blok, Aleksandr. 1981. *Teatr*, edited by Pavel Gromov (Leningrad: Sovetskii pisatel', 1981)

Blok, Aleksandr and Andrei Belyi [Boris Bugaev]. *Aleksandr Blok i Andrei Belyi. Perepiska* (Moscow: Goslitizdat, 1965).

Blok, Aleksandr and Valerii Briusov. "Perepiska Bloka s V.Ia. Briusovym (1903-1919)," edited by Iuliia Blagovolina. *Aleksandr Blok. Novye materialy i issledovaniia*, 1: 466-524.

Blok, Aleksandr, Anna Gorodetskaia, and Sergei Gorodetskii. "Perepiska s A.A. i S.M. Gorodetskimi," edited by Vladimir Enisherlov. *Aleksandr Blok. Novye materialy i issledovaniia*, 2: 5-62.

Blok, Aleksandr and Vladimir Piast [Pestovskii]. "Perepiska s Vl. Piastom," edited by Zinaida Mints. *Aleksandr Blok. Novye materialy i issledovaniia*, 2: 175-228.

Blok, Aleksandr and Aleksei Remizov. "Perepiska s A.M. Remizovym (1905-1920)," edited by Antonina Iulova. *Aleksandr Blok. Novye materialy i issledovaniia*, 2: 82-128.

Bongard-Levin, Grigorii. "Kalidasa u Aleksandra Bloka." In Boris Piotrovskii (ed.). *Sovetskaia kul'tura. 70 let razvitiia: K 80-letiiu akademika M.P. Kima* (Moskva: Nauka, 1987), 70-82.

Bonneau, Sophie. *Le Drame Lyrique d'Alexandre Blok.* Thèse Complémentaire proposée à la Faculté des Lettres de l'Université de Paris pour le Doctorat ès Lettres (Paris: Maurice Lavergne Imprimeur, 1946).

Bowra, Cecil Maurice. *From Virgil to Milton* (London: Macmillan & Co., 1945).

Chałacińska-Wiertelak, Halina. "Fenomen Teatru Błoka," *Zeszyty Naukowe Wydziału Humanistycznego Uniwersytetu Gdańskiego, Filologia rosyjska*, no. 14 (1985): 51-7.

Chałacińska-Wiertelak, Halina. "Poetyka sugestii: *Małe tragedie* Puszkina, *Buda Jarmarczna* Bloka." *Studia Rossica Posnaniensia*, vol. XVIII (1986): 57-63.

Chekhov, Anton. *Polnoe sobranie sochinenii i pisem v tridtsati tomakh* (Moskva: Izdatel'stvo "Nauka," 1974-83).

Chulkov, Georgii. "*The Puppet Show*," *Pereval*, 4 (1907): 51-3

Clayton, J. Douglas. *Pierrot in Petrograd* (Montreal and Kingston: McGill-Queen's University Press, 1993).

Clowes, Edith. "Characterization in *Doktor Zhivago*: Lara and Tonja." *Slavic and East European Journal* 34, no. 3 (1990): 322-31.

Debreczeny, Paul. *The Other Pushkin: A Study of Alexander Pushkin's Prose Fiction* (Stanford, CA: Stanford University Press, 1983).

Diez, Friedrich. *Leben und Werke der Troubadours: Ein Beitrag zur nähern Kenntnis des Mettelalters* (Zwickau: Gebruder Schumann, 1829).

Dinesman, Tat'iana (ed.). "Pis'ma k Bloku uchastnikov postanovki dramy 'Roza i krest'". *Aleksandr Blok. Novye materialy i issledovaniia*, 5: 69-84.

Dobuzhinskii, Mstislav. *Vospominaniia* (Moskva: Nauka, 1987).

Dolgopolov, Leonid. "Primechaniia." In Blok 1960-3, 4: 553-96.

Dolinskii, Mikhail. 1976. *Sviaz' vremen* (Moskva: Iskusstvo, 1976).

Dolinskii, Mikhail. 1985. *Iskusstvo i Aleksandr Blok* (Moskva: Sovetskii khudozhnik, 1985).

Donchin, Georgette. *The Influence of French Symbolism on Russian Poetry* (The Hague: Mouton and Company, 1958).

Dostoevskii, Fedor. *Polnoe sobranie sochinenii*, 30 vol. (Leningrad: Nauka, 1972-88).

Dostoevsky, Fyodor. *The Brothers Karamazov*, translated by Richard Pevear and Larissa Volokhonsky (New York: Random House, 1991).

Dujardin, Édouard. *Le Monologue Intérieur* (Paris: Albert Messein, 1931).

Èfros, Nikolai. *Moskovskii khudozhestvennyi teatr 1898-1923* (Moskva-Peterburg: Gosudarstvennoe izdatel'stvo, 1924).

Èlik, Maiia. "Notografiia proizvedenii na stikhi i siuzhety A. Bloka." In Maiia Èlik (comp.). *Blok i muzyka* (Moskva-Leningrad: Sovetskii kompozitor, 1972), 246-79.

Èllis [Lev Kobylinskii]. "Pis'ma Èllisa k Bloku," edited by Aleksandr Lavrov. *Aleksandr Blok. Novye materialy i issledovaniia*, 2: 273-91.
Ershov, Petr. "Simvolicheskaia lirika na stsene." *Novyi zhurnal*. 67(1962): 98-117.
Fedorov, Andrei. *Teatr A. Bloka i dramaturgiia ego vremeni* (Leningrad: Izdatel'stvo Leningradskogo universiteta, 1972).
Fedorov, Andrei. *Al. Blok – dramaturg* (Leningrad: Izdatel'stvo Leningradskogo universiteta, 1980).
Fel'dman, Oleg, Tat'iana Pavlova, Evgeniia Dubnova, and Grigorii Khaichenko. "Teatral'naia zhizn'". In Iurii Dmitriev, Tat'iana Rodina, Oleg Fel'dman, Efim Kholodov, and Tat'iana Shakh-Azizova (eds.). *Istoriia russkogo dramaticheskogo teatra v semi tomakh* (Moskva: Iskusstvo, 1987), 7: 254-416.
Fevral'skii, Aleksandr. *Puti k sintezu. Meierkhol'd i kino* (Moskva: Iskusstvo,1978).
Freidkina, Liubov'. *Dni i gody Vl. I. Nemirovicha-Danchenko. Letopis' zhizni i tvorchestva* (Moskva: Vserossiiskoe teatral'noe obshchestvo, 1962).
Frolov, Vladimir. "Teatr Bloka." In his *Sud'by zhanrov dramaturgii* (Moskva: Sovetskii pisatel', 1979), 135-53.
Gaidarov, Vladimir. *V teatre i v kino* (Moskva-Leningrad: Iskusstvo, 1966).
Galanina, Iuliia. "Blok v Peterburgskom dramaticheskom kruzhke." *Aleksandr Blok. Novye materialy i issledovaniia*, 5: 35-45.
Gerasimov, Iurii. "Aleksandr Blok i sovetskii teatr pervykh let revoliutsii." In Iurii Lotman (ed.). *Blokovskii sbornik: Trudy konferentsii, posviashchennoi izucheniiu zhizni i tvorchestva A.A. Bloka, mai 1962 goda*, [vol. 1], (Tartu: Tartuskii gosudarstvennyi universitet, 1964), 321-43.
Giamatti, A. Bartlett. *The Earthly Paradise and the Renaissance Epic* (Princeton, NJ: Princeton University Press, 1966).
Gogol, Nikolai. *Dead Souls*, translated by David Magarshack (Harmondsworth, England: Penguin Books, 1978).
Goldin, Frederick (trans. and ed.). *Lyrics of the Troubadours and Trouvères: An Anthology and a History* (Garden City, NY: Anchor Press/Doubleday, 1973).
Green, Michael, trans. 1986a. *The Puppet Show*, by Aleksandr Blok. Michael Green (ed. and trans.) *The Russian Symbolist Theatre* (Ann Arbor, MI: Ardis, 1986), 45-57.
Green, Michael, trans. 1986b. *The Rose and the Cross*, by Aleksandr Blok. Michael Green (ed. and trans.) *The Russian Symbolist Theatre* (Ann Arbor, MI: Ardis, 1986), 59-107.
Greene, Thomas. *The Descent from Heaven: A Study in Epic Continuity* (New Haven: Yale University Press, 1963).
Griffiths, Frederick T. and Stanley J. Rabinowitz. "*Doctor Zhivago* and the Tradition of National Epic." *Comparative Literature* 32 (1980): 63-79.
Gripich, Aleksei. "Uchitel' stseny." In *Vstrechi s Meierkhol'dom. Sbornik vospominanii*, edited by Liubov' Vendrovskaia. (Moskva: Vserossiiskoe teatral'noe obshchestvo, 1967), 114-45.
Gromov, Pavel. 1961a. "Iz tvorcheskoi istorii 'Rozy i kresta'." In his *Geroi i vremia* (Leningrad: Sovetskii pisatel', 1961), 522-78.

Gromov, Pavel. 1961b. "'Pesnia sud'by' v tvorcheskoi èvoliutsii Bloka." In his *Geroi i vremia* (Leningrad: Sovetskii pisatel', 1961), 482-521.
Gromov, Pavel. 1961c. "Trilogiia liricheskikh dram 1906 g." In his *Geroi i vremia* (Leningrad: Sovetskii pisatel', 1961), 388-481.
Gromov, Pavel. 1981. "Poèticheskii teatr Aleksandra Bloka." In Aleksandr Blok, *Teatr*, edited by Pavel Gromov (Leningrad: Sovetskii pisatel', 1981), 5-56.
Gzovskaia, Ol'ga. "Aleksandr Aleksandrovich Blok." In her *Puti i pereput'ia. Portrety. Stat'i i vospominaniia ob O.V. Gzovskoi* (Moskva: Vserossiiskoe teatral'noe obshchestvo, 1976), 243-56.
Hopkins, Gerard Manley. "Poetic Diction." In his *Journals and Papers*, edited by Humphry House and Graham Storey (London: Oxford University Press, 1959)
Hubert, Merton Jerome and Marion E. Porter (trans.). *The Romance of Flamenca* (Princeton: Princeton University Press, 1962).
Ireson, J.C. "Towards a Theory of the Symbolist Theatre." in J.C. Ireson, I.D. McFarlane, and Garnet Rees (eds.), *Studies in French Literature: Presented to H.W. Lawton by Colleagues, Pupils, and Friends* (Manchester: Manchester University Press, 1968), 135-56.
Iutkevich, Sergei. "Kak my nachinali svoi put' v iskusstve." In Konstantin Mardzhanov [Kotè Mardzhanishvili]. *Tvorcheskoe nasledie, pis'ma, vospominaniia, i stat'i o K.A. Mardzhanishvili* (Tbilisi: Literatura da khelovneba, 1966), 520-32.
Ivanov, Evgenii. "Zapisi ob Aleksandre Bloke." In Iurii Lotman (ed.). *Blokovskii sbornik: Trudy konferentsii, posviashchennoi izucheniiu zhizni i tvorchestva A.A. Bloka, mai 1962 goda*, [vol. 1], (Tartu: Tartuskii gosudarstvennyi universitet, 1964), 389-424.
Ivanova, Evgeniia. "Blok v teatral'no-literaturnoi komissii i TEO Narkomprosa." *Aleksandr Blok. Novye materialy i issledovaniia*, 5: 134-222.
Ivashkin, Aleksandr (comp.). "Katalog sochinenii." In Aleksandr Ivashkin (comp.). *Besedy s Al'fredom Shnitke* (Moskva: RIK "Kul'tura", 1994), 262-98.
Jakobson, Roman. 1987a "Linguistics and Poetics." In his *Language in Literature*, edited by Krystyna Pomorska and Stephen Rudy (Cambridge, MA: Belknap Pr., 1987), 62-94.
Jakobson, Roman. 1987b. "Marginal Notes on the Prose of the Poet Pasternak." In his *Language in Literature*, edited by Krystyna Pomorska and Stephen Rudy (Cambridge, MA: Belknap Pr., 1987), 301-17.
Jakobson, Roman. 1987c. "The Statue in Puškin's Poetic Mythology." In his *Language in Literature*, edited by Krystyna Pomorska and Stephen Rudy (Cambridge, MA: Harvard Univ. Pr., 1987), 318-67.
Jones, W. Gareth. "*Commedia dell'arte* : Blok and Meyerhold, 1905-1917." In David J. George and Christopher J. Gossip (eds.). *Studies in the Commedia dell'arte* (Cardiff: University of Wales Press, 1993), 185-97.
Joret, Charles. "La légende de la rose au moyen âge chez les nations romanes et germaniques." In *Études romanes, dédiées à Gaston Paris* (Paris: Émile Bouillon,1891; rpt., Geneva: Slatkine Reprints, 1976), 279-302.
Karpova, G.I. "Znachenie kategorii 'muzykal'nosti' v poètike liricheskoi dramy ('Neznakomka' A. Bloka)," *Khudozhestvennoe tvorchestvo i literaturnyi protsess* [Tomsk] 7 (1985): 52-68.

Kemball, Robin. *Alexander Blok: A Study in Rhythm and Metre* (The Hague: Mouton, 1965).
Khoprova, Tat'iana. *Muzyka v zhizni i tvorchestve A. Bloka* (Leningrad: Muzyka, 1974).
Kipnis, L. M. "O dramaticheskoi poème Aleksandra Bloka 'Pesnia sud'by'." In Aleksandr Ninov (ed.), *Russkii teatr i dramaturgiia èpokhi revoliutsii 1905-7 godov* (Leningrad: Leningradskii gosudarstvennyi institut teatra, muzyki i kinematografii, 1987), 73-95.
Klein, Karen. *The Partisan Voice: A Study of the Political Lyric in France and Germany, 1180-1230* (The Hague and Paris: Mouton, 1971).
Kogan, Petr (ed.). *Briusovu — Sbornik posviashchennyi 50-tiletiiu so dnia rozhdeniia poèta* (Moskva, 1924)
Konechnyi, Al'bin. "'Roza i krest' v teatral'no-literaturnom komitete." In *Aleksandr Blok. Novye materialy i issledovaniia. Literaturnoe nasledstvo*, 5: 85-7.
Kotrelev, Nikolai and Aleksandr Lavrov (eds.). "Vstupitel'naia stat'ia." In Aleksandr Blok and Sergei Solov'ev. "Perepiska Bloka s S.M. Solov'evym (1896-1915)," *Aleksandr Blok. Novye materialy i issledovaniia*, 1: 308-407.
Kotrelev, Nikolai and Roman Timenchik (eds.). "Blok v neizdannoi perepiske i dnevnikakh sovremennikov (1898-1921)." *Aleksandr Blok. Novye materialy i issledovaniia*, 3: 153-539.
Kristeva, Julia. *Le Texte du Roman* (The Hague: Mouton, 1970).
Kuzmin, Mikhail. "Pis'ma M.A. Kuzmina k Bloku i otryvki iz dnevnika M.A. Kuzmina," edited by Klara Suvorova. *Aleksandr Blok. Novye materialy i issledovaniia*, 2: 143-74.
Lakshin, V. "Blok i Stanislavskii. Neizvestnye pis'ma A. Bloka." *Russkaia literatura*, no. 4 (1958): 191.
Lenchik, L.E. 1971. "Drama A. Bloka *Neznakomka* v vyskazyvaniiakh sovremennykh literaturovedov." Novosibirskii gosudarstvennyi pedagogicheskii institut. Nauchnye trudy, vypusk 65. *Voprosy russkoi, sovetskoi i zarubezhnoi literatury*, (Novosibirsk: Novosibirskii gosudarstvennyi pedagogicheskii institut, 1971), 159-65.
Lenchik, L.E. 1972. "Simvolika siuzhetno-obraznykh sviazei v drame A. Bloka *Korol' na ploshchadi.*" In Zinaida Mints, et. al. (eds). *Blokovskii sbornik*, vol. II, (Tartu: Tartuskii gosudarstvennyi universitet, 1972), 206-17.
Lewitter, L.R. "The Inspiration and Meaning of Aleksandr Blok's *The Rose and the Cross.*" *Slavonic and East European Review* 35 (1957): 428-42.
Mallarmé, Stéphane. *Œuvres complètes* (Paris: Bibliothèque de la Pléiade, 1945).
Mandel'shtam, Osip, "Buria i natisk", in his *Sobranie sochinenii v trekh tomakh* (New York: Mezhdunarodnoe Literaturnoe Sodruzhestvo, 1967-71), 2: 339-51.
Markov, Pavel. *V Khudozhestvennom teatre* (Moskva: Vserossiiskoe teatral'noe obshchestvo, 1976).
Medvedev, Pavel. *Dramy i poèmy Al. Bloka: Iz istorii ikh sozdaniia* (Leningrad: Izdatel'stvo pisatelei, 1928).
Meierkhol'd, Vsevolod. 1968a. "Balagan", in his *Stat'i, pis'ma, rechi, besedy. Chast' pervaia 1891-1917.* (Moskva: Iskusstvo, 1968), 207-229.
Meierkhol'd, Vsevolod. 1968b. "Iz vystupleniia na diskussii 'Tvorcheskaia metodologiia Teatra imeni Meierkhol'da' 25 dekabria 1930 g.", in his

Stat'i, pis'ma, rechi, besedy. Chast' vtoraia 1917-1939. (Moskva: Iskusstvo, 1968), 229-240.

Meierkhol'd, Vsevolod. 1968c. "Ob oformlenii stseny v 'Zoriakh'." In his *Stat'i, pis'ma, rechi, besedy. Chast' vtoraia 1917-1939*. (Moskva: Iskusstvo, 1968), 18-9.

Meierkhol'd, Vsevolod. 1976. *Perepiska 1896-1939* (Moskva: Iskusstvo, 1976).

Mendeleeva-Blok, Liubov'. "Facts and Myths about Blok and Myself." In Lucy Vogel (ed. and trans.). *Blok: An Anthology of Essays and Memoirs* (Ann Arbor: Ardis, 1982), 8-63.

Meyer, Paul (ed. and trans.). *Le roman de Flamenca* (Paris: A. Franck, 1865).

Mints, Zinaida. 1971. "Blok i Dostoevskii." In Vasilii Bazanov and Georgii Fridlender (eds.). *Dostoevskii i ego vremia*. (Leningrad: Nauka, 1971), 217-47.

Mints, Zinaida. 1986. "V smyslovom prostranstve *Balaganchika*." *Uchenye Zapiski Tartuskogo Universiteta*, 720 (1986): 44-53.

Mints, Zinaida. 1988. "V 'khudozhestvennom pole' *Balaganchika*." In Morris Halle, Krystyna Pomorska, Elena Semeka-Pankratov, and Boris Uspenskij (eds.). *Semiotics and the History of Culture: In Honor of Jurij Lotman. Studies in Russian*. UCLA Slavic Studies, vol. 17. (Columbus, OH: Slavica, 1988), 400-7.

Mochulsky, Konstantin. *Aleksandr Blok*, translated by Doris V. Johnson. (Detroit: Wayne State Univ. Pr., 1983).

Morderer, Valentina and Aleksandr Parnis (eds.). "Darstvennye nadpisi Bloka na knigakh i fotografiiakh." *Aleksandr Blok. Novye materialy i issledovaniia*, 3: 5-152.

Mukařovsky, Jan. "The Poet." In his *The Word and Verbal Art*, translated and edited by John Burbank and Peter Steiner (New Haven, CT: Yale University Press, 1977), 143-60.

Nabokov, Vladimir. "L'Inconnue de la Seine". In his *Poems and Problems* (New York: McGraw-Hill Book Company, 1970), 82-5.

Nemirovich-Danchenko, Vladimir. *Izbrannye pis'ma*, 2 volumes (Moskva: Iskusstvo, 1979).

Nicoll, Allardyce. *The World of Harlequin: A Critical Study of the Commedia dell'Arte* (Cambridge: Cambridge Univ. Pr., 1963).

Ogneva, E.A. "'Roza i krest' Aleksandra Bloka (avtobiograficheskaia osnova)," *Russkaia literatura* 19, no. 2 (1976): 136-43.

Orlov, Dmitrii. *Kniga o tvorchestve* (Moskva: Vserossiiskoe teatral'noe obshchestvo, 1962).

Osokin, N.A. *Istoriia srednikh vekov* (Kazan': Imperatorskii universitet, 1889), vol. 2, part 1.

Pinskii, Leonid. *Realizm èpokhi Vozrozhdeniia* (Moskva: Goslitizdat, 1961).

Poliakova, Elena. "Akterskoe iskusstvo". In Iurii Dmitriev, Tat'iana Rodina, et. al. (eds.). *Istoriia russkogo dramaticheskogo teatra v semi tomakh*. (Moskva: Iskusstvo, 1987), 7: 189-253.

Polkanova, Mariia. "O podgotovke spektaklia 'Roza i krest' v Khudozhestvennom teatre." *Aleksandr Blok. Novye materialy i issledovaniia*, 5: 56-68.

Pollak, Seweryn. "Błok dramaturg." Aleksander Błok, *Utwory dramatyczne*, translated by Seweryn Pollak and Jerzy Zagórski (Krakow: Wydawnictwo Literackie, 1985), 214-35.

Pound, Ezra. "Langue d'Oc". In his *Personæ: The Shorter Poems of Ezra Pound*, edited by Lea Baechler and A. Walton Litz (New York: New Directions, 1990), 169-75.

Prikhod'ko, I.S. 1993. "Mifopoètika 'Pesni sud'by' A. Bloka." *Izvestiia Akademii Nauk. Seriia literatury i iazyka* 52, no. 6 (1993): 38-51.

Prikhod'ko, I.S. 1994. "Skrytye smysly dramy A. Bloka 'Roza i krest.'" *Izvestiia Akademii Nauk. Seriia literatury i iazyka* 53, no. 6 (1994): 36-51.

Pyman, Avril. *The Life of Aleksandr Blok, Volume I: The Distant Thunder 1880-1908* (Oxford: Oxford University Press, 1979).

Pyman, Avril. *The Life of Aleksandr Blok, Volume II: The Release of Harmony 1908-1921* (Oxford: Oxford University Press, 1980).

Reeve, Franklin D., trans. *The Puppet Show*, by Aleksandr Blok, in Franklin D. Reeve, ed. and trans. *Twentieth Century Russian Plays* (New York: W.W. Norton & Company, 1963), 163-7

Richardson, William. Zolotoe runo *and Russian Modernism, 1905-1910.* (Ann Arbor, MI: Ardis, 1986).

Rodina, Tat'iana. *Aleksandr Blok i russkii teatr nachala XX veka.* (Moskva: Nauka, 1972).

Rubtsov, Aleksei. *Dramaturgiia Aleksandra Bloka* (Minsk: Vysheishaia shkola, 1968).

Rudnev, Petr. "O stikhe dramy A. Bloka 'Roza i krest'". *Uchenye zapiski Tartuskogo universiteta* 251(1970): 294-33.

Rudnitskii, Konstanin. 1978. "V teatre na Ofitserskoi." In Liubov' Vendrovskaia and Aleksandr Fevral'skii (eds.). *Tvorcheskoe nasledie V.È. Meierkhol'da.* (Moskva: Vserossiiskoe teatral'noe obshchestvo, 1978), 137-210.

Rudnitskii, Konstanin. 1987. "Rezhisserskoe iskusstvo." In Iurii Dmitriev, Tat'iana Rodina, et. al. (eds.). *Istoriia russkogo dramaticheskogo teatra v semi tomakh* (Moskva: Iskusstvo, 1987), 7: 101-8

Rudnitskii, Konstanin. 1990. "Tairov i Kamernyi Teatr." In his *Russkoe rezhisserskoe iskusstvo, 1908-17* (Moskva: Nauka, 1990), 201-38.

Salmon, Amédée. "Remèdes populaires du moyen age." In *Études romanes (dédiées à Gaston Paris par ses élèves français et étrangers*, deuxième partie (Paris: Émile Bouillon, 1891; rpt., Geneva: Slatkine Reprints, 1976), 253-66.

Sébillot, Paul-Yves. *La Bretagne pittoresque et légendaire* (Paris: H. Daragon, 1911).

Shelud'ko, Dmitrii. "Ob istochnikakh dramy Bloka 'Roza i krest'". *Slavia* IX (1930): 103-38.

Sholomova, Sof'ia. "K istorii pervoi postanovki dramy 'Roza i krest'". *Aleksandr Blok. Novye materialy i issledovaniia. Literaturnoe nasledstvo*, 5: 46-55.

Smirnov-Nesvitskii, Iurii. "Tragicheskii spektakl' Vakhtangova." In Vakhtangov, Evgenii. *Evgenii Vakhtangov*, edited by Liubov' Vendrovskaia and Galina Kaptereva (Moskva: Vserossiiskoe teatral'noe obshchestvo, 1984), 521-50.

Smolenskii [Aleksandr Izmailov]. "Dramaticheskii teatr. ('Balaganchik'. 'Chudo strannika Antoniia')". *Birzhevye vedomosti*, no. 9673, 1 January, 1907, 6.

Stanislavskii, Konstantin [Konstantin Alekseev]. *Sobranie sochinenii v vos'mi tomakh* (Moskva: Iskusstvo, 1960).

Stroeva, Mariana. *Rezhisserskie iskaniia Stanislavskogo 1898-1917* (Moskva: Nauka, 1973).

Stroeva, Mariana. *Rezhisserskie iskaniia Stanislavskogo 1917-1938* (Moskva: Nauka, 1977).

Superfin, Gabriėl' [M. Bronnyi, pseud.] and Roman Timenchik. "K istorii neosushchestvlennoi postanovki dramy A. Bloka 'Roza i krest.'" In Zinaida Mints, Valerii Bezzubov, Iurii Lotman, and Dmitrii Maksimov (eds.). *Blokovskii sbornik II. Trudy vtoroi nauchnoi konferentsii, posviashchinnoi izucheniiu zhizni i tvorchestva A.A. Bloka* (Tartu: Tartuskii gosudarstvennyi universitet, 1972), 411-5.

Symons, James. *Meyerhold's Theatre of the Grotesque* (Coral Gables, FL: University of Miami Press, 1971).

Tairov, Aleksandr [Kornblit]. *Zapiski rezhissera. Stat'i, besedy, rechi, pis'ma* (Moskva: Vserossiiskoe teatral'noe obshchestvo, 1970).

T-ch [Georgii Chulkov]. "Teatr V.F. Komissarzhevskoi." *Tovarishch*, no. 154, 1 January, 1907, 6.

Thomas, Antoine."Vivien d'Aliscans et la légende de Saint Vidian." In *Études romanes (dédiées à Gaston Paris par ses élèves français et étrangers*, deuxième partie (Paris: Émile Bouillon, 1891; rpt., Geneva: Slatkine Reprints, 1976), 121-35.

Thomson, R.D.B. "The Non-Literary Sources of *Roza i krest.*" *Slavonic and East European Review* 45, no. 105 (July 1967): 292-306.

Thompson, Ewa. "The Development of Aleksandr Blok as a Dramatist." *Slavic and East European Journal* 14, no. 3 (1970): 341-51.

Timenchik, Roman. "Vstupitel'naia stat'ia." In Rem Shcherbakov. "Neizvestnaia stat'ia N.S. Gumileva 'Teatr Aleksandra Bloka'". In *Aleksandr Blok. Novye materialy i issledovaniia. Literaturnoe nasledstvo*, 5: 23-31.

Tolstoi, Lev. *Polnoe sobranie sochinenii*, edited by Vladimir Chertkov. (Moskva: Khudozhesvennaia literatura, 1928-58).

Vakhtangov, Evgenii. Letter to Vsevolod Meierkhol'd, Vsekhsviatskii Sanitorium, November 10, 1920. In *Evgenii Vakhtangov*, edited by Liubov' Vendrovskaia and Galina Kaptereva (Moskva: Vserossiiskoe teatral'noe obshchestvo, 1984), 326-7.

Veltrusky, Jiři. *Drama as Literature*. (Lisse: The Peter de Ridder Press, 1977).

Verigina, Valentina. 1961. "Vospominaniia ob Aleksandre Bloke." *Uchenye zapiski Tartuskogo gosudarstvennogo universiteta. Trudy po russkoi i slavianskoi filologii* (Tartu, 1961), 4: 310-71.

Verigina, Valentina. 1974. *Vospominaniia* (Leningrad: Iskusstvo, 1974).

Vilenkin, Vitalii. "Kommentarii." In Nemirovich-Danchenko, 1: 479-601, 2: 557-685.

Vinogradskaia, Irina (ed.). *Stanislavskii repetiruet. Zapisi i stenogrammy repetitsii* (Moskva: Soiuz teatral'nykh deiatelei RSFSR, 1987).

Vogak, Konstantin. "Aleksandr Blok. 'Roza i krest'." *Liubov' k trem apel'sinam* 1 (1914): 56.

Vogel, Lucy, trans. 1983. *The Rose and the Cross*, by Alexander Blok. *Slavic and East European Arts* 2, 1 (fall, 1983): 119-49

Vogel, Lucy. 1987a. "Dichotomies in Blok's Drama *The King on the Square*." *Slavic and East European Journal* 31, 3 (1987): 322-33

Vogel, Lucy, trans. 1987b. *The King on the Square* by Alexander Blok. *Russian Language Journal* XLI (winter-spring, 1987): 283-312

Vogel, Lucy, trans. 1990. *The Puppet Show*, by Aleksander Blok. *Canadian-American Slavic Studies* 24, no. 2 (1990): 181-98.

Volkov, Nikolai. 1926. *Aleksandr Blok i teatr* (Moskva: Gosudarstvennaia akademiia khudozhestvennykh nauk, 1926).

Volkov, Nikolai. 1929. *Meierkhol'd*, 2 vol. (Moscow-Leningrad: Academia, 1929).

Westphalen, Timothy C. 1991. "The Dialogization of the Lyric: Elements of Carnival in Aleksandr Blok's Trilogy of Lyrical Dramas". Ph.D. dissertation, Harvard University, 1991.

Westphalen, Timothy C. 1992. "The Ongoing Influence of V.S. Solov'ev on A.A. Blok," *Slavic and East European Journal*, 36, no. 4 (1992): 435-51.

Westphalen, Timothy C. 1993. "The Carnival-Grotesque and Blok's *The Puppet Show*," *Slavic Review*, 52, no. 1 (spring 1993): 49-66.

Wörn, Dietrich. *Aleksandr Bloks Drama "Pesnja sud'by" ("Das Lied Des Schicksals")* (München: Otto Sagner, 1974).

Zaborova, Roza. "Novoe ob Aleksandre Bloke." In *Knigi. Arkhivy. Avtografy. Obzory, soobshcheniia, publikatsii* (Moskva: Kniga, 1973), 29-56

Zarovnaia, V. "Liricheskaia drama A. Bloka 'Balaganchik'". *Voprosy russkoi sovetskoi i zarubezhnoi literatury* (Khabarovsk), vyp. 1 (1972): 125-46.

Zelentsova, N.S. "Nekotorye osobennosti èvoliutsii Bloka-dramaturga." *Uchenye zapiski Tartuskogo gosudarstvennogo universiteta*, (*Blokovskii sbornik* VII), vol. 735 (1986): 32-47.

Zhirmunskii, Viktor. *Drama Aleksandra Bloka 'Roza i krest'. Literaturnye istochniki* (Leningrad: Izdatel'stvo Leningradskogo universiteta, 1964).

Zolotnitskii, David. *Akademicheskie teatry na putiakh Oktiabria* (Leningrad: Iskusstvo, 1982).

INDEX OF NAMES

Other titles in the Russian Theatre Archive series:

Volume 11
Meyerhold Speaks/Meyerhold Rehearses
by Aleksandr Gladkov
translated, edited and with an introduction by Alma Law

Volume 12
Moscow Performances
The New Russian Theater 1991–1996
John Freedman

Volume 13
Lyric Incarnate:
The Dramas of Aleksandr Blok
Timothy C. Westphalen

Volume 14
Russian Mirror:
Three Plays by Russian Women
edited by Melissa Smith

Volume 15
Two Comedies by Catherine the Great, Empress of Russia:
Oh, These Times! and *The Siberian Shaman*
edited and translated by Lurana Donnels O'Malley

Volume 16
Off Nevsky Prospect:
St Petersburg's Theatre Studios in the 1980s and 1990s
Elena Markova

Additional volumes in preparation:

Russian Theatre and Movement: the 1920s
Vladislav Ivanov

The Theatre of Poets
Dmitry Milkov

This book is part of a series. The publisher will accept continuation orders which may be cancelled at any time and which provide for automatic billing and shipping of each title in the series upon publication. Please write for details.

